WATCHING WHAT WE EAT

The

EVOLUTION

of TELEVISION

COOKING SHOWS

WATCHING WHAT WE EAT

The
EVOLUTION
of TELEVISION
COOKING SHOWS

Kathleen Collins

continuum

NEW YORK • LONDON

2009

The Continuum International Publishing Group Inc
80 Maiden Lane, New York, NY 10038

The Continuum International Publishing Group Ltd
The Tower Building, 11 York Road, London SE1 7NX

www.continuumbooks.com

Printed in the United States of America

Library of Congress Cataloging-in-Publication Data

Collins, Kathleen, 1965–
 Watching what we eat : the evolution of television cooking shows / Kathleen Collins.
    p. cm.
 Includes bibliographical references.
 ISBN-13: 978-0-8264-2930-8 (hardcover : alk. paper)
 ISBN-10: 0-8264-2930-0 (hardcover : alk. paper) 1. Television cooking shows—United States—History and criticism. I. Title.

PN1992.8.C67C65 2009
791.45'6564—dc22

CONTENTS

ACKNOWLEDGMENTS

The idea for this book was hatched in 2001. While the project itself experienced many stops and starts and iterations along the way, the idea never quit, and drawing on the knowledge, skills, and patience of a big handful of very good people, it has finally come to fruition. I would like to extend a heartfelt thank you to Rob Snyder for his close reading and vital suggestions from hatching through final manuscript draft. Lorraine Glennon, Celia Hartmann, Rachel King, Regina Marchi, Nancy MacDonell, and Ted Weinstein also provided support and helpful ideas in the proposal stages. For general psychic reinforcement and idea-bouncing, Dirk Burhans, Tim Kinnel (who provided the book's primary title), Regina Marchi, and Adam Ried were indispensable.

For generously sharing information and resources, I thank Milly Abrams, Laura Brounstein, Stephen Chen, LaDeva Davis, Anne de Ravel, Michaela DeSoucey, Joe Langhan, Bob Lape, Krishnendu Ray, Kate Rohmann, Signe Rousseau, Megan Steintrager, Susan Stellin, and members of the ASFS and Newslib listservs.

In my archival research and photo searching odyssey, I was kindly assisted by people at various organizations, including those at the General Mills Archives, Photofest, and the UCLA Film and

Television Archive. Leigh Montgomery at the *Christian Science Monitor*, Glenn Griffin at the HBI Archives, and Karen King at the National Public Broadcasting Archives were especially helpful. The librarians at the Schlesinger Library—Sara Hutcheon, Diana Carey, and Ellen Shea—deserve awards for being far beyond good at their jobs and for making it an extra pleasure to do research there.

I am grateful for a PSC–CUNY grant, which funded trips for research to see cooking show videos and for securing the images in these pages.

My editor, David Barker, has left this first-time book author with the surely mistaken impression that all writers must organically find their way to the right editor. I thank him for his positive and encouraging attitude from the get-go. I am also grateful to others at Continuum—John Mark Boling, Emma Cook, Katie Gallof, Max Novick, Gabriella Page-Fort—and copyeditor Angela Chnapko, for their enthusiasm and stellar work in bringing this book to fruition.

My sincere thanks goes to everyone who spent the time to let me interview them. Their voices and insights are the heart of this book.

The biggest slice of the gratitude pie is reserved for my partner, Gerard Trimarco, who made this book—and who makes everything—better.

We humans are the only cooking animal; we long ago turned our eating from natural history into culture by cooking our food.

—Sidney Mintz

Louisa recounted, word for word, a cooking program she'd been watching on TV. "First he put the veal shanks endwise in a pot. Then he poured over them a sauce made of tomato paste, lemon zest, bits of celery . . . but everything was cut up ahead of time! *Naturally* it looks easy if you don't have to witness all the peeling and chopping. . . ."

"There's not enough real life on television," Louisa said.

"That's the whole point," Brindle told her.

"I'd like to see him try scraping the tomato paste out of that little tiny Hunt's can, too."

—Anne Tyler, *Morgan's Passing*

INTRODUCTION

A few years ago, I was struck by two casual observations. First, I witnessed my great uncle, a man of eighty-plus years whose only cooking experience has been at the backyard grill, lingering on the Food Network almost as long as he normally does on *This Old House* or MSNBC. A couple of days later, I was on an airline flight where a good number of passengers—including myself—were tuned into the Food Network on their personal TV screens. The young man next to me, wearing a Yankees cap and whom I would have pegged for an ESPN watcher, seemed to be content watching *Mario Eats Italy* with his hand nowhere near the channel changer. Curious, I thought, that we three demographically different people seemed to be drawn to the same kind of TV show. How did it come to be that a genre originally intended for housewives sixty years ago is still alive, kicking, and capturing the attention of so many?

I have been watching TV cooking shows since the early 1970s. While dwelling in the public broadcasting neighborhood where I watched *Sesame Street*, I met and—like most viewers—was immediately charmed by Julia Child. With her as my model, I would narrate the preparation of my after-school snack, describing the ingredients of peanut butter and crackers to my invisible audience. She began to affect my life in a small and personal way while simultaneously affecting American culture in a substantial and far-reaching way. She was not the first cook on television, but as the first to prop open the door to culinary progressivism, she may have been the most important.

Today, more and more children are playing "cooking show" like I did. In part, that is due to the great field of programs from which they have to pick their material, but it is also a telling sign that food and cooking have become mainstreamed in American life in an unprecedented way. The more I paid attention to the interest in cooking shows, and the more I thought about the combined forces of food and television—two of my abiding loves—the more I was sure there was an enlightening story to be told about the place where they meet. And while the cable channel that started in 1993 can take much of the credit for the mainstreaming, there was life in food television before the Food Network and I wanted to know more about it.

The story begins on the radio, where homemaking shows hosted by the likes of Betty Crocker and the United States Department of Agriculture's Aunt Sammy instructed women and kept them company in the kitchen from before the Great Depression to the end of World War II and after. Cooking via broadcasting was already a staple for American housewives by the time television emerged. Ever since the first boxy black-and-white TV sets began to appear in American living rooms in the late 1940s, we have been watching people chop, sauté, fillet, whisk, flip, pour, arrange, and serve food on the small screen.

In the post–World War II years, cooking shows, which were hosted for the most part by home economists, provided information for housewives to help them perform their kitchen duties well. Hosts James Beard and Dione Lucas were exceptions to this model, and their gourmandise illustrated a mindset split of the era—is cooking a science or an art? Is food a vehicle for nutrition or a pleasurable pastime? (Though the questions may have changed, polemics about food continue to engage us today.) American middle-class families headed for the suburbs, cultivating a culture of uniformity and consumerism. Women—whether they worked at home or in the office—spent money on nifty new products and heeded timesaving ideas by tipsters like Josie McCarthy, Alma Kitchell in her Kelvinator Kitchen, and "can opener queen" Poppy Cannon. Such early cooking mentors taught the June Cleavers of Levittown how to fulfill their feminine roles with pragmatism and confidence, and clearly made the point that men belonged in the workforce and women belonged in the kitchen (ideally in heels and a smart dress).

Betty Friedan's *The Feminine Mystique* would eventually reveal that many postwar suburban women felt devalued and unfulfilled by their lot as homemakers. As part of the social upheavals of the 1960s, the ripplings of feminism allowed women and men to begin shedding restrictive roles. Taking cues from the already established civil rights movement, as well as an overall atmosphere of social activism, women took a stand against the status quo and moved into the workforce with gusto. At the same time, the Kennedys' enviable Camelot made dining—especially on French food—fashionable, and a growing middle-class wanderlust created an even more vigorous interest in international culture. As an open-minded, socially conscious mood pervaded the nation, Americans' growing urge for adventure and creativity found its way into the kitchen. Cooking shows began to reflect a broadminded departure from the standard, dry format and attempted to add spice to a bland culinary landscape.

On public broadcasting's *The French Chef* starting in 1963, Cordon Bleu alumna and *Mastering the Art of French Cooking* coauthor Julia Child was a liaison between the average home cook and the world of sophisticated French food. Her popularizing of the cuisine was revolutionary, not to be considered separately from the larger rebellious and egalitarian impulses expressing themselves in all kinds of ways around the country at the time. Child wanted Americans to be empowered in the kitchen and to enjoy the pleasures of food for its own sake. She also wanted viewers to benefit from cooking as a leisure time hobby, and, luckily, the country was finally ready to embrace the ideas espoused by Beard and Lucas in the 1940s. The concept of "gourmet" crept into the cultural mindset in the 1960s and 1970s, and cooking took on a new role. As novice home cooks felt more at ease in their kitchens and knowledge of food and cooking were woven into American culture inch by inch, producers of cooking shows took the cue that there was more room for fun. The time was ripe for Graham Kerr, host of *The Galloping Gourmet*, which premiered in 1969. Entertainment—as opposed to teaching—was the primary intent, and Kerr's personality and humor were the major components of the show's success. He related to his viewers—including the first in-studio cooking show audience—in a non-pedantic, intimate manner. Like a Pied Piper, Kerr invited even more Americans to climb aboard the culinary bandwagon. During the "me decade," food and cooking became associated with a personal sense of self.

After the belt-tightening of the 1970s, people were ready to spend good money on frivolous activities like eating out. The words "pesto," "polenta," and "nouvelle cuisine" became increasingly familiar to the average Joe in the 1980s. Americans were becoming interested in who was cooking in restaurants, with Wolfgang Puck one of the decade's icons. Workaholism and greed ruled the day, allowing pre-pared foods, microwaves, and haute cuisine to share the stage. All the while, Cajun cook Justin Wilson helped to spread the word about an unpretentious regional cuisine, and "Frugal Gourmet" Jeff Smith made it his mission to teach viewers about the food and peoples of nonsuperpower countries.

Cable television and its resulting niche-ification created a need for more attention-grabbing fare to compete for viewers' interest, and programmers eagerly fed the beast by providing a swarm of choices. Eventually there would be a TV program for just about every demographic and every segment of American life. In 1993, the Food Network joined the growing narrowcasting panoply, and cooking and food got an entire network all to themselves. The Food Network was both a culmination of the incipient "foodie" culture as well as an instigator. The cable network gradually revamped the traditional instructional cooking program, adding live bands, participatory studio audiences, science, travel, and game shows, making the genre a microcosm of television and entertainment itself.

Presently, reality and competition shows—wildly successful on other channels—have made their inevitable way into the cooking/food show genre. Popular home renovation shows like *Kitchen Accomplished* and *While You Were Out* signal the elevated stature of the kitchen. Such innovations prove beyond any lingering doubt that cooking shows and their audiences demand far more than recipe instruction. Perhaps most telling, the hosts of many of these shows—on the Food Network and other broadcast and cable channels—have become celebrities. Emeril Lagasse and Rachael Ray exemplify the host-driven hallmark of the modern cooking show, and they are but two of the stars in the vast firmament.

More than just a how-to or amusement, cooking shows are a unique social barometer. Their legacy corresponds to the transitioning of women at home to women at work, from eight- to twenty-four-hour workdays, from cooking as domestic labor to enjoyable leisure, and from clearly defined to more fluid gender roles. As the role of food changed from mere necessity to a means of self-expression and a conspicuous lifestyle accessory, the nature of cooking shows has shifted from didactic to entertaining. The genre has changed considerably since the first cooking shows began appearing in the late 1940s and even more since the debut of *The French Chef*. But in some profound ways the programs still serve the same purpose. Then as now, cooking shows teach viewers not simply how to cook but how to live. Common throughout the genre's history, too, is the specter of consumption. We are ardent consumers of food, of television, and of the products springing forth from both.

The egoism of every age is that its inhabitants believe they are the first to encounter certain experiences or events. But very little is ever really new. The cultural patterns and behaviors we saw in the twentieth century and are seeing now have occurred before. Nineteenth century dinner clubs, for instance, predated gourmet clubs of the 1960s and 1970s. There is a common misconception that food suddenly became intertwined with lifestyle in the 1980s and 1990s and that food is a new cultural trend. But both food and media trends have come and gone and come back again in United States history. What was new in the twentieth century was the combination of food and television, and this book covers the period of time where television had—and is still having—its influence. Interest in food has been a relative constant for two centuries. Television transformed it into a phenomenon.

Our collective adulation of cooking shows is in large part a result of television's eminently powerful allure. A turned-off television set is a passive, neutral agent—literally a fair and balanced information outlet. But once it's turned on, whatever fills the screen has the potential to captivate, even if it's someone making mashed potatoes—it seems these days, *especially* if it's someone making mashed potatoes or any other food. We might not choose to sit in the kitchen and watch our spouse cook mashed potatoes, but many of us find watching someone do so on TV a perfectly fine—even enjoyable—way to pass the time. This book aims, in part, to explore why that is.

The place where food and television meet is a dynamic and bubbling place because food and TV command central roles in our lives. Food would be impossible to live without, but many would melodramatically say the same about television. Because food and television are both all-pervasive in American culture, their existence and effect on our lives are often taken for granted. But they are both arenas in which our attitudes and behaviors reflect who we are as individuals and as a society. Because everyone eats and virtually everyone has access to television, they purport to be democratic and potentially unifying cultural forces. Both have been venues for learning, entertainment, and experimentation, whether for a home cook attempting a new recipe in the kitchen or broadcasters rolling out a new educational series for preschoolers. When learning, entertainment, and experimentation happen at the same time in food and TV, the result is the narrative of food television over the past half-century.

Most homemaking programs in the 1940s and early 1950s were shot live and were mere ephemera designed as promotional conduits for appliance and utility companies. Certainly no one imagined that one day they might be interesting cultural artifacts, and, as a sad result, very few remain. To research some of the older programs I discuss, I relied on newspaper and magazine articles from the period as well as archival documents, cookbooks, and memoirs. For shows that were taped and that are still in existence and accessible, I used my own eyes and ears. And for those shows I actually remember watching, I also called on my personal memory collection. To examine programs old and current and the genre as a whole, I drew on the expertise and experience of others' eyes, ears, and memories, too, through two dozen interviews with scholars, program hosts (or their family members), and television producers and executives.

The arrival of three successive noteworthy entities—television, Julia Child, and the Food Network—provides a clear outline of the evolution of television cooking to the present day. These three occurrences demarcate what I see as the early, middle, and modern periods. The early period (1946–1962) begins with the advent of television where cooking instruction showed up in short order. The middle period (1963–1992) begins with the appearance of Julia Child on *The French Chef* and lasts until the premiere of the Food Network in 1993. We are currently in the modern period. A theretofore organized decade structure to the chapters falls apart once I hit the 1990s, but there would be no way to justify writing one or even two chapters

on the past fifteen years of food television given not only the expo-
nential growth of programs but also the momentous changes that
have taken place. There has been an immense amount of journalism
and blogging, and more than a modicum of academic writing on the
modern period content—mostly on specific programs and hosts. My
goal in the last four chapters is to highlight the dramatic shift in the
genre, provoked by the Food Network, and to look beyond the shows
to the larger forces at work and play.

The use of "evolution" in the book's subtitle emphasizes my view
that the genre has survived because it has adapted to changes in the
environment. Just as in scientific evolution, elements that are beneficial to the genre have developed over time and others have died out.
As our needs and desires changed, the shows mutated. Americans
have adapted, too—we have in many ways been changed by cooking
shows. Though it reveals a historical perspective, the book is not a
"history" in the purest sense because it is not a detailed chronicle.
And by no means is it an encyclopedia. There are dozens, if not hundreds, of cooking shows (probably just on the Food Network alone)
that are not even mentioned. I chose to focus on the archetypes—
James Beard, Dione Lucas, Julia Child, Graham Kerr, Jeff Smith,
Martha Stewart, Sara Moulton, Emeril Lagasse, Rachael Ray—as well
as a few unsung but emblematic hosts, like Joyce Chen and LaDeva
Davis. My intention is to show, by pertinent examples, how and why
the genre has changed over the past sixty-plus years.

There is no other television genre, especially an initially routine,
low-production-value type like the cooking show, that has experienced
such a triumphant fate. There is compelling evidence to believe that
the genre shows little danger of extinction, and in the last chapter
some of those intimately involved with the world of food and television share their predictions for the future.

The historical arc of TV cooking shows reflects an evolution of women's roles from homemakers to coworkers; food as a way to feed ourselves to a way to express our creativity and cultural capital; a shift from a culture of conformity to one of diversity; and a change in focus—from a social life centered inside the home, to one outside the home, to a desire to have a foot in both. Meat and potatoes gave way to boeuf bourguignon, which gave way to grass-fed Kobe beef burgers. This progression reflects the public's growing knowledge about food and nutrition, as well as a trend toward conspicuous consumption in contemporary America and our desire to emulate the sophisticated "good life."

Cooking shows have taught us, changed us, and changed with us. At the beginning of the twenty-first century, they have evolved to satisfy our yearning for quality, affordable, environmentally and health-conscious, easy-to-prepare yet sophisticated food. And while many viewers may not have the time to execute the lessons nor the money to afford the high-end ingredients or appliances used by cooking show hosts, these shows prevail because everyone eats, knows something about food, and can relate to the endeavor. With the exception of the nail-biting reality subgenre, cooking shows are generally predictable, and we undoubtedly watch them in part for a connection with something traditionally associated with home and comfort.

The following pages contain three essential ingredients: food/cooking, television, and consumer culture. The book is about how these ingredients interact, how they affect us, and how we affect them. While variety shows, westerns, and live, scripted dramas have gone the way of rabbit-ear antennae, cooking shows are still being watched, on airplanes as well as on high-definition plasma screens via TiVo. This book will illuminate how cooking shows have both reflected and shaped significant changes in American culture, and it will explore how their wide appeal and our shared interest tells us quite a bit about the optimism and aspirations that we share as individuals and as a society.

EARLY PERIOD
(1945–1962)

CHAPTER 1

Stirrings:
Radio, Home Economists, and James Beard

In a culture like ours, long accustomed to splitting and divid-
ing all things as a means of control, it is sometimes a bit of a
shock to be reminded that, in operational and practical fact,
the medium is the message.

—Marshall McLuhan

Cooking on the Airwaves

Aunt Sammy began her radio career in October 1926. She was a fig-
ment of the Farm Radio Service of the United States Department
of Agriculture, which used radio to communicate with farmers in
various parts of the country. More than one hundred stations carried her fifteen-minute *Housekeeper's Chat*, and dozens of women
from around the country played the role of Aunt Sammy, all reading
from the same script adapted with local speech patterns and regional
accents. For nearly a decade, she doled out advice on pest control,
floor care, laundry, nutrition, vitamins, and uses for leftover pickle
vinegar, and assured listeners that garlic *is* eaten by respectable people and that onions do *not* cause drowsiness. One of the show's regular segments, "What Shall We Have for Dinner?" was "concerned

with the problem the average homemaker must solve 365 times a year," said the *Chicago Daily Tribune*. She shared recipes for standard dishes such as scalloped potatoes, broiled chicken, apple turnovers, meatloaf with green beans, and lemon jelly dessert. Some of her listeners' favorite recipes also included blackberry flummery, cider gelatin salad, rice and liver loaf, cooked lettuce, fried cucumbers, and stuffed beef heart.

Morse Salisbury, radio service chief, was credited with livening up the show so that Aunt Sammy would deliver her tips with more levity and less lecture. He believed it was important that the audience felt "talked to" and "visited with." "The first injunction laid upon the radio speaker is to be entertaining and natural and friendly," said Salisbury. Aunt Sammy would tell jokes and comment on current events and the comings and goings of people like

Courtesy National Archives, photo no. 16-G-93-46501B

"Aunt Sammy"—here played by Nan Dumont, with USDA officials—delivered recipes and nutritional information to housewives via radio.

Mrs. Hoover and Mrs. Roosevelt. "Queen Marie of Rumania is visiting my town this week," announced Aunt Sammy on one broadcast. "She didn't come to America especially to see me, but I thought she might drop in to discuss household problems. I have a new recipe, called Peach Dainty, that I've been saving for her. I am sure the King would like it, and the Prince and Princess, too."

Cooking instruction has a history as old as that of humans and fire. Cookbooks have been around for hundreds of years—the first original American cookbook, written by Amelia Simmons, was published in 1796. Food writing and recipes began to appear in American newspapers and magazines like *Ladies' Home Journal* and *McCall's* in the mid- and late-nineteenth century, and cooking schools cropped up as well. More informally, cooking advice was osmotically transmitted from mother to daughter, verbally from farmer's wife to farmer's wife and domestic servant to domestic servant and so on. When

radio programs were first broadcast in the early 1920s, suddenly there was a new channel for transmitting culinary advice. Though media theorist Marshall McLuhan might not have explicitly envisioned sharing canning tips, this was a manifestation of the global village he later referred to when he explored the social effects of electronic media.

Radio offered a new way for housewives to share recipes.

Courtesy of General Mills Archives

Radio cooking programs combined the informality of the verbal and the formality of the recipe, creating a virtual coffee klatch. As described in the *Washington Post* in 1925,

> Radio has brought about a national exchange of cooking recipes. When Mrs. New York is a little bit in doubt about the meringue for her pie, she is just as likely to ask Mrs. California or Mrs. Minnesota for advice as she is her next door neighbor. If young Mrs. Wisconsin can't get her baked beans quite as brown as mother use to bake them, she can call upon the famed authority on the subject, Mrs. Boston. If a contemplated Southern dinner is on the mind of Mrs. Michigan, she can get suggestions for it from her friend, Mrs. Missouri.

The real (albeit fake) famed authority at the time was Betty Crocker. Like Aunt Sammy, she was fictional, but unlike civil servant Sammy, Betty was a commercial mascot. Though Betty was invented in 1921 by the flour purveyor Washburn Crosby Company to address home cooks' baking quandaries via friendly letters, according to *Fortune* magazine, "The radio made Betty." She began local radio programs in 1924 (preceding Aunt Sammy), went to national networks broadcasting in cities across the U.S. two years later and stayed there nearly three decades. Letter writer Betty was, in reality, a team of home economists employed by Washburn Crosby. Radio Betty was impersonated by various actresses telling listeners "how to buy, what to buy, how to make the best with what is available," said the *Chicago Daily Tribune.* She gave "new ideas to old cooks and old ideas to new cooks." Mondays and Wednesdays were devoted to household problems including food preparation and proper menus, and Friday was devoted to her enormously popular radio cooking school, which boasted graduates from nearly every state. For many housewives, Betty filled the role of a nonjudgmental, wise friend or family member providing advice to those nervous or lonely in the kitchen.

Recipes by Radio!

WINTER PROGRAM
By Betty Crocker
GOLD MEDAL FLOUR
HOME SERVICE DEPARTMENT
Washburn Crosby Company
Minneapolis, Minnesota

Courtesy of General Mills Archives

In addition to Betty and Sammy, there was another well-known women's program in the 1920s. If the "happy homemaker" moniker brings the *Mary Tyler Moore* show's Sue Ann Nivens to mind, you need to travel back about a half a century to the original, Ida Bailey Allen. Her first show, *Hospitality Talks,* aired in 1923 in Medford, Massachusetts, followed by *The Homemakers Hour* in New York City in 1926 and then across the U.S. via CBS on the *National Radio Homemakers Hour* in 1929. Unlike Betty, Sammy and successor-in-name-only, Sue Ann, Ida was quite real. A trained dietician, cooking school instructor and author of more than twenty books on food, cooking, and home economics, Ida was one of the most respected women in early radio.

Women's Work

Though image-free, radio was an effective mirror for domestic culture in the between-the-wars era, particularly with regard to perceptions of gender roles. One newspaper article announced:

> Uncle Sam has taken unto himself a helpmate. The old boy who worried along in a state of single blessedness for considerably more than a century, and who was a pronounced women-hater for so long, has finally capitulated to the fair sex, and with the mingled pride and embarrassment of the traditional benedict he is presenting to his enormous family of nephew and nieces their new "Aunt Sammy."

Uncle can scarcely be blamed for relinquishing his bachelorhood for such a gem, but *she* could only have succumbed to the old chauvinistic curmudgeon out of a sense of public service. A stereotypical man-wife dynamic ensued. From one Aunt Sammy broadcast:

> By the way, some of you have begun to listen in quite recently. You may not have copies of the loose-leaf *Radio Cook Book* Uncle Sam is sending to homemakers. I want to give Uncle Sam all the credit due him, but the cookbook was not his idea at all. After he saw how neat it was, and how easily extra pages could be added, he waxed enthusiastic—he really did. His only regret was that he didn't originate the idea himself. Isn't that just like a man?

She fed the *Chicago Tribune* this line, which could only have been suggested by a pragmatic and generous husband: "The housekeepers' program has a dual purpose, according to Aunt Sammy. It aims to help the housewife in the intricate and vastly important task of managing a home, and to show her how, by careful planning of meals and saving steps and labor, she may have more leisure for what are broadly termed 'cultural activities.'"

Did the radio powers-that-were really think women needed so much instruction, so many tips and suggestions to do what they'd been doing for centuries? Probably not, if they were honest about it, but radio cooking programs served advertisers and programmers quite well, as they were simple to produce and were directly tied to consumer products. But the media, in some instances, unabashedly insulted women on this front. A 1925 *Hartford Courant* article heaped praise on the new radio show's tackling of women's work. "The blunt truth is that American women are poor cooks even with a greater variety of food available and more money to spend for it than any other nation," wrote the unidentified author. "The radio is amazingly hastening a change in American women's knowledge of cookery because the isolated millions of women in city and country, who read no papers and stay at home most of the time, have through radio come in contact with educational forces." A nice plug for the service that radio can provide—but anonymous went on to say,

> Nine-tenths of the women of the country either had to get their knowledge haphazardly or to learn it from print, which is notoriously hard for the average woman, especially when attempted all by herself. . . . Women are going to benefit far more than men from radio. . . . It brings the greatly needed up-to-date trade knowledge for their chief profession of cookery, homemaking, child-raising so vital to any nation . . . Radio is going to lift the level of woman's intelligence; lift the level of American cookery to a point where we need not be quite so ashamed of it as now, and lift child health to a higher point.

It wasn't just women in the home kitchen every hour of the day, but when men did intentionally amble in, it was a lark—not their "chief profession" by any means. Encouraging men as food hobbyists was even advocated by some. In 1939, the *New York Times*'s Kiley Taylor reported that the imagination and efforts of men interested in cooking as a hobby could potentially improve American cuisine. These men cook what they like, to please themselves and each other (not to feed the kids lunch), noted Taylor, and women should be patient and grateful that they get a partner in the kitchen. If a man shows interest, she wrote, "his wife is flying directly in the face of providence if she fails to encourage him," even though said partner is admittedly like "Ferdinand in a china shop." Betty Crocker declared that widowers and single men from all over wrote to her upon listening to her radio show. "Many men are genuinely proud of their culinary skill," she said, "and see nothing undignified or unmasculine in being able to turn out a batch of fluffy biscuits."

While a small number of men enjoyed cooking as a pastime at home, they were running the prestigious restaurant industry (as they are for the most part today). There was, however, at least one professional who crossed over into the home via radio. In the early 1930s, New York restaurateur George Rector hosted *Our Daily Food Recipes* wherein he discussed food, menus, school lunches, and, once, the machinations of a grape juice factory.

Mixed messages were directed at women from multiple directions. As historian Doris Kearns Goodwin described in her book *No Ordinary Time: Franklin and Eleanor Roosevelt: The Home Front in World War II*, Rosie the Riveter was pushed aside after the war's end by images of women reclaiming their rightful place at home. Goodwin provides accounts of magazine interviews with women who willingly, and sometimes with relief, left the workforce, making way for men looking for work. She wrote, "Magazines that had once given prominent display to products such as Heinz soup and GE cleaners, which allowed women to fly through their chores at home so they could rush to their work in the factory, now featured menus that took a full day to prepare." So while some women reluctantly went back to the stove, others embraced the homemaker role and took recipe collecting and cooking seriously, whether for their own edification or for the well-being of their families. The impetus to do well at such tasks would add to a motivated audience for cooking instruction on radio, and then television.

Radio's Mission

It is quaint to imagine that radio broadcasters produced programs to instruct and to provide a networking outlet for housewives, and, publicly, that was the mission. But then as now, the objective of any broadcasting organ is to sell products for its advertisers. Food and kitchen appliance companies figured out that cooking shows were a super way to market their products. Proctor & Gamble began advertising on the radio in 1923, for instance, providing an ideal forum for radio programs featuring recipes using Crisco. In a stark representation of commercial broadcasting's bottom line, cooking instruction was literally a byproduct.

With the media bashing women's impoverished cooking skills and the advertisers compelling them to sing the virtues of what was often essentially junk food, women were at an impasse. *The Mary Lee Taylor Show*, broadcast from the PET Milk experimental kitchen for two decades starting in 1933, was hosted by the eponymous home economist (actually a pseudonym for Erma Proetz). On one installment, listeners could hear Miss Taylor interacting with a male counterpart, perhaps to disabuse listeners of the idea that Mary might just be brazen enough to make stuffed vanilla wafers for herself. "If you could look into this PET Milk kitchen through your loudspeaker, I know you'd think that the stuffed vanilla wafers I've been putting together look mighty festive," Mary said. "The creamy yellow filling, bristling with coconut, certainly has a come hither look. Mr. Cole is reaching for a second one with a look on his face that makes me think the first one just hit the right spot." She read the recipe very slowly and repeated each part for dictation: "Melt over boiling water. [Pause.] Melt over boiling water." Miss Taylor emphasized the nutritional charms of this recipe that required only four grocery staples: PET milk, coconut, marshmallows, and vanilla wafers. "Let young daughters try their wings with this recipe, easy and most wholesome," chirped Mary. "All PET Milk is irradiated to add vitamin D to help teeth and bones grow properly." Maybe the idea was that one nutritious element casts a healthy glow over the whole operation. The desire for women's cooking or the nation's health to improve was at odds with the advertisers' agenda, a dynamic that is often at work today. Competing messages and far-fetched nutritional spin were ever thus.

American-born women weren't the only targets of persuasion. Being as much of a middle-class American as possible was of major importance in the early twentieth century, no matter who you were. "Radio has been a boon, especially to the millions of foreign-speaking women, rather unused to American ideas, and coming from parts of Europe primitive in ideas of cookery," reported the *Hartford Courant* in 1925. "They are learning modern cookery by radio with splendid results in home nutrition. This kind of Americanization is practical and productive and will be reflected in better national health." As historian Mary McFeely wrote about cookbooks,

> As agents of our consumer culture, [cookbooks] speak . . . to American ethnic groups: Italian Americans, Asian Americans, African Americans, Hispanic Americans, and indeed to all working-class Americans, saying, "this is what you ought to aspire to." While aspirations may be difficult to achieve or alto-gether unsuitable, they nonetheless are presented as goals.

As more people were listening to radio than ever before in the years surrounding World War II, these messages were sure to reach a mass audience loud and clear.

During the war, hundreds of thousands of women took off their aprons, marched into the workforce, and volunteered in the Women's Auxiliary Army Corps (WAAC). For many women, cooking and domesticity were put on the back burner. Those ineligible to be a WAAC or paid labor force worker, however, might feel powerless and constrained. A *Christian Science Monitor* article in 1943 depicted such a war wife:

> While she has been peeling potatoes, washing dishes, exchanging ration stamps for groceries with the delivery boy . . . the radio has been telling her of the WACS (Women's Army Corp), the WAVES (Women Accepted for Volunteer Emergency Service), the men on the beachhead near Naples, the dogfights in the air over the South Pacific. . . . Of course she does her bit in the war activities, but somehow all the italics in her life seem to come out of the cook book instead of the military manual.

In addition to the myriad benefits described above, during World War II radio homemaking programs served to rally women stuck at home to play their part in the war effort. Often referred to as "captain" or "general" of the kitchen, it was de rigueur to impel women to grasp the importance of their roles, not just to feed their families but also to promote the strength of the nation. If you're not with us, you're against us, ladies. Nowadays during times of crisis we're nudged to go shopping. Back in the day, these women were instructed to stay home and conserve.

Some radio shows may have highlighted what women were missing, but others helped to loop them in. Indeed, women had their hands full managing rations of sugar, coffee, meat, and canned goods, and saving valuable resources for the war effort. To compensate for the scarcity of meat, homemakers were encouraged to cook casseroles or meatless dishes. To make up for the shortage of fresh vegetables, many started victory gardens on empty lots or in backyards. Their efforts, they were assured, could help the military cause in direct ways. Saved kitchen fat, tin cans, lipstick containers, razor blades, and nylons could be used to make bullets, tanks, rifle cartridges, gunpowder bags, and machine guns. In 1941, New York's local public radio station, WNYC, spent nearly half of its programming time on such war preparedness segments as ration announcements and on-air war bond drives, and at other times during the war New York City Mayor La Guardia himself shared, via radio, recipe tips for breakfast coffee and making pasta fagiole from leftovers.

At the same time that conservation and rationing were being advised, however, there was another sentiment in certain quarters simmering just below the surface. For most Americans, the year 1941 brings to mind a pastiche of images that include British fighter planes, U-boats, and Pearl Harbor. Though it depends on one's proclivities—it was, after all, a banner year for Joe DiMaggio, Glenn Miller, and Orson Welles—what is unlikely to come to mind is a cornucopia of vernal mirth and lavish feasts. As it happens, though, 1941 was a critical year in that regard. In January, magazine publisher Earle MacAusland trotted out a magazine called *Gourmet: The Magazine of Good Living*. These fit-to-bursting words were penned by food writer Clementine Paddleford in the May edition of *Gourmet*'s inaugural year:

> Spring moves in, splashing the town with gay color. Overnight, sidewalk tables pop up, abloom with colored umbrellas. Windows are open again. . . . Elbows are out on window ledges. . . . Chestnut carts have put away their charcoal burners to carry a burden of lilacs. . . . California's black cherries glow deep as embers, blushing over their price, no doubt— around 75 cents a pound. These fat Fancies are the advance guard bringing word that more cherries are coming.

War? What war? Life is just a bowl of cherries! In later issues Paddleford suggested tips on whipped cream substitutes as a nod to sacrificing (and much of her reporting did focus on the wartime kitchen), but the contents of the magazine were directed at those not accustomed to skimping—on anything—and the publication served as a forum for musing about life's fine trappings, including dining. MacAusland proclaimed that there had never been a time more fitting for such a publication. As food writer Betty Fussell wrote, MacAusland ". . . had to defend his depiction of lush food in posh surroundings from outraged patriots and purists by claiming that he showed things that were 'worth fighting for.'" To his credit, it was certainly one way to symbolically put the Great Depression up on a closet shelf, and it was an indulgent diversion from the creeping threat of war.

While *Gourmet's* gestalt had everything to do with pushing adversity to the back of the collective mind, the U.S. government's plan was to address it head on. President Roosevelt took action in hopes of remedying the undernourishment of the nation's citizens, so the Food and Nutrition Board of the National Academy of Sciences was charged with creating a set of standards so that people would know if they were getting the right amount of nutrients required for good health and, of immediate concern, good fightin'. Consequently, the same month that Paddleford waxed giddy about fat cherries, the public first got wind of the entity known as the Recommended Dietary Allowance (what we know now as the Reference Daily Intake).

Over at a neighboring government agency, the Federal Communications Commission, there was another kind of development in the works. Two months after the RDA was announced and six months after *Gourmet* hit coffee tables, commercial television was born. As the director of the Metropolitan Museum of Art auspiciously commented at the time, "Television will be the instrument which will create as complete a revolution in the education of the future as the discovery of movable type and the invention of the printing press 400 years ago." RCA president and television visionary David Sarnoff likewise voiced optimism as well as patriotism: "It is our earnest hope that television will help to strengthen the United States as a nation of free people and high ideals." Sarnoff, who died in 1971, never got to experience the unrestrained and exemplary era of reality TV, but his democratic heart was in the right place.

It is impossible to ignore the significance of this constellation of events, given the mighty convergence of food and television today. Or maybe it's simply a convenient beginning to the story. In 1941, *Gourmet* (playing the role of the id) and the U.S. government (cast as the superego) began telling us (literally recommending, in both cases) what we should eat and how we should live, albeit advocating two somewhat divergent attitudes. These were not the first illustrations of paradoxical, conflicting messages surrounding food in modern America, and they most certainly would not be the last. Add television, that most potent of persuaders, and you only intensify the overt and subliminal signals that still seduce, amuse, and confuse us today. (In another admittedly overdetermined coincidence, homemaking expert Martha Stewart was also born in 1941.)

In a short span of months in 1941, the seeds of the future of our relationship to food and TV were planted. Those elements that would burrow into our individual and collective psyches were available and ready for use in countless ways. Though rocky at first, it was the beginning of a long relationship that not only thrives today but also affects our lives in more ways than we can possibly realize.

Turn on the Television

Though television sets first appeared during World War II, the medium had yet to make a dent in the American home in the early 1940s. After the war ended, it was still a rare novelty. By 1950, only 9 percent of homes had a set. Stakes were relatively low in the early days, so programming results were hit or miss. The television industry was like a big clunky science and technology lab. In 1944 *Television* magazine declared, "The program end of television has been an arid wasteland, almost devoid of imagination, showmanship, and (what is more important) any indication of any knowledge of the nature of television." The use of the word "wasteland" rings out, here predating Federal Communications Commissioner Newton Minow's famous 1961 characterization of television as a "vast wasteland." Knowledge of a medium's nature, as we've seen most recently with our experience of the Internet, does not come bundled with the owner's manual. In the pre-network days, there was almost no use of live studio programming, almost no sponsors and very few actors. That's because there was no audience. If you were fortunate enough to find yourself in front of a TV set, you would most likely be looking at a sports event with no option of changing the station. Rather than a wasteland, in 1944, it was just undeveloped land.

Since radio had made cooking instruction a known quantity and it was cheap and easy to produce, the new medium of television immediately took up the genre. One early experimental pilot was *The Queen Was in the Kitchen* (a line from the nursery rhyme "Song of Sixpence"), broadcast by the DuMont Network in 1945. It was hosted by radio personality Allen Prescott, who had previously hosted a radio show called *Wife Saver*, and it was sponsored by American Central Manufacturing Company, the makers of American Kitchens products. The show's purpose was not to promote cooking skills but to showcase, via comedy skits, narration, and films, what the kitchen of the near future would look like.

In May 1946, NBC broadcast television's first regularly scheduled program, *Radio City Matinee*, which, like most of the early TV programs, had been adapted from radio. Radio's George Rector had a cooking demonstration spot on the show, alongside a milliner, a flower arranger, a comic, an architect giving home decorating tips, and an artist who gave drawing lessons. These anthology shows were common on television through the 1940s and 1950s, and most of them had a cooking or homemaking segment. There was never any question that these were directed at women. Because television sets were out in the public sphere and not in private homes where they would eventually assume their mantle of tyranny, however, these segments often missed their intended audience.

Dean of Television Cookery?

As men gathered in bars to watch the *Friday Night Fights* on the new medium, they were an unlikely audience for the first nationally televised program devoted to cooking. The host of that show, James Beard, may have been unfamiliar to the men on the barstools, but he was known among the *Gourmet* set. By 1945, Beard had published three of the more than two dozen cookbooks that he would publish over the course of his life. His prolific nature was only part of the reason that he came to be considered the dean of American cookery. So among those who paid attention to such things, his name meant something, even back then.

Though Beard had dabbled as a theater actor in the 1920s, he had no designs on becoming a television actor. But as he related in his autobiography, *Delights and Prejudices*, in late 1945 he ran into a friend who informed him that NBC wanted to see him. One unexpected turn led to another, and, within several months, Beard found himself on the small screen. In August of 1946, the Elsie the Cow company, Borden, sponsored a fifteen-minute show called *Elsie Presents James Beard in "I Love to Eat."* Beard intended to combine instruction and fun—the pattern for nearly every successful TV chef who came after him. As he wrote in his autobiography, "At last—a chance to cook and act at the same time."

Unlike the purely instructional shows that were more prevalent at the time, Beard's was meant to be entertaining to watch, perhaps enough to capture the attention even of those whose only relationship to the stove was passing it on the way to the refrigerator or some of those fellows who claimed cooking as a hobby. "By then the heavyweight champion (in all sense of the term) of American gastronomy, [Beard] loomed as an emblematic figure in the flickering screens of the nation's saloons," wrote Jay Jacobs in *Gourmet* in 1984.

Beard wrote of a letter he received signed by twenty-six viewers of the televised fights who said they stuck around after the sportscast when "Elsie" came on and found that show enjoyable as well. Prior to Beard, no one on radio or television knew quite how to—or didn't think or care to—make a pure cooking show entertaining. For Beard, serving good food was always more than a matter of sustenance or proper nutrition; it was a performance. "Put on a fine show!" he wrote. "I think if I have done nothing else, I have taught people to enjoy making food."

With Beard's appearance, there now existed two strains of cooking shows—the one full of instruction for housewives (superego) and the other sort of which Beard's was the sole representative at the time (id). The title of the show alone—*I Love to Eat*—went against the grain of the contemporaneous conventional wisdom of eating to live versus living to eat.

According to veteran food and dining broadcaster Bob Lape, Beard summarized the menu for *Elsie Presents* as "anything showy and, secondly, things that would please the sponsor." He "merrily falsified his ingredients," wrote Jay Jacobs in *Gourmet*, "substituting more photogenic or more durable substances, such as ink for the natural veining of Roquefort cheese and mashed potatoes for ice cream, as the exigencies of the then-primitive new medium dictated." Correspondingly, makeup artist Dick Smith said that one of his jobs was to pencil in hair on Beard's scalp. "Television wasn't sharp enough to pick them up as pencil strokes," he said.

Jacobs's summation of the show in his *Gourmet* paean cast a different image than what some others said about him. He said that for the brief time Beard was on television,

[H]is image crystallized as *the* American icon of gourmandise. He was the first professional cook in the country to receive nationwide visual exposure, and he played the role to the hilt. At long last his theatrical and gastronomic talents had come into play simultaneously. . . . In the nearly four decades since his video debut . . . no one else even remotely has personified the pleasures of the kitchen and table as convincingly as he.

By Beard's own assessment, too, the show was a success. "One didn't talk to Jim about failure," said cookbook author and former Beard teaching colleague Barbara Kafka. Both Julia Child and cookbook author Marion Cunningham, however, recalled that he was a bit stiff and awkward on camera. Child said he had a great personality but "froze up in front of the camera." One to mince garlic more than words, Kafka said, "Jim was a terrible

James Beard on the set of the first nationally televised cooking show, *Elsie Presents James Beard in "I Love to Eat."*

actor and desperately wanted to be an opera singer. It was never in the cards. . . . Jim had a very healthy ego. He wanted to be a star. He had charisma. He could have been a good producer or director if he didn't want to be the star."

Rarely awkward off screen, Beard's charisma was a central facet of his being. "At the end of our cooking classes, people felt they were having a class with James Beard and were enormously involved with him," said Kafka. "If he had been able to mobilize that on TV, he would have had a roaring success. It just didn't come across." The show was expanded to thirty minutes but cancelled by a new sponsor, Birds Eye, the following spring when parent company General Foods decided to take a breather from television.

As far as sponsorship went, Beard had no quarrel with acting as a commercial conduit. "A new medium inaugurated a new theater of cooking and new 'cuisines of advertisement,'" wrote Betty Fussell.

Some have criticized Beard for working too closely with the food industry, for endorsing products like Omaha Steaks and Camp Maple Syrup. But that's the kind of purism that Beard laughs off as loudly as he does prissiness. People take food too damn seriously, he said. "It's something you enjoy and have fun with, and if you don't, to hell with it. It's no ritual; it's . . . good and amusing and a pleasant part of life."

As Beard biographer Robert Clark wrote in the *Journal of Gastronomy*,

> The cooking and serving of food was still viewed by most Americans as a means rather than an end, a means to which turn-of-the-century feminists and reformers had tried to bring dignity by insisting that it required the skills of the scientist-manager to assure its correct, economic preparation and consumption. The thought that cooking, eating, and drinking might become an aesthetic, social, and intellectual pleasure for middle-class Americans was at best nascent, and as yet no 'personalities' had appeared to inculcate them as such.

It was easily a couple of decades before the American populace would embrace any such sentiment on a large scale. Ahead of his time on television, the attitude that Beard promoted on the show was more akin to what we see today than it was to his peers.

Home Economists Populate the Small Screen

And just who were Beard's peers? Quite different from *I Love to Eat*, the era's hallmarks were those cooking programs to which we ascribe mental-hygienic properties and which were hosted by stereotypical, earnest home economists. These shows—almost always produced by local broadcast stations—were instructive and prescriptive, teaching housewives how to perform their kitchen duties with pragmatism and confidence. The number of television stations around the country grew from fewer than twenty in 1948 to over three hundred in 1954. The late 1940s and early 1950s consequently saw the emergence of dozens of regional cooking shows—or home-making shows with cooking segments—from Chicago, Nashville, Omaha, and Providence to Milwaukee, Honolulu, Rochester, and Greensboro. On the late 1940s Milwaukee-area program *What's New in the Kitchen*, host Breta Griem shared commonsense tips on food preparation and budget planning. The daughter of a county agricultural agent, she was a dyed-in-the-wool home economist. Shows like hers were legion, and Griem's enjoyed unusual longevity. In cases where hosts were not local home economists, they were former radio performers, repackaged into television cooks by net-work managers.

In the ranks with Griem were Louise Leslie with *Homemaker's Exchange*, *Jessie's TV Notebook*, Marjorie Abel's *Hot Points in the Kitchen*, Betty Adams's *Sugar 'N Spice*, the Minneapolis–St. Paul pro-gram *The Bee Baxter Show*, Ruth Bean's *Shop, Look and Cook*, Ruth Crane's *The Modern Woman*, Scoot Kennedy and his *New Orleans Cookbook*, Helen Ruth's *Menu Magic*, Wilma Sim's *Homemaking with KSD-TV*, and Mary Wilson's *Pots, Pans and Personalities.* There were multiple shows produced in the same view-ing area: *Cooking with Roz* and *Cooking with Philameena* in New Haven, and *Chicago Cooks with Barbara Barkley* and *Chicago Cooks with Kay Middleton*. *Menu Magic* with Edith Green ran daily in San Francisco for years. Betty Furness, perhaps best

In addition to hosting *The Bee Baxter Show*, Baxter (left) wrote, produced, and directed a variety of radio and television shows in the 1940s and 50s.

Courtesy of KSTP-TV, LLC

known for demonstrations of Westinghouse products on *Studio One*, though she later headed New York State's Department of Consumer Affairs, hosted *Meet Betty Furness*. It was not strictly a cooking show, though one of her regular sets was a "magnificent Westinghouse kitchen." Betty Crocker segued from radio to the small screen, too, finally attaching a walking, talking figure to the fictional but eminently trusted name. First represented by actress Adelaide Hawley, Betty starred in *Betty Crocker Magazine of the Air* in the late 1940s and appeared in TV shows throughout the 1950s, serving as a model for efficiency—but not necessarily creativity— in the kitchen.

A 1953 clip from Philadelphia's *Television Kitchen* embodies the style of such programs. Florence Hanford, thin and tidy in an uncluttered kitchen furnished with tied-back curtains and white appliances, stirs a bowl of white batter while adding sugar. "I don't like to give you the exact recipe," she said, "because it takes too long. It takes too long for me to give it and it takes too long for you to copy it. Besides that, I might not give it just right or you might not copy it just right and then you wouldn't have perfect results and of course we want you to have perfect results." Hanford's menus included dishes like broiled sausage lamb chops, tri-fruit salad, frankfurters with sauerkraut, and apple lime chiffon cake, the recipes for which viewers could request by writing to the local station.

Perhaps the longest running local cooking show was Los Angeles's *Cooking with Corris* (called *Tricks and Treats* for the first half of its life, beginning in 1947). Each show had a theme, such as "Chuck Wagon Supper," "The Boss Comes to Dinner," or "Hawaiian Luau." Guy was the director of consumer services for Helms Bakeries, the show's sponsor, and she would promote cakes, donuts, and breads during the show—even if they didn't quite jibe with the episode's theme. Local manifestations of these programs tended to last longer than those that moved to the big time. A national show might be subject to more pushing and shoving by executives and advertisers, the higher stakes environment making them vulnerable as programming increased. But the longevity was also likely due to the neighborly relationship viewers developed with local hosts. "I'm not there to be a teacher," Guy told the *Los Angeles Times* upon beginning her third decade on TV in the 1960s. "All I want is to exchange recipes with friends." Guy, with her subdued, friendly but down-to-business manner and her demonstrations of exceptionally simple and economical recipes, was a perfect emblem of the cooking shows that populated the early period.

These shows, according to Jane and Michael Stern, taught viewers how to make the likes of turkey pot pie, butterscotch nut rolls, and vanilla crumb refrigerator cake. All that plus household tips and endorsements for a Hotpoint kitchen and Sunsweet Prunes. As the Sterns listed in *American Gourmet*, these shows promoted "Wonder Shredders, Chop-o-matics, juicerators, electric skillets, deep fat fryers. . . . In this way, the advertisers contributed untold nuances to the elevation of America's culinary consciousness in the 1950s." Creating tantalizing, authentic (from scratch) cooking was apparently not high on the priority list since many of the ingredients consisted of canned and processed foods, but they were cheap airtime fillers (usually fifteen to thirty minutes long), made excellent vehicles for advertisers, and reminded everyone of proper gender role expectations.

"American women are making a strong, concerted effort to bring new flavors and tastes to the daily meals they serve their families," wrote William Kaufman in *Cooking with the Experts*, a collection of recipes from local television cooking shows published in 1953. "The popularity of the television cooking show attests to this fact. Women look to cooking more and more as a real outlet for their creative and artistic drives. I doubt if there was ever a cooking school in the world that had as large an attendance as one cooking program seen on television in the smallest area in the United States."

Despite the era's rigid gender roles, home economics television did offer some housewives newfound opportunities for spinning their domestic skills into a profession. Where Kaufman's book promoted the artistic side of cooking, Ellen Pennell, an associate professor of technical journalism at Iowa State College, offered a more scientific approach and even more ambitious possibilities. In 1954, Pennell published *Women on TV*, a manual for women to apply their domestic skills in the exciting new medium on both sides of the camera. The foreword begins, "Men may design women's hats or sell them cars but when it comes to the subjects that reach deep into the heart of the home—women believe women." Pennell provided specific guidelines, such as the number of people who should appear on a show, rehearsal time, script preparation, demo tables, lettering on charts, vocabulary, clothing, kitchen colors, the use of props (they increase interest, the manual told readers), choosing products for sponsorship, and the importance of voice (sounding "too sexy" was bad; sounding "like a good cook in her own home" was good). The message was encouraging and conveyed the idea that the television industry needed women's talents.

The notion that domestic skills could be useful outside of the home was novel in the early 1950s. Edna Vance (aka "Aunt Susan") was an example of such atypical professional success for women. Vance started the *Aunt Susan's Cooking School of the Air* radio show in Oklahoma City in the 1930s. In 1946 and 1947, she oversaw *Betty Crocker Magazine of the Air*, a radio show that aired on nearly two hundred ABC stations across the U.S., and she later became home economics director for the DuMont Network. She coproduced several television shows with her husband, and hosted *Kitchen Fare* and *Susan Adams' Kitchen*, the latter of which ran for more than five years and boasted over 100 sponsors.

While most cooking programs were hosted by women in the early period, Beard, Rector, and Prescott weren't the only male hosts. In May 1947, Swift and Co. had an hour-long cooking and homemaking show called *At Home* starring actress and model Jinx Falkenburg and her husband, radio host Tex McCrary. Broadway restaurant owner Vincent Sardi hosted *Home on the Range* in 1948, using actors to prepare meals. Chef Jack Cardini, a San Francisco Bay Area restaurateur, hosted *Chef Cardini* in 1951. Joseph Milani hosted *Chef Milani Cooks* in Los Angeles in the 1940s and 50s, and Eddie Doucette presided over *Home Cooking* in Chicago, starting in 1952. Carson Gulley, cookbook author and a senior chef (noteworthy, too, because he was African American) at the University of Wisconsin residence halls, hosted *What's Cookin'* with his wife Beatrice on WMTV in Madison, Wisconsin, starting in the 1950s.

Francois Pope and his wife Antoinette operated the Antoinette Pope School of Fancy Cookery in Chicago for decades. *Creative Cookery*, which featured Francois and his sons, Frank and Robert, debuted in 1951 and lasted through the decade. The Pope family found Italian food to be so popular they started selling their own frozen pizza and spaghetti sauce. In another shining sign of the times (and completely contrary to Ellen Pennell's stance that "women believe women"), the *Chicago Tribune* reported that after years of dreary home ec hosts, "housewives discovered they preferred men as teachers of this oldest art in the world, and women have mostly disappeared from this branch of TV." As Francois told a *Tribune* reporter in 1960,

> Fancy cookery is everyday cookery dressed up. One of the main reasons for our success in television is the formality projected by a father and sons teaching women how to cook, and we found it more dignified to wear a business suit. Cooking is not a job or a chore and women can more easily see this when men act as their teachers. The finest cooks in the world are men.

According to this unfounded theory, somewhere along the line, someone made a mistake putting women in the kitchen. As a result of this historical error, the theory would have, scores of men have had to suffer at the hands of their inferior cook wives, and men had to begin to take the offensive. A *Los Angeles Times* reporter likewise described Chef Milani's show as something for which men like him should be grateful and that "we should, every one of us, give three cheers for the man who has taken a difficult job off our hands; the project of teaching our wives how to cook."

Pope's wearing of a suit may or may not have commanded more attention from women, but it did seem to inspire kudos from reviewers—at least those television critics who happened to be men, as most of them were at the time. A 1951 full-page *Variety* ad featuring a photo of Francois and the boys claimed that *Creative Cookery* was "the most remarkable cooking program in the history of radio and television." One male reviewer wrote,

> This culinary offering rates as a strong argument that service shows aimed at special audiences can find a niche alongside the broader-angled "entertainment" formats. This is a cooking show, pure and simply, with no gadgets or gimmicks, but it should strike a responsive chord with the hausfrau hankering to keep hubby happy with her scullery art.

Another male reviewer was impressed by the Popes's demonstration of a complete meal in sixty minutes, in this case shrimp de Jonghe (a local Chicago specialty involving garlic, sherry, and breadcrumbs), a "Pope-invented cheese and mushroom concoction," and a German pancake for dessert.

"Even without the aid of color or smell, the food took on an appetizing appearance," wrote the reviewer.

> To save time a good deal of the food is prepared beforehand so that the Popes have merely to repeat methods of preparation, reserving most of their time for explaining little tricks that make the food palate more pleasing. Camera work was excellent, with a prism lense [sic] on the camera permitting mouth-watering close-ups of the food.

These details do not reveal what made it superior to other programs of its ilk, but it is notable that even as early as 1951 there were critics discussing cooking show production values. And at the time, demonstrating tricks instead of technique was likely considered preferable by many viewers.

The Product Is the Message

In the early, post–World War II years, the function of food was, for most people, sustenance, as unambiguous a role as those assigned to men and women—the former to bring it home, the latter to fry it up. Marsha Cassidy, author of *What Women Watched: Daytime Television in the 1950s*, said,

> In the earliest days of cooking shows, an attempt was made to "professionalize" homemaking, as more and more women were prevailed upon to stay home and return to traditional women's work. Thus, cooking shows of the 1950s created friendly experts who gave viewers the modern information they needed to raise families and create a happy home life. The family—artfully nurtured by a glamorous, efficient homemaker—gained an exulted place in the rhetoric of the 1950s. It was even seen as an antidote to Communism.

Photofest

Alma Kitchell hosted *In the Kelvinator Kitchen* in the late 1940s—an emblematic cooking show touting the sponsor's product.

According to Cassidy, home economists saw television as a powerful teaching tool, more effective and far-reaching than the in-person demos that had previously been their outlet.

As Pennell explained in *Women on TV*, however, television ratings indicated that home-service programs were not in high enough demand to simply stand on the merit of their own content. "Many sponsors admit that demonstrations are much more forceful in small doses," she wrote. "As a result, home economics practices are employed for commercials. . . . In this field the home economist is in demand since the sponsor and the studio technicians realize they need her technical skill."

In 1947, singer and radio talk show host Alma Kitchell gave up her radio career to host a network television series called *In the Kelvinator Kitchen*, that ran for two years. A *New Yorker* writer carped about a few inaccuracies that occurred during the program, including the misnaming of pieces of beef that were shown via slides as Kitchell narrated. She executed her tasks in a "fine, white modern kitchen" donated by Kelvinator, such blatant sponsorship being a common practice at the time.

In his 1953 study on the development of television network programs, Robert Hammel Stewart described television's approach as "honestly commercial. . . . In some instances listeners must regret even today that the same care, skill, attention and imagination has not been devoted to programs as has been expended in the preparation of commercial announcements." Clearly a soothsayer, Stewart's comment stands the test of time and helps explain why many of us watch the televised Super Bowl with no interest whatsoever in the football game but for the creative and costly ads that punctuate the event. Though we are now accustomed to sports arenas and concert halls named after corporate sponsors, there was a time when this was the case for television shows whose existence was indebted to a single sponsor and often bore its name.

The shows' sponsors loomed as a big-brother presence throughout each episode, a feature that has long since given way to distinct, expensive advertising and strategic product placement. Just a few years shy of the time when networks would assert control over programming, advertisers were still footing the bill and calling the shots. Sponsors would often script and produce an entire show and hosts would unabashedly shill for products. This integrated advertising practice would seem jarring and offensive today, because even though we *know* TV is for selling, we tend to ignore the reality. Up through the 1970s, show hosts like Johnny Carson would promote Alpo dog food or Lucky Strike cigarettes right on the set. We are almost back to the early days with the current groundswell of seamless advertising. As Bob Lape wrote, echoing Beard's working philosophy, "Today's aims are anything that would interest an audience, sell a book, and—also—please a sponsor."

Appliances were not the only products being promoted, of course. The end of World War II was a watershed in terms of changing attitudes about food. Broadly stated, before and during the war there was a hunger for whatever was scarce, and not long after the war there was a hunger for whatever was new and smacked of convenience. Whereas victory gardens resulted in increased consumption of fresh vegetables during the war, just a few years later, canned vegetables topped the grocery list along with Cheerios, frozen orange juice, and cake mixes. If the civilian force wanted canned green beans, it had earned that right. These novel items were speedily worked into cooking programs. Josephine McCarthy, host of a 1953 NBC cooking program and author of *Josie McCarthy's Favorite TV Recipes*, praised packaged foods. Some of the most requested recipes included in her book were calico soup with ham dumplings, Chinese plum duck, roast stuffed spare ribs with sausage forcemeat stuffing, frankfurter salad bowl, two crust lemon pie, Mexican wedding cookies, fried Greek tea cookies, panned scallops with herbs, and young turkey cacciatore. In the introduction to her 1958 cookbook, which samples some of the thousands of recipes she had offered over the air, she wrote, "Many are old-fashioned, slow to make, but, to my mind, worth the trouble." Her from-scratch advocacy did not contradict her praising of time-saving convenience foods. She didn't include them in her book, she explained, because they came with their own foolproof instructions on the package.

In 1957, Josie appeared again in a daily segment of NBC's *Hi, Mom!*, hosted by puppeteer and ventriloquist Shari Lewis and her constant companion, Lambchop. *Josie's Kitchen* offered viewers practical menus, such as beef stew, spoon bread, hot vegetable salad, and a tutti frutti sundae. Josie made a point of assuring viewing moms that the meals could be put together from staples sure to be already in the house. She peppered her monologue with, "Had ya thought that now?" when delivering a handy tip like cobbling together leftovers. Josie, a pleasant, solid lady with short curly hair and a nice modest suit, notably apronless, simply showed ingredients in various stages and verbally took viewers through the process, as many a segment was forced to do in the interest of time. "It's a beautiful menu even though it's a plain Jane menu . . . a nice meal for a man to come home to, wouldn't ya say?" Shari interrupted with an ad for Reddi-wip: "When you're very busy and need an extra pair of hands to whip the cream, I'd like to tell you that you have whipped cream the modern way with Reddi-wip. . . ." As she squirted it on a chocolate tart and some fruit, she said, "I'm happy to tell you mothers that Reddi-wip is wholesome cream. It was put in this container by your dairyman. . . . You get about a pint and a half from each red, white and blue container." Other housewifely ads played during the show for Chock full o' Nuts, Dash detergent, a pointy brassiere, and Lestoil cleanser. The program ended with Shari's "Goodbye, mommy. We'll see you tomorrow."

Lighten Up

These early cooking shows were not all purely medicinal—some were laced with a spoonful of sugar. After Milton Berle hit it big in 1949 with "Texaco Star Theater," the comedy-variety show became a television staple, and sparks of entertainment even found their way into cooking shows and segments. James Beard was not the only one trying to have some fun. Late 1940s' Los Angeles was a relative hotbed of locally produced cooking shows, and two in particular incorporated a more entertainment-oriented element than the genre was used to.

Chef Milani was equal parts entertainer and chef. During World War II, Milani was the food director for the first incarnation of the

Hollywood Canteen, the legendary servicemen's club cofounded by actors Bette Davis and John Garfield and volunteer-staffed by movie stars. During the 1940s, Milani had a string of bit parts in movies wherein he usually played a chef or another food or restaurant-related role. By the time he had his cooking show on Los Angeles's ABC affiliate, starting in 1949, show biz was his lifeblood. In a 1950 episode for the 4th of July, while the camera painstakingly watched Chef Milani festoon a ham with canned pineapple and maraschino cherries ("the eye is what catches the stomach," said Milani as he labored over his masterpiece), the kitchen behind him buzzed with activity: his plump, smiling, and servile wife ("she's a good girl," said Milani in his thick Italian accent. "We been married thirty-five years and never had a fight."), the impish helper Bobby (praised by Milani because he loved his mother as all good boys should), the interjecting emcee Luigi (played by radio and TV personality Lou Marcelle), all bustling, joking, laughing, and making noises about how good the kitchen smelled and wondering aloud when it would be time to eat. The effect was a strange, semi-functional stand-in for an Italian-American family.

The episode was in essence an extended advertisement for Hunts canned foods, Western-Holly Gas, and Wilson Tender Made Ham, all of which Milani touted continually. When he asked Bobby to hand him a can of peas, Bobby comically dropped the can. Milani spewed an angry tirade of Italian at Bobby (including biting his face) while Luigi said to the camera, "For the benefit of those of you who do not speak Italian, Chef Milani just told Bobby that he must be more careful in the way he handles Hunts fresh garden tender peas." Because decorating a ham and composing a salad of canned vegetables did not require much time, the rest of the show consisted of Bobby waking from a furtive nap singing "A Dream Is a Wish Your Heart Makes," a trio of ladies playing and singing the polka ditty "Hoop-Dee-Doo" and an Italian minuet, and a leggy, blonde "Television Queen of the Month" (selected by the Los Angeles Art Directors Guild), who said she was there "to point out the importance of television" and came bearing a cake she had baked.

If you lived in Los Angeles in 1949, you could have also watched Monty Margetts hosting *Cook's Corner*. Despite (or likely because of) the fact that Margetts knew nothing about cooking—she had to ask a friend what "marinate" meant—the NBC station director believed that Margetts's charming personality and ease on the air could carry the show.

Margetts recalled a friend from KFI television station coaxing her into cooking television: "We want to try out some commercials. We've had a home economist doing a show, but they're so deadly dull. Would you like to try it?" She did a commercial for Iris canned peaches. "Naturally, I had trouble with the can opener and sort of a comedy show was born." She was reluctant to call the show *Cook's Corner* because she wasn't a cook. "I'm not a dizzy dame, I'm just interested in a hell of a lot more things than cooking, and I made no secret about it. I always did my best, but nobody knew at the end of the show whether it was going to come out, least of all me."

It was an immediate success. Margetts was frank and candid with her audience, creating an interpersonal intimacy that was not only new to the young genre, but unexpected, given that homemaking shows were not typically associated with frankness and candidness—and certainly not comedy.

She flaunted her naiveté and, in a reversal of a typical instructional show's intention, actually learned from viewers. This was perhaps a harbinger of the call-in show, but at the time such give and take was unorthodox. As Margetts recalled, "[T]hey started writing in, these nice people, telling me how to do things. So I started reading their letters, and taking their advice. Because I figured, if you're smart enough to take their advice, and tell the world that you're taking it, they will buy anything you sell them. . . . And that's what made the show turn very successful." She also got letters from people disturbed by her licking her fingers. "I read them on the air, too. I said, 'It hadn't occurred to me that I was doing anything wrong. I'm awfully sorry.' Then I got letters like, 'Monty, pay no attention. Tell that person to take a long walk off a short bridge.'"

Creating a trusting, friendly relationship, like sharing recipe tips, forged many a woman's bond. "So I think that was it: especially housewives who were tied down with children and that. The attitude seemed to be, they were so glad to have a friend to talk to them for half an hour," said Margetts, just like Shari Lewis and Lambchop who assured mom-viewers that they would all be back tomorrow. At their foundation, these shows were comforting, soothing, and reassuring. If a mom or housewife learned a thing or two to make their lives easier, all the better. At the same time, Monty never lost sight of her essential role, to sell. Like many a cooking show host of today who is not a chef, she was a conduit for information, which is neither better nor worse. And like every cooking show today, personality was the most important factor to her success. As any Food Network executive would tell you, find good talent, and you're way more than halfway there.

Formerly a radio comedian, Ernie Kovacs hosted a local cooking show in Philadelphia in 1950 called *Deadline for Dinner*, which he called "dead lion for dinner." The show consisted of cooking tips from guest chefs, but improvising once when a guest stood him up, Kovacs whipped up "eggs Scavok," his name spelled backwards. *Cooking with the Bontempi's* featured Fedora the cook, Pino the accordionist, and a dog. The husband and wife team prepared Italian meals, interviewed guests, and sang. These more jocular, lighthearted productions were a glimmer of the future of cooking shows.

Though not acknowledged as such in the early days of television, a nascent medium still finding its way, a genre was born—or rather, reborn. These early cooking programs were spawned out of practicality, but they seemed fitting as a part of the return to harmonious domestic life. They can be seen as the predecessors to the phenomenon we see today, but in many ways they were a different specimen altogether. No matter what the tone of the show, the advent of television merged the public and private domains in an unprecedented way, giving rise to transformative changes in the American home as well as the American public.

CHAPTER 2

La Cuisine and Canned Soup:
Dione Lucas vs. Convenience

Canned soups can be magnificent, the lowly meatball wildly
exciting, and old-fashioned corned beef hash an emotional
experience.

—*Cosmopolitan*, 1952

There is a tendency to whisk in and out of the kitchen, to be
lured by dishes that can be made most quickly. Cooking cannot be relegated to the same category as dishwashing or making beds.

—Dione Lucas

Home, Sweet Home

Just a few years after World War II, with soldiers returned from abroad
and Rosie the Riveter having resumed her place at the kitchen stove,
the heart of America could be found at home. As if a starter's gun had
gone off, the middle class migrated en masse to the suburbs where
newly ensconced neighbors unfailingly found themselves surrounded
by people just like them. To be sure, the late 1940s and the lion's share
of the 1950s are often remembered for the appreciation of conformity,
with images of Levittown and its brethren providing the cover art.

The postwar emphasis on family togetherness as well as the magnetic force of television itself converged to make home the "it" place. The 1950s saw a steep and rapid rise in saturation of the television medium as well as a greatly expanded programming repertoire. In 1940, there were fewer than 4,000 TV sets in the U.S., while, by 1960, there were some 45 million with 90 percent of homes owning at least one set. Sets were becoming ubiquitous—all the better to kill family conversation, said some critics, but they were ideal companions for housewives and a perfect forum for cooking instruction.

Both programming and advertisements portrayed compelling cultural models, the images people presumably wanted to see when they looked in the mirror. Sitcoms such as *Leave It to Beaver, Father Knows Best, Donna Reed, Make Room for Daddy,* and *The Adventures of Ozzie and Harriet* had all the elements of an ideal postwar family, and both real-life suburbanites and their TV counterparts were living in an American Dream world. Their protagonists included the dad/husband prototype who went to an unidentified but important job with his briefcase and who had little interaction with his children other than delivering stern admonishments or wise counsel. The mom/wife was devoted to housework and child rearing. The kids (never just one) were communicative and bright, if rambunctious at times. They all ate dinner together at the same time. Backyard fallout shelters were often the only things puncturing the perfect picture, a sign of the Cold War tremors that allowed Senator Joseph McCarthy so much airtime during the decade.

As Rockwellian as the family unit appeared to be, the postwar mentality also encompassed a taste for bright shiny newness befitting the richest population in the world. Americans clamored for new labor-saving technological advances, many of which found their way into the kitchen. As Laura Shapiro wrote in *Something from the Oven,* "Canned soup casseroles were thriving everywhere, and it was hard to beat the thrill of watching Reddi-wip unfurl in a swoosh from beneath a fingertip." Media images of the homemaker and the changing reality were increasingly at odds in the 1950s. New food products, their advertisements, and most cooking programs reinforced the traditional notions of gender roles. But more women were working outside the home than these stories acknowledged. Growing numbers of women were looking for ways to lighten their workload at home to make time for their own careers and leisure pursuits, so, despite the outmoded sensibility, they embraced the convenience of new products.

The national appeal of a bevy of new products meant that a greater number of people were eating and preparing the same foods the same way. Despite the rise of the suburb and the ensuing geographical dispersion, the likes of TV dinners and Jell-O salads—whose popularity and promotion were aided enormously by television—brought Americans closer together in a culinary sense and created a standardized quasi-national quasi-cuisine. The chemically creative but woefully soulless attitude toward food and cooking in the 1950s was unflatteringly yet accurately described by food historian Harvey Levenstein as a time of "culinary gridlock." Levenstein also noted that "this tie-in with the era's TV boom allowed consumers to rationalize the obvious lowering of dining standards with the excuse that they were intended to be eaten in untypical circumstances—in front of TV set—even though this was rarely the case."

At the same time, soldiers returned home from Europe and the Pacific with the scent of something new on their jackets. Though most troops had little occasion to dine in the areas they served, internationalism may have begun to pique the interest of the bourgeoisie. Armed with the cockiness of a superpower, Americans developed a desire to visit foreign countries and taste new, exotic foods. They felt bold but still apprehensive about European sophistication.

Sarah Bernhardt of the Kitchen Stove

James Beard's contemporary, the Cordon Bleu–trained Dione Lucas, may have seemed out of place when she first appeared on the small screen in 1947, but her TV longevity surpassed Beard's by a decade.

Imagine a formidable high school science teacher, one who scared the daylights out of you but for whom you had quivering respect. Your teacher handled poisonous chemicals and fragile test tubes with ease and confidence. She provoked the desire to gratify and impress; she was inspiring yet daunting. You wanted to flee from her yet also to be embraced against her bosom, which you were certain had an essence of humanity deep within. Lucas was like that. Despite her science teacher qualities, she was one of the rare proponents in the postwar period of cookery as art. As one newspaper headline read: "Dione Lucas Abhors Jiffy Techniques in Cookery: Believes 'more art and less chemistry' makes for finer cooking." The mentality of food and cooking commingling in the realm of art is a European sensibility, one that Lucas espoused intrinsically but that was only beginning to catch on with some segments in the U.S.

Throughout American history and to the present day, the art-or-science stance on food and cooking has waxed and waned and coexisted. Most Europeans, who have always embraced a peaceful union of the two perspectives, have long raised eyebrows when observing our attitudes toward gastronomy. Puritans though we were raised to be, our forefathers themselves expressed more passion for culinaria than most of their descendants in the first half of the twentieth century. Puritan minister Cotton Mather, Ben Franklin, George Washington, and Thomas Jefferson were ardent gastronomes. *The New Female Instructor*, a guide to household management for young ladies in good standing, first published in 1817, included an "Art of Cookery" section (though this was a matter of semantics given the real purpose of the book). During the Depression and World War II, when our collective minds should have been focused on the barest essentials, to fetishize cooking would have seemed frivolous. There were always those renegades, however, who preached art over science. In addition to Beard and Lucas, NBC's *Mystery Chef* enlisted viewers to "[a]lways be an artist at the stove, not just someone who cooks."

Amidst the swirl of frozen and canned foods, breakfast cereals, and electric appliances that heralded the changes in the world of cooking in the 1940s and 1950s, Lucas was an anachronism. While home economists, cookbook authors, and housewives themselves were pushing for economy in the kitchen during the postwar era, Lucas urged homemakers to spend even more time there. Now, however, that time was to be spent for their own fulfillment instead of completing a prescribed chore. After watching an episode of Dione Lucas on TV, a New Orleans newspaper reporter declared, "This seems to us like no ordinary cooking show." Similar to Beard, Lucas's show was nothing like the other cooking shows on at the time. As Lucas wrote in her *Cordon Bleu Cook Book*, "Preparation of a good food requires time, skill and patience, and the results mean the difference between eating to exist and the satisfaction derived from one of the major pleasures of life." She was a reminder that we needn't succumb to the forces of technological progress, and she glorified cooking in a way that made housewives feel like *artistes*. Lucas unapologetically saw herself as an artist and was known to refer to her spatula as her palette knife. She hoped to bequeath this attitude to home cooks. A 1949 *Life* magazine writer said that Lucas "argues that cooking is one of the few creative outlets left for a modern housewife and that a fine recipe, almost as intricate as a Bach fugue, deserves just as much rehearsed skill and unhurried execution." Though the *New York Post*'s Jo Coppola found it unusual that Lucas would comment that " '[t]he beef,' she said as she larded it with salt pork, tongue, and truffles, 'is so beautiful on its own,' " such observation about fundamental ingredients is standard for anyone discussing food today.

Born in Italy and raised in France and England, unschooled in the traditional sense, Lucas was trained first as a jewelry maker, then as a cello player. Cooking came as a necessity when her father became ill and she, the youngest of four children at age nineteen, had to look for work to bolster the family finances. She soon recognized cooking as an art form in its own right, and, as she wrote in the introduction of her *Cordon Bleu Cook Book*, "The preparation of good food is merely another expression of art, one of the joys of civilized living." In the 1930s Lucas was one of the first female graduates of the Cordon Bleu cooking school in Paris. Her ensuing professional experience, which consisted mainly of catering for an A-list clientele, included working as a hotel chef in Hamburg where she was often called upon to prepare Adolph Hitler his favorite meal—stuffed squab. Along with her friend Rosemary Hume, she founded the Au Petit Cordon Bleu restaurant and cooking school in London in 1933. When the Germans attacked London in 1940, she fled to North America with her two young sons and eventually ended up in New York. By 1942 she had opened another Cordon Bleu restaurant in Manhattan. There, in a 40-by-20-foot basement, she held classes for amateur gourmet pioneers, imparting the various intricacies of cooking in the celebrated Cordon Bleu way.

Lucas's mission was to bring her sophisticated skills and seemingly arcane knowledge to the good but culinarily disadvantaged people of New York. Cookbook author Barbara Kafka, who had worked with James Beard, said of Lucas, "She was the big deal in town." Indeed, Lucas, whose *Cordon Bleu Cookbook* was published in 1947, soon became too popular for her confining kitchen. She had brought her antimodern philosophy and no-monkey-business approach stateside and then—ironically via the ultra-modern television—nationwide. *The Dione Lucas Show*, originally called *To the Queen's Taste*, began as a local prime-time program on WCBS in New York in 1947. The decision to broadcast her teaching classes was practical and, arguably, benevolent—she simply wanted to reach more students. Her original program was shot on location in the same basement where she had already been teaching ladies and gents, the skilled and buffoons alike. Like Beard's *I Love to Eat*, Lucas's show appeared during the evening, which was unusual for any cooking show on network TV through the rest of the twentieth century. By the mid-1950s, the show was airing nationally five nights per week, and Lucas was traveling around the country giving her renowned cooking demonstration classes.

Lucas appeared on the airwaves just as they were first reaching American homes, when fewer than 1 percent of them had TV sets. According to 1949 Hooper ratings (the proto-Nielsens of the day),

Lucas edged out the glamour-laden *The Gloria Swanson Hour* (which itself included a segment featuring New York chefs) with twice as many viewers. Approximately 63,000 families watched Lucas's prime time show, which represented about half the number of television sets in the U.S. at the time. Granted, it was broadcast during prime time for much of its run, and in the pre-cable 1950s, there were only three or four programs on television for viewers to choose from at any given time. Even a bad show could generate a large audience under such favorable conditions. Her relative popularity, however, was telling.

Dione Lucas—artist and reluctant scientist in one culinary teacher.

It was a revelation for most people to watch someone cook—or do anything, for that matter—on a television screen. A 1948 *Variety* reviewer referred to Lucas's show as "a natural type of women's show for video . . . which gives femmes a chance to see a theoretical recipe being worked out in practice with perfect clarity." With the exception of Beard's short-lived show a year earlier or an occasional segment on a variety show, Lucas—who was much more popular and widely watched than Beard—was likely the first person most people saw cooking on national television. The *Variety* reviewer continued, "Mrs. Lucas has enough wit and charm to make this program acceptable to noncooking males. Under normal procedure, however, this type of show should be slotted for afternoon viewers." "Normal" is a bit hard to figure in 1948, since TV was brand new to home viewers. Presumably the reviewer meant that under normal societal expectations, this program should be shown during the day when only women were around. But, sure enough, women weren't the only ones who watched. Men might have been "abnormal" or incidental viewers, given the paucity of programs and number of sets in the house, but Lucas caught their attention, too. *New York Times* television critic Jack Gould offered Lucas's 1958 program *Gourmet Club* a backhanded compliment, implying that Lucas was not the usual airhead in an apron.

> If the average cooking show makes the gentleman viewer shudder a trifle, Dione Lucas . . . may prove an exception. The lady obviously knows what she is about, and her directions are so specific that they almost have the fascination of a science. If, incidentally, she inspires a distaff companion to more varied efforts in the kitchen, it is well worth the masculine initiative to tune her in.

The masculine initiative surely generated a few "darling, why don't you make that?" comments, too.

As a television personality Lucas's appearance was game for commentary. After she slimmed down a bit at one point, a New York City police officer on his beat near the Cordon Bleu Restaurant reportedly stopped by to tell Lucas that he and his wife, both television fans, "thought she looked a lot better for it." In May of 1949, Angelica Gibbs of the *New Yorker* wrote, "Her undeniable good looks are, rather, of the type favored by painters of the Italian Renaissance school. Her eyes, which are hazel, sparkle only on rare occasions, and her chin is sharply defined. She wears her straight, reddish-brown hair pulled ruthlessly back from her face and wound into an enormous bun on her neck." She brings to mind the stern shopkeeper Mrs. Olsen from *Little House on the Prairie*, not quite an artist's muse. Nevertheless, she had a powerful presence, and it is a challenge not to be transfixed by her powerful presence. As Jo Coppola wrote of *Gourmet Club*, "even if you can't boil water, you'll find Miss Lucas at the skillet an impressive sight."

Though art was her métier, she employed a daunting meticulousness. She coached viewers through recipes with *precise* step-by-step instruction. All well and good, but she also managed to give the impression, with her science-teacher demeanor, British accent, and the easy, dexterous way she tossed an omelet (her specialty) in its pan, that this was "la cuisine," and cooking for elites. Many of her recipes were complex and time-consuming—not exactly everyday fare for Betty homemaker. She sprinkled in some helpful hints—for example: put flour and sugar in small containers that are easily accessible instead of big canisters on hard to reach shelves—which were welcomed by beginners and the crazy busy (a yet undefined but existing demographic). But watching with laser focus and even taking notes was far from enough to be able to imitate her. As Jo Coppola wrote, "I must say that an evening cooking show—especially one conducted by Miss Lucas—is an excellent idea. At least the audience can get the details of her culinary masterpieces and then have a good night's rest to sort of work up to trying them."

Her intentions were charitable, but unlike her successor, Julia Child, who made it acceptable if not advantageous to blunder in the kitchen, Lucas had that dubious skill of unwittingly provoking palpable anxiety. One of her cookbook coauthors, Marion Gorman, recalled one of Lucas's sons telling a story about Lucas making a soufflé on her show. When she removed the paper collar from it, the soufflé collapsed. "The star was utterly mortified," wrote Gorman, "but the incident precipitated a deluge of mail that continued for weeks from happy viewers, pleased to know that Dione Lucas could make a mistake." She mastered dishes like lemon meringue pie, Caesar salad, chicken Kiev, mimosa salad (beets and vegetables with hard-boiled eggs and mayonnaise), gnocchi Parisienne, and sole Marguery. As New York *Daily News*'s Ben Gross wrote, "She's a caviar, champagne and crepes suzettes gal, and her intent is to make you as expert in concocting the deluxe dishes presiding over the ranges in the town's most elegant food dispensaries. Watch her—and before you know it, you may be an Escoffier." While much of her repertoire was French-leaning, she also made meatloaf, veal goulash, fish shashlik, ravioli, baked Alaska, and apple pie, referring to the latter as "the traditional *American* (Ah-MED-i-kin) apple pie, the most beautiful dessert you've ever had in your life." Lucas would sometimes unabashedly share her preferences, while also revealing current food trends. "Never use olive oil," she commanded while demonstrating how to make salad dressing. "It's much too strong." It's hard to imagine, but there was apparently a time when shoppers didn't belabor origin or grades of extra virgin.

Lucas never appeared to break a sweat, despite her constraining, starched poplin blouses, apron cinched at the waist, and pleated skirt billowing out in a Mrs. Olsen, bustle-suggesting way. Her directions were often so regimented and devoid of conversational annotation that she sounded like she was just dictating a recipe—or penance. Brimming with injunctions and admonitions, many of her directions were cautionary—if you don't do this, you'll get a lumpy dough; if you don't do that, it will taste horrid. The dark forecasting could either turn off an inexperienced cook or provide a comforting structure welcomed by many a desperate newbie cook or insecure homemaker. Milly Abrams, a young housewife in New York City in 1952, was inspired rather than deterred by Lucas's prowess. "Dione Lucas was the first person I ever saw cooking on TV," she said. "I was a Jewish girl brought up in the Bronx. This was cooking you knew nothing about. Dione was an innovator."

In one particularly awe-inspiring episode, Lucas made an apple strudel using a recipe requiring enormous confidence and circus-freak skill. Lucas went at it with the nonchalance of someone about to make one-bowl brownies. Among other feats, the recipe required stretching dough over the edges of her work table, like a fitted sheet over a mattress. That which would incite tears or cursing in one's own kitchen did not even elicit a slight sheen of perspiration from Lucas. Watching Lucas might answer the question as to why people who don't cook would ever watch a cooking show. Though she was a real woman undertaking real tasks, she was transformed by the magic of TV into a performer. Jo Coppola described her as "a far cry from the meat-and-potato cooks who populated the channels. . . . Even then, with all the competition, Miss Lucas was in a class by herself. She is, you might say, the Sarah Bernhardt of the kitchen stove."

Lucas's instructions were laced with deliciously dry witticisms, seamlessly woven into her tutorial and delivered perfectly deadpan. In fact, she rarely cracked a smile. When making omelets, she told viewers to "add a thousand grains of salt. Put it in your hand so you can see you've got a thousand grains." When making crepes suzette, she coached, "Use a little rum, or a lot of rum, depending on the conditions of the bottle—and of yourself." In the spirit of European gourmandise, she offered: "If you get distracted, if someone wants to ask you a very important question or you want to read the headlines, then you'll get a very good goulash because you've added more cream than you meant to. If it's a heaping cup of sour cream, it's very good"—she kisses her fingers—"If it's a cup, it's good. If it's three-quarters of a cup"—she screws up her face and shakes her head "—no, no good." There's the sparkle in the eye.

Other instructions, however, were more ambiguous. After mixing pastry dough and forming it into a ball, she instructed the viewer to beat it one hundred times. "You'll get a very good strudel if you do it one hudred times," she said, as she whacked it forcefully onto her table. "You'll get a very mediocre dough if you do it ninety-eight times." It was impossible to tell if she was earnest. It's easy to imagine a young housewife in 1953 dutifully noting the tip like an eager pupil, counting intently as she beat her own dough, then wondering halfway through if she was being taken for a ride while still worrying that she had lost count.

Likewise, when making chicken pot pie, she told the viewer to pat the kneaded dough twice, which she did, as if it were a baby's bottom. "Is she serious?" viewers must have wondered. Best just to do it, they probably concluded like doubting Catholics, just in case. Such moments of secretly elbowing the viewer were part of her charm. "I get her," one might think. Her subtle, semi-jokes enhanced an exclusive feeling of intimacy with us, the viewers, a crucial element to any good television show host. Once a viewer got to know Lucas, he or she would recognize her playfulness. Reading the words of Marion Gorman, one might conclude that the sarcasm about precision might have been Lucas's way of flying in its face. "Some of the recipes she used called for 'a little of this or that ingredient' (although in teaching, she had to but often was frustrated in having to be precise.)," wrote Gorman. As Lucas wrote in her *Cordon Bleu Cook Book*, "The kitchen is the heart of the Home and should not be regarded as a scientific laboratory where each ingredient is accurately measured, much as the druggist compounds a formula."

Lucas's scholarly and genteel air was unusual for a cooking show host—sui generis, she might herself say. Before kneading a ball of dough in one episode, she suggested removing "impedimenti" as she took off her watch. When making French onion soup, she lectured on the history of the soup's origin via Louis XIV. You could imagine how she operated in her restaurant, as she would hand bowls and pans to an employee offstage with a polite yet authoritative, "If someone would be kind enough to take that, thank you very much." She signed off her shows with, "I do hope you've enjoyed this demonstration, and as always I thank you for your patience. Good-bye and God bless you all." She commanded respect, yet she did so diplomatically, indirectly, and ingratiatingly. Such conspicuous politeness and formality can be forbidding and is probably not what most people raised in regular, messy families are used to. She would likely cluck her tongue disapprovingly at Emeril's "bams" and everybody else's "likes" and "y' knows"—not to mention blanch visibly at Rachael Ray's "yum-o's."

Writer and former production coordinator for *The Dione Lucas Show* Rose Dosti wrote in the *Los Angeles Times* that Lucas was a "no nonsense type with an intimidating air of Captain Cook, [who] often snatched the dish out of the inept hands of her charges and finished it off with a proper professional flourish. No dish would leave her presence without a final Dione Lucas stamp." Her erudite and worldly manner may have beguiled those viewers who were pushovers for her European background. According to food and pop culture writers Jane and Michael Stern in their book *American Gourmet*, she was a purist, playing "the role of television's supreme European epicure; and for those pioneers of the gourmet revolution who sought authentic and precise instruction more than entertainment, she remained a beacon of culinary excellence."

Despite abundant evidence to the contrary, Lucas was not a snob; she did not insist on fine china or blather on about proper etiquette. She didn't *mean* to seem so posh. Lucas's preferred meal was allegedly a broiled hamburger and tossed salad. Because of her Cordon Bleu indoctrination and formal presentation, she could seem hard at first blush, but she was more flexible than she let on. She was not so prim that she wouldn't illustrate a cut of meat via her own hip. She was capable of humility. When it was necessary, for certain strudel-type acrobatics, to put her back to the camera, she self-deprecatingly excused her "large back." While there was a sense that she would cuff you with a rolling pin if you were too afraid to try something—she clearly valued fortitude and likely did not suffer cowards gladly—she promised challenge and, if you had it in you, a good time. On an episode of *Gourmet Club*, she ordered the show's producer, Horace Sutton, to bring over some red wine to thin a sauce. Jo Coppola reported Lucas's reaction in the *New York Post*: "'That,' she said as he sprinkled some into the sauce, 'is the most Scottish tablespoon I ever saw in my life. A little more wine,' she commanded."

Similar to many cooking shows of the period, Lucas's shows were sponsored by utility companies, her patrons being the Brooklyn Union Gas Co. and Caloric Appliance Corp. "She didn't have the whole 30 minutes to give to the beef as she devoted quite a bit of time selling gas ranges for the sponsor," wrote Coppola. *The Dione Lucas Show* opened with that especially generic, jaunty, canned 1950s TV show theme music and was visually accompanied by a simple animation of a pan over a flame. Text rolling over a red background read, "To encourage the American housewife to enhance one of her most creative talents, by bringing glamour to the dinner table through artistry in the kitchen with the aid of GAS—the Modern Cooking Fuel."

In a typical episode, just after the opener, the camera showed a close-up of Lucas cooking an omelet. She silently finished the procedure, looked into the camera, gave a slight bow, and said, "Welcome to my beautiful Caloric gas kitchen." To all appearances of her own free will born of genuine love for her stove (not the sponsor's directive), Lucas made quite a show of periodically reminding viewers about her beautiful Caloric gas kitchen. Occasionally she would stop whatever she was doing and provide a full advertisement for her stove. She made promises, which would seem utterly forced and insidious today: "If you use gas, you'll have a good result every time." She called the Caloric gas range the "best, easiest, and prettiest to cook with" and harped on its even heat. When she gave a recipe's cooking temperature, the camera would zoom in on the oven dial, with the Caloric logo in its full glory. Lucas was dubbed the "nation's leading saleswoman of gas appliances" in a 1953 promotional packet for utilities companies. The text indicated that a "national TV show [was] available to utilities for sponsorship at the local level as part of a complete package to sell gas cooking to the American housewife." While she was also called "TV's queen of culinary experts" by the same "Operation Blue Flame" promotion team, it was clear that like the other shows of the time, the actual content of the show was a side dish to accompany the main course of product promotion.

On another episode, Lucas promised viewers she would show them a trick but that first they had to "go out and buy a gas range" to enact it themselves. She clearly and slowly and teacherly (more kindergarten now than high school) enunciated the words *gas* and *range*. At the end of that same episode, after making an apple pie, she even addressed the stove directly: "Now I don't know what you think, Mr. Caloric Gas range, but I think it's a pretty beautiful apple pie and I think you'll agree with me." In the intimidating apple strudel episode, Lucas pulled the dough so thin that the checked tablecloth of her work table was clearly visible through it. To both flaunt the feat and appease the sponsor, she held a print ad for an automatic Caloric gas range under a piece of the overhanging dough and read it aloud. It was a clever plug opportunity that had the mischievous distinction of being invented by Lucas herself.

Lucas did not believe in shortcuts. (Unable to resist the powerful consumer forces, however, she developed her own line of canned soups by 1956.) Nor did she believe that women belonged in the kitchen as opposed to the workplace. Unlike her peers, she encouraged women to feel empowered by their kitchen skills instead of bound to them. Fans appreciated Lucas reducing gourmet cooking to simple ingredients, prepped, assembled, and ready for cooking on her "readiness tray," perhaps a concession to the convenience-seekers. Part of her appeal, they said, was that her menus related to the working woman as well as to the classic dinner-party giver. Detractors said the opposite, that her cooking was too highbrow and complicated and was only feasible for already skilled cooks with an abundance of free time.

Reminiscences of Lucas vary from adulatory to scathing. Presumably it was ever thus that anyone in the limelight would be seen through garishly colored lenses. *New York Times* food writer Marian Burros called her a great showman and a great teacher. Laura Shapiro, on the other hand, speculated that Lucas wasn't a teacher at heart.

"She could be actively dislikable," said Barbara Kafka. "Technically she was extremely good, she worked like a beast. You could see her in her restaurant. She was standing there, hardly a young woman, veins popping, making omelets herself. She had the technique but not the charm, no sense of theater." Kafka obliquely compared her to James Beard, who she conceded had the requisite charm and talent but an inability to convey it on television. "Her show was terrible," she said of Lucas. Of both Beard's and Lucas's shows Kafka said, "They were more liable to poison something than promote it."

Julia Child's biographer, Noel Riley Fitch, wrote, "Lucas was a crisp and neurotic woman whose apprentices thought her bossy. Others alleged that she was a veritable soap opera of eccentricities, dramatics and migraines, exacerbated by drugs and alcohol." The suspicion that alcohol might have been a problem for Lucas was a perennial. Marian Burros wrote in *Cooking for Comfort*, "When she taught before a large group, she loved to sample whatever alcohol was to be used in cooking—directly from the bottle—more than once."

In 1970, Lucas developed plans for another television show that never came to fruition. Unfortunately, Lucas's life ended in business chaos and illness. Though she enjoyed a relatively long period of success in her field, she left little lasting impression. She was well-respected by her peers—James Beard called her a "superb teacher" and "one that can measure up against the masters," the *New York Times*'s Craig Claiborne called her "the high priestess of high cookery," and as another newspaper article warned, "She is a cooking mistress no self-respecting gourmet dare ignore." But history dared to ignore her. "Her influence never ran very deep," Laura Shapiro wrote. It's quite likely that Food Network junkie, TV history buff, or all-around know-it-all though you may be, you have just been reading about her for the first time. By the time Julia Child arrived on the scene and galvanized the cooking show genre, Lucas was virtually eclipsed.

Maybe it was just bad timing, in terms of the convenience food craze and the newness of television. But by any account, Lucas was at the very least instrumental in beginning to popularize French and gourmet cooking in the U.S.—a decade before Julia Child had her way with it. Child herself referred to Lucas as "the mother of French cooking in America." Lucas's universal appeal could largely be attributed to the fact that viewers liked watching the artist at work, an element that in part explains the sustained appeal of cooking shows over the course of the next fifty years.

Magazines of the Air

Women's programming was big business in the 1950s, and the lady of the house was the dream marketing target. "Formats with feminine appeal" were popular with viewers and broadcasters, and the home-making show was the most common type. According to a 1952 Iowa State College survey, almost three quarters of the country's 108 operating television stations were producing homemaking programs, and more than half of those presented food as a subject. In addition to food and cooking, other topics included clothing, home furnishings, time management, gardening, childcare, hygiene, and family relations.

As Lynn Spigel wrote in *Make Room for TV*, her treatise of women's daytime viewing habits, television was in itself a "consumer educator," teaching housewives not only to consume advertisers' products but how to consume television itself. Likewise, *What Women Watched* author Marsha Cassidy said:

> Cooking shows of the late 1940s and 1950s served as an important way to draw women to their TV sets during the day. They were also easy to sponsor and self-sustaining economically. During this period, viewers frequently had access to only one or two channels. These were important reasons why the early cooking shows became a standard genre of American television.

Programmers tried to transmute the popularity of women's magazines like *Ladies' Home Journal*, *Good Housekeeping*, and *McCall's* into TV shows. The concept of a magazine-style format in broadcasting has been credited to Ida Bailey Allen's radio show in the 1920s. The nature of broadcasting was conceived by some radio programmers as a magazine of the air partly because many stations were owned by newspaper companies. The idea regained popularity on television in the 1950s, when networks starting controlling programming and sponsors couldn't afford whole shows. Much of women's programming lent itself to segments, corresponding to the projected rhythm of an average woman's weekday at home. In one survey, however, a housewife said she had work to do and didn't have time to sit and watch TV—she could be cleaning the kitchen instead of watching someone telling her how to do it. According to anthropologist Sidney Mintz, despite labor-saving appliances, housewives spent more time washing clothes, cooking, and shopping than their mothers or grandmothers. Sociologist Juliet Schor has noted similar patterns. "Between the 1920s and 1960s, food preparation fell almost ten hours a week," wrote Schor,

> but was offset by a rise in shopping, managerial tasks, and child care. Certain innovations were labor saving on their own, but led to new tasks. The refrigerator eliminated the need for daily shopping and storing ice at home, but helped drive the door-to-door vendor out of business, thereby contributing to the rise of the supermarket with its self-service and greater travel time.

A homemaking show's format supposedly allowed a housewife to drop in and out of the show without committing to a full thirty or sixty minutes, conveniently allowing her to tend to household tasks in pieces. As Robert Hammel Stewart wrote of the women's daytime variety program format, "[A]long with the slower pace is a lesser emphasis on the visual aspects of the program. The housewife can do her work while she listens and enjoys the program without the insistent demand that she also watch imposed by visual antics." Perhaps that was the idea, but the visual is what TV is all about. With cooking, especially, "seeing is believing" as Susan Adams, host of *Susan Adams' Kitchen Fare*, broadcast on the DuMont Network in New York, Pennsylvania, Connecticut, and New Jersey in 1952, avowed. Adams's viewers wrote in that once they had seen a recipe prepared on screen, they could do it right themselves. Even though we may often leave the set on just for the companionship of sound today, there is little doubt that women did not treat television like radio, captivated as everyone was by the introduction of moving pictures into their very homes. TV demands visual attention.

Drumming up fresh "visual antics" was and is the job of every television programmer. Hosted by "editor-in-chief" Arlene Francis and her junior editor Hugh Downs, *Home*, though not strictly a cooking or even purely homemaking show, provides an apt illustration. The brainchild of NBC president Sylvester "Pat" Weaver, *Home* relied on the increasingly popular magazine show format and an unusual set to emphasize it. A *New York Times* ad for *Home* called it "[t]he electronic magazine for women." Weaver had introduced the morning talk show *Today* in 1951, anchored by Dave Garroway and the late-night talk show *Tonight* in 1954, hosted by Steve Allen. Both shows relied on celebrities to grab viewers, and even though *Home* was a midday women's program, it followed the same proven strategy with familiar faces and casual conversation. The show, which first aired on March 1, 1954, was on live every weekday. *Home* addressed the traditional homemaking segments—gardening, fashion, beauty, home decorating, child rearing—but placed them in an uber-modern circular revolving stage. Francis, known for her panelist role on the game show *What's My Line* and radio and Broadway stints, assumed the editor-in-chief role with aplomb. Seated comfortably in her swivel chair while her associates performed before her, like writers or underling editors pitching story ideas, she thoughtfully and pointedly removed her glasses while speaking, taking the air of a real-life editor who goes to important meetings all day but rarely has to roll up her sleeves.

Home also embodied all the trappings of what we continue to associate with talk/news shows. Poking-fun banter ensued between Francis and Downs, similar to what goes on with Meredith and Matt or Regis and Kelly. Lawrence Laurent panned the show in the *Washington Post*, criticizing its dumbing down of Arlene Francis as a purveyor of "piffle." Laurent wrote, "Miss Francis, in person a woman of great calm and a biting sense of humor, is dedicated at *Home* to imitating the over 80 women commentators in American radio and TV."

Laurent also critiqued the show's cooking segment. "There is also Kit Kinne, an experienced home economist," he wrote. "She . . . is slowly catching on to the nonstop bombardment *Home* requires in food demonstrations. All the recipes, I might add, are quite simple; inevitably described as 'glamorous, lots of fun to make, easy to prepare.'" Food featured on the show ranged from meatloaf to pots de crème. On the show's final episode, a be-toqued Chef Philip cut some cake for tea. Meanwhile Francis extolled, "Chef Philip has made some of the most imaginative and intricate dishes that have ever been put forth for human consumption. He is an artist supreme. . . . We don't know what we're going to do about adding a little MSG and a little *bo*kay *gar*ni from now on." Downs waxed equally hyperbolic: "I think you're the only man living who can whip up a gourmet's delight out of a hamburger or frankfurter or anything." Much of the food prepared on the show was not for the homemaker but for people interested in what chefs do in restaurants, revealing a budding social trend.

For part of *Home's* three-year run, the food department was overseen by Poppy Cannon. As a popular magazine food writer and editor, she was deemed the "can opener queen" and became one of the best-known faces of the zealous appetite for convenience. In the 1950s, kitchen shortcuts were novel, sought-after, and thought to be clever, making tipsters like Cannon into heroines. Canned tomato sauce, canned beef gravy, canned cream of mushroom soup, and bouillon cubes all figured prominently in her *Can-Opener Cookbook* recipes. A store-bought angel food cake is an ingredient in a dessert recipe. Her final chapter, "How to open . . . ," is concerned with the types of can openers available and what to look for in a good one. "As any vaudevillian will tell you," she wrote, "the opener is crucial." James Beard described Cannon as a "very brilliant advertising woman" and a "commercialist." Cannon, while living a sophisticated, intellectual life with her husband, NAACP president Walter White, likely embraced such a description. In a 1952 issue of *Cosmopolitan* she wrote, "Armed with a can opener, I become the artist-cook, the master, the creative chef."

There was a veneer of glamour to the set and in the gestures of the hosts, as if it were a cocktail hour in the middle of the day. A stark departure from the buttoned-up, dry, home economical quality of local programs, what *Home* did that other women's programming did not do was to take seriously women's right to be entertained—and feel part of the larger world—in addition to providing a service. Francis addressed divorce and the inner city school crisis as well as traveling on assignment to Europe and Asia. Homemaking bits were mixed in with segments on civic and world affairs—Middle East unrest, segregation, community activism, and interviews with writers, artists, and political leaders.

Charlotte Curtis, reporting on the 1961 American Women in Radio and Television convention for the *New York Times* wrote, "Today's woman, according to television critics as well as audience analysts, is interested in politics, economics, art, music, drama, housing and foreign news, as well as fashion, food, home furnishings and teaching Johnny to read." Where Ellen Pennell's *Women on TV* manual (published the very year that *Home* premiered) enthusiastically touted the potential for women in television, Pennell's was a specific and imminently outmoded exercise—though she probably did not expect her acolytes to aspire beyond the local level. Emphasis on the domestic arena alone could be a death knell for a national show and a career-stopper for a woman. It was now imaginable that women could aim higher, perhaps even to executive. "Most of the women seemed hopeful about the future," wrote Curtis, "but many of them still remember the not too distant past when a woman's place was in the radio or television kitchen."

According to Marsha Cassidy, *Home* promoted "upper-middle-brow aspirations" with its urbane style and attention to intellectual topics. There was a resistance to such aspirational programming, however. NBC executive Charles Barry was concerned about the highbrow content and wrote to a colleague in 1954: "Maybe you can improve tastes, but gosh would somebody please tell me how to cook corned beef and cabbage without any smell?" A casualty of the network's desire to target a more mass audience, Poppy Cannon was let go from the show because her recipes—mostly French—were deemed too sophisticated for the NBC viewers. Her vichyssoise, however, was made with frozen mashed potatoes, a leek, and a can of Campbell's cream of chicken soup. Lynn Spigel wrote: "The television producer could educate the housewife beyond her means, but only through mixing upper-class fantasy with tropes of averageness." In other words, keep those dreams in check, ladies. A viewer may be able to emulate one of Kit Kinne's recipes, but she certainly doesn't live in a Park Avenue apartment. Similarly, it's fine to see Martha Stewart making potato salad, nevertheless when she not only tells you that she grew all the ingredients herself, but then shows you the very Giverny-esque garden where they were born and plucked, you may—some programmers fear—throw up your hands and stop watching. Others understand that the dream is part of the attraction. It's the reflection of who we are situated beside the reflection of who we want to be that seems to be the magical combination. This is no less true today.

Feminine Mystique

The 1950s have been flattened and pressed into a scrapbook, repeatedly characterized as too conformist, uncreative, suppressed, and all-around boring. Of course, things were not so simple. Even Norman Rockwell addressed fomenting racial issues. As writer and law professor Ben Stein enumerated in an article called "Those Fabulous Fifties," the decade was far from stagnant. Nation-changing activities were underway in every area of life, politically, technologically, and culturally. The Korean War, the Rosenbergs' execution, the Brown v. Board of Education decision, Rosa Parks, Sputnik, Army-McCarthy hearings, *The Caine Mutiny*, *Cat on a Hot Tin Roof*, Miles Davis, Elvis Presley, Jack Kerouac—hardly a banal lot.

Likewise, women's roles became flattened and pressed. As technology historian Ruth Schwartz Cowan wrote, "[T]he industrial revolution in the home seems to have heightened the emotional context of the work, until a woman's sense of self-worth became a function of her success at arranging bits of fruit to form a clown's face in a gelatin salad." This is the era from whence the *Feminine Mystique* sprang, Betty Friedan's revelation about the stultifying life of a housewife, describing the experience of her peers. Clearly there was more beneath the surface. This may have seemed several steps back from first wave feminism, but we can imagine the calm before the storm, gearing up for wave two.

In retrospect, the competing messages sent to homemakers are manifest. One set of messages implied that cooking was difficult and time-consuming and prevailed upon housewives to take full advantage of the new crop of convenience foods and appliances. Another set of dispatches made it seem that programmers and advertisers were conspiring to make housework seem like a lark. Programs were increasingly formatted to combine labor with leisure, and advertisements portrayed happy, nicely dressed, satisfied women undertaking or just completing a household task and sitting down to enjoy a magazine or relax with a cup of coffee. Though many people today have televisions in their kitchen, the attempted introduction of the TV-stove, an example of the "conflation of labor and leisure" as Lynn Spigel noted, took the cake.

In total, the expectation that women's place was in the home, perhaps because it was in danger of being challenged, was reemphasized in every arena. The persuasive campaign extended beyond making housework look fun. Just as housewives in the previous decade were deemed patriotic as they toiled away in their kitchens, so housewives in the 1950s served as conduits to display national progress. Technological advances gave license to put emphasis on the kitchen. And the famous 1959 "Kitchen Debate" between Vice President Richard Nixon and Soviet Premier Nikita Khrushchev illustrated the place that the kitchen held in the American psyche.

Home in many ways typified the 1950s in its unwitting mimicry of the confusing female role models that were bred during the era. The show spoke to a woman viewer because it recognized that she was more than just a mother and a wife. As Cassidy wrote, "Francis was ideally situated to uphold emerging standards of suburban domesticity and consumerism at the base of postwar womanhood, but her urbanity and her reputation as a career woman destabilized the feminine mystique on a daily basis." That is to say, she was all right and all wrong for the part. On the one hand, she presented useful service items to women viewers, but simultaneously her unabashed urbanity and elegance—her off-the-shoulder dresses, her rich voice, her effortless segueing from toddler care to an interview with Pearl Buck—had the potential to alienate. In addition, wrote Cassidy, the "modernist stage set . . . weakened homey naturalism."

Home was a compilation of mixed messages that either mirrored or added to the ambiguity simmering beneath the surface of many a Helene Curtis–hairsprayed coiffure. It could be argued that the show lacked a model for a suburban woman's real life, but it could also be lauded (and criticized) for exposing her to alternatives. The societal expectations that she would be a good housewife rubbed up against the itchiness to be more than that, creating a discomfort that had few outlets for release. Hadn't she been in the workforce just ten years before, and hadn't her grandmother gotten out of the house more?

The entire middle class itself was experiencing an indeterminate transformation. A healthy postwar economy led to increased social status for a number of people and traditional social hierarchies were beginning to fray. Both men and women were beginning to question their roles as they entered into the 1960s.

Women's service shows themselves were in question. *Home* lived a short life, especially in comparison to its bookends *Today* and *Tonight*, and was cancelled in 1957. Advertisers and network executives put their heads down and tried to learn from it. Some concluded that cooking just didn't do well on TV. "Women in the audience never seemed to like getting recipes when they had to write them down—even when they also got a demonstration of how to cook it," said one. "I think these shows [cooking and fashion] failed because women want to have something they can refer back to for instruction. And, of course, that means magazines and newspapers." So in 1962, some influential players were calling time of death for the television cooking show. Though the observations were valuable and accurate to a large degree, it was Arlene Francis who seemed to truly understand and foretell a turning point: "I think that perhaps women just want to be entertained—not instructed—on television." Women didn't want to take notes like they were in class, they wanted to be entertained. And well, cooking just isn't entertaining, is it? Less than a year later, however, Julia Child was on the air and didn't leave for three decades. Somehow, with cooking as her only topic, Julia Child managed to satisfy the desire for both learning and entertainment.

MIDDLE PERIOD
(1963–1992)

CHAPTER 3

Julia Child and Revolution in the Kitchen

Now it was time to give television a whirl.

—Julia Child

Accidental Queen of Small Screen Cuisine

When conjuring up a historical (that is, pre–Food Network) lineup of television chefs, it is usually Julia Child's name that first passes anyone's lips. She certainly didn't mean to obliterate anyone, but her popularity and uniqueness were such that all those before her and many of her contemporaries and even successors have paled in comparison. Every cooking show since the advent of *The French Chef* in one way or another tips a hat to Child. Journalists and scholars have spent much energy noting her contributions to American culture, but her contribution to television cooking itself is not to be overlooked. Though many people mistakenly assume she was the first television chef, in some sense they are right.

The way in which she came to television was a mere twist of fate. Child (an American), along with Louise Bertholle and Simone Beck (both French women), had published the now-classic tome *Mastering the Art of French Cooking* in 1961. One of the places where she showcased it was *I've Been Reading*, a local book review program on Boston's public station, WGBH. "Julia was coming through town promoting her book," recalled *French Chef* producer Russ Morash, then a cameraman at WGBH.

Morash remembered the first conversation he had with Julia. He happened to answer the phone for the producer one day, and "she called the office and said that she would require a hot plate. And I said, 'well madam'—I didn't know her of course—I said, 'that would be highly irregular, I've never seen any props like that being used. It's a pretty straight laced show.'" Though *Mastering* was perhaps interesting to the *Gourmet* magazine types who might watch public television book review programs, promoting a cookbook on the show was also highly irregular and certainly, Morash thought, this was a one-off lark. "I thought she was a real pip, and I passed the note on that she required a hot plate."

"She comes on the show," said Morash,

She has a proper omelet pan, which in Boston in those days was totally an unknown quantity as were fresh fish, leeks, ground pepper, all of these were to come following her lead, but, at the time, unh unh, you wouldn't find any of that in Boston. She made Professor Duhamel [the show's host] an omelet, and it was a big hit. There but for the grace of god, you know, collisions occur and nobody sees them. It's amazing how the whole thing came about.

Morash is one who thinks of her as *the* pioneer. "There was no cooking on television before Julia, really, and there wasn't for a long time thereafter." Describing the home economist–hosted programs he said, "Every TV studio had a kitchen because they were peddling food items. They were doing cheap cookery programs. When the kitchen wasn't doing anything, like selling appliances, you could do cookery stuff." He even dismissed the one Child herself referred to as the mother of French cooking in America: "They make a big deal out of Dione Lucas and all this. There was nothing."

Certainly there is a difference between "nothing" and *nothing*. Modifying Morash's view—and he is not alone in holding it—Child was inarguably the first of her kind. She was one of the first to present a purely food-centered cooking show as opposed to a homemaking show, and, at the same time, as if by accident, a host-centered cooking show. Of her antecedents in the genre, she is most closely related to Lucas and Beard, both of whom had distinctive personalities and advocated fine food and cooking as a non-chore. But Beard's personality did not translate to TV and Lucas's could be perceived as off-putting. And they both suffered from showing up too early to the party. They just didn't have all the essential elements, whereas Child very much did. She was the first serious cook who was fun to watch and who arrived at the right moment. Geoffrey Drummond, who later produced a *Cooking with Master Chefs* series with Child, said, "Julia Child was the first iconic television cook. She opened cooking for a generation of people who had gotten *The Joy of Cooking* as wedding gifts but here they got to see somebody cooking beyond backyard down home American cooking."

With Morash tapped as producer-director, WGBH decided it would make a few pilot episodes with this unlikely TV personality "to see whether there might be a real cooking audience out there over the airwaves," wrote Child in her 1968 *The French Chef Cookbook*. The first pilot episode appeared in February 1962. There was most certainly an audience, one who almost seemed to be waiting for Child to show up.

"The pilots were immediately successful," said Morash. "People who'd seen it thought she was a real eccentric character from Cambridge. But classy. She was very clever because she used very simple recipes, and if you followed the directions you'd get an instant success." On the three pilot episodes, she demonstrated omelettes, coq au vin, and a noncollapsible soufflé. "People thought she was British even though she was from Pasadena," said Drummond. This confusion may have added more cachet to the host than a regular-sounding Californian would evoke, and the fact that she seemed both vaguely continental *and* accessible added to her appeal.

Child described herself in the *French Chef Cookbook* in retrospect, acknowledging the improbability of such a phenomenon: "There was this woman tossing French omelettes, splashing eggs about the place, brandishing big knives, panting heavily as she careened around the stove, and WGBH-TV lurched into educational television's first cooking program."

WGBH queried viewers about the pilots with results that spurred not only hefty sacks of letters riddled with refrains of "more please!" but additional monetary contributions to the station. "Not only did I get a wonderfully refreshing new approach to the preparation and cooking of said poultry," wrote Irene from Cambridge as she praised Child's coq au vin recipe, "I loved the way she projected over the camera directly to me the watcher. . . . And her to-do about the brandy-firing was without parallel for that rare tongue-in-cheek sort of humor the viewer longs for in this day of the over-rehearsed ad-lib. . . . I certainly will be watching for another Pots and Pans wing-ding by Julia Child."

A nerve had been touched, and Morash was sent out to do a thirteen-episode series. The first regular show aired February 11, 1963. Among those pioneering episodes, Child demonstrated boeuf bourguignon, French onion soup, lobster a l'Americaine, and crepes suzette. When he watches them occasionally now, Morash said, "It's as good today as it was then. She really grabbed onto the camera and believed that the camera was a person, which is the whole key to communication on television." Despite her enormous accomplishment in writing *Mastering*, it wasn't until her TV show that the book really sold in great quantity and she was catapulted to stardom. Just as radio had made Betty Crocker, TV made Julia Child. Unlike Betty, Julia was very real but in many ways just as much a character and certainly a pop culture icon. Biographer Laura Shapiro equates Child's true peers not to other homemaking show hosts but to Lucille Ball, Steve Allen, and Milton Berle, other television performers who made a lasting impression on the culture.

She was tall (six foot two) and, while attractive, was not of the mold favored by Hollywood producers. She was sometimes awkward and never tried to feign a TV persona. Child biographer Noel Riley Fitch wrote, "Luckily, she found an audience before the television image-makers could discover that she was 'all wrong' for television. Certainly today she would probably not have a chance at

"The French Chef," Julia Child, unwittingly in the process of becoming a legend.

breaking into television. Despite the warbles, gasps, and breathlessness, she could keep talking—a considerable talent for a live demonstration—and speak in full sentences interspersing narratives and effective references to France and to food."

Like Dione Lucas, Child was schooled at the Cordon Bleu, but in neither manner nor verbiage did she advertise her classical training. The mere fact that she began as an amateur in her late thirties was inspiration enough for the tentative but enthusiastic cook. Before becoming the famous Julia Child, Julia McWilliams was a research assistant at the Office of Strategic Services (a precursor to part of the Central Intelligence Agency), followed by other increasingly responsible posts with the outfit. She met her future husband, Paul Child (also with the OSS as a cartographer), when she was posted in Ceylon (now Sri Lanka), and when they moved to Paris for Paul's foreign service assignment, the rest of her life began. Though Child admittedly began her culinary training in large part to keep herself busy, learn French, and please her husband, her earnestness and passion for the challenge went far beyond satisfying those desires. But even without knowing her background, viewers felt comfortable trying Child's tricks in their own kitchens. She was neither fussy nor intimidating. She was sloppy and folksy and exposed her blunders with whimsy (though according to those close to her, she got quite upset when she made them). She put her hands in the poultry and plopped the innards on her countertop. She'd bone a chicken with a Band-Aid on her finger. She was genuine. She took fancy cooking down a notch, to where we lived.

She had, in the words of one fan, an "unassuming, unruffled manner." She was not prissy—she would stick her fingers in the sauce to taste, lick spoons, drop ingredients, and then toss them into the stew pot. As different as she was from her predecessors, so she was from her progeny. Today's cooking shows groom their hosts for celebrity-hood. For nonlive shows, any dropped utensils or unsanitary peccadilloes can be edited out. Those imperfections, however, were a crucial element to Child's persona.

"Don't you ever get awfully tired of just baked, boiled, mashed, and fried potatoes?" Child began her "Potato Show" episode in 1963. She described one of her potato dishes, a large pancake, as "simple-minded but very good." Then she delivered one of her characteristic nuggets of can-do counsel: "When you flip anything you just have to have the courage of your conviction." As she attempted said flip, some of the potato missed the pan and the pancake broke. Without missing a beat, she said, "When I flipped it, I didn't have the courage to do it the way I should have. . . . You can always pick it up." Then she uttered the famous aphorism: "If you're alone in the kitchen, who is going to see?" That line has been repeated ad nauseum for decades, though in the retelling the potato on the stovetop often becomes a chicken or some other large food item on the floor. She continued with her spirited, contagious philosophy: "The only way to learn to flip things is just to flip them."

Just a few details from her crepes suzette episode illustrate the tone of the show. Julia told us that "no stick-em pans" are the best to use. When tasting the orange butter she'd made, she ate a big teaspoonful. While waiting for the butter to carmelize, she put on her glasses halfway down her nose and read the recipe proportions from a piece of paper, suggesting that viewers get a pencil to jot it down if they wanted to. She suggested telling the history of crepes suzette to entertain your guests while waiting for the butter to finish. "You have to be a good raconteur," she said. "When you serve this you will 'épater les bourgeois,'" she said, then translated that to "excites [pause] people." In translating "bourgeois" to "people" instead of "middle class" or even "*the* people," she allows the phrase to refer to us, the viewers, but seems to want to save us from seeing ourselves as the masses.

Even though masses (albeit of the PBS sort) were watching her, she had a way of making the viewer feel like she was the only one, as if she were simply sitting in Julia's kitchen watching her talk to herself as she prepared dinner. "Where's my draining equipment?" she said, seemingly to herself at one point. Another time: "Oh, I did want to remind myself to set the timer," then thinks about the time as she sets it. "I've got so many burners on, I'm hot," she said as she grabbed multiple sheets of paper towels and wiped down her face with two hands. The informality and the quiet (no studio audience) created intimacy. There was not even the sense of a crew except for the occasional odd camera shot that was common in the early days. She might lurch her face toward the camera, and the camera jerked as it moved in and out. At times it was evident that she was stalling for time, and the cameraman would pan around the dining room for something to fill the interminable TV minutes.

As Morash said, comparing former and current production methods,

I'm a dinosaur. Our shows will never be repeated because today's television producer doesn't sense the need to econo-mize his resources. He goes out and gets much more money than I ever did and wants to have all these toys around him, but I don't think it makes the show any better. We made one tape, and it was live on tape. You couldn't make any mistakes or your mistakes showed. They now isolate each camera so they end up with four tapes, and they can go back and at their leisure they can edit in the right shot. My view? It takes something away from the performance of it.

Child was fully aware of the unavoidable performance aspect of her role. While she refers to herself as "an absolutely amateur performer," according to Karen Lehrman in *US News & World Report*, "she played herself." Laura Shapiro wrote, "Julia had no gift for artifice: she could perform but she couldn't pretend." After watching the potato pancake episode, New York area chef and restaurateur Dan Barber said, in comparing *The French Chef* to something like one of Rachael Ray's shows today, "When you see that, a lot's been lost."

"Unless the sky fell in, the cameras failed, or the lights went off, there would be no stops, and no corrections—just straight thirty minutes from start to finish . . . I hate to stop," Child wrote.

I lose that sense of drama and excitement which the uninterrupted thirty-minute limitation imposes. Besides, I would far prefer to have things happen as they naturally do, such as the mousse refusing to leave the mold, the potatoes sticking to the skillet, the apple charlotte slowly collapsing. One of the secrets of cooking is to learn to correct something if you can, and bear with it if you cannot.

One time they did stop the cameras:

I found I had no sense of timing whatsoever, 1 minute or 5 minutes meant nothing to me as sadly illustrated by our second show and first try at "onion soup." . . . I rushed through that program like a madwoman but I got everything in, only to find that when I carried the onion soup to the dining room I had gone so fast we still had 8 minutes left. Agony. I had to sit there and talk for all that time.

The French Reign

In addition to her unmatched personality Child also had the zeitgeist on her side, a benefit not afforded James Beard or Dione Lucas. The interest in French food was peaking. Articles about French cooking in U.S. magazines increased by roughly 60 percent from June 1958 to April 1969 compared to the 1945–1958 period. Nearly one hundred cookbooks about French cuisine were published between 1959 and 1969, an increase of 68 percent compared to the number from 1940–1958. The Kennedy's Camelot had captured the nation's fancy and had a strong hand in making food and dining fashionable. They even hired a French chef for the White House, Rene Verdon. Child herself cited the Kennedys as introducing food as "in" to the nation. Though ethnic foods were not yet on the radar for average nonimmigrant Americans, a middle-class travel revolution was in progress and interests were developing. In the late 1950s and early 1960s the syndicated *Continental Cookery* hosted by husband and wife Fedora and Pino Bontempi featured Italian cooking, for instance, but French cooking went down especially easy with the American public.

French food was perceived to be the very essence of sophistication and worldliness in the 1950s and 60s. Child's intent was to take French cooking from high society to the suburbs, from Park Avenue and the Champs Elysees to Elm Street. Taking the initiative to learn the elite art of gastronomy and then ultimately share it with a mass audience via the non-elite medium of television may not be an act worthy of a peace prize, but it was a benign form of Robin Hoodism and democracy in action. Whereas her predecessors simply set out to teach people how to prepare meals and did so with a more teacherly and sometimes pedantic attitude, Child set out to popularize. She continued the legacy of Dione Lucas in raising the status of home cooking, but what she did in addition, much as the eccentric Fanny Cradock had done with aristocratic British food in England the previous decade, was, in the words of Karen Lehrman, to "[knock] classic cuisine, formerly seen as a haughty masculine preserve, off its high horse." And whereas Dione Lucas's crisp demeanor and proper British accent underscored her Cordon Bleu techniques and gave the impression that French cuisine was complex cooking for sophisticates, Child wanted to demystify the arcane process of French cooking. The word "demystify" seems to be the favorite word choice of writers in this context, but Child herself put it best: "The idea was to take the bugaboo out of French cooking."

A clip from her bouillabaisse episode perfectly captures Child's mission and populism. She extolled the wonders of the fish soup but lamented that

> when you get a famous recipe like this, the *gourmets* get a hold of it, and they fancy it up so much and say, "do this," "do that," or "that's not the real thing" that us ordinary people feel that it's impossible to do and terribly expensive. But you can make a bouillabaisse out of any kind of fresh, lean fish that you want. And it's wonderful to eat and everybody enjoys making it and particularly eating it, and there's nothing very difficult about it.

"Can you imagine, at that time French food was close to esoteric," said notable French chef and friend of Julia, Jacques Pépin. To allay fears of the unknown, Child wished "to demonstrate that it is not merely good cooking but that it follows definite rules." Rules are comforting because they can be followed. In other words, you may not have congenital culinary skills, but you can learn to cook well nonetheless. Glancing at one page of *Mastering the Art of French Cooking* is sufficient evidence to the fact. Seeing it on television, perhaps, took removing the bugaboo one step further.

Duke University Romance Studies professor Alice Yaeger Kaplan observed that "the French food invasion started as an upper middle-class diversion" and cited *Mastering the Art of French Cooking* and *The French Chef* as instigators. "A country which has had so much trouble promoting the serious study of foreign languages, seems suddenly to promote French *as consumption*—or perhaps as consumption instead of French." *Gourmet* magazine had fueled the invasion even earlier. "In the postwar climate," wrote Betty Fussell, "[*Gourmet* editor MacAusland] could confess openly that his 'dream-like cookery' appealed to fantasy and snobbery with food never meant to be eaten from recipes never meant to be cooked. It was the beginning of gourmet chic and the cuisine of the *moi* generation."

The besotted American attitude toward French food waned to some extent over the course of the 1970s, 80s, and 90s, before reaching its nadir in 2003 with U.S. reaction to French president Chirac's criticism of the U.S. policy on invading Iraq (the provenance of "freedom fries"). The nation's appetite gradually became more curious and its palate more diverse. Classic French cooking all but disappeared from television cooking shows, especially as health trends sent people away from rich foods and toward lighter dishes. If any one country was thought to take its place, it would have to be Italy with its reliance on simple recipes and fresh ingredients.

"I don't think people like the French very much," said native Frenchman Pépin, laughing. "Especially in the last ten to fifteen years." He clearly sees its influence on the U.S. over the years, invoking those besides Child who championed the cuisine on television— Madeline Kamman, Pierre Franey (*Cuisine Rapide*), himself. "Even James Beard when he was cooking at the beginning was French." Pépin firmly stands by its wisdom. In addition to being in vogue, in the professional realm French cooking techniques were and are thought to be a good—the only, many say—foundation for cooking properly. Referring to the New York City culinary school where he teaches master classes, Chef Pépin said,

> We are the French Culinary Institute because the structure of what we teach, the culinary techniques, are French. But people who come out of here, like Bobby Flay or Wylie Dufresne who are great chefs now on their own, don't do French

food. The body of work that we teach here can go back to *Le Cuisinier* of La Varenne from the seventeenth century. And at least there is a consensus, at least we as professionals agree on this, whether it's a julienne or brunoise or a mirepoix or whatever. At least you agree on that body of work and then you can move in whatever direction.

Impact on America

Aside from her high likeability rating on television, Child's influence on the way Americans ate was considerable. In addition to demonstrating sophisticated cooking techniques, she introduced viewers to new ingredients and products—items that most Americans took for granted by the 1990s. Geoffrey Drummond recalls an early episode where Child was making garlic mashed potatoes: "She said, 'This is a garlic. And if you can't find this in the supermarket try to go to an Italian grocery store or an Italian green grocer.'" Cooking equipment stores, which were just beginning to appear (Williams Sonoma was founded in 1956) began to blossom around the time *The French Chef* appeared. "Fish poachers, charlotte molds, chefs knives, and copper beating bowls became best-sellers," wrote Sylvia Lovegren in *Fashionable Foods; Seven Decades of Food Fads.* "Wire whisks sold out in Pittsburgh after one of her shows. A butcher who usually sold seven geese a year reported selling sixty-five after Julia cooked a goose on television."

In a marked departure from the 1950s, when the kitchen buzz was around labor-saving gadgets and new convenience foods and it was considered unseemly to have anything to do with the food one served at a dinner party, as journalist Nora Ephron declared, "Food became, for dinner party conversation in the 60s, what abstract expressionism had been in the 50s." Child may have seemed to be alone in the TV dining room set at the end of her show as she prepared to serve nonexistent guests food and wine by candlelight, but as Lovegren wrote, "Everyone seemed to be in the kitchen with Julia in the sixties."

As food historian Harvey Levenstein explained the cooking-as-status-symbol phenomenon, baby boomers, in seeking self-fulfillment, rejected family-centric traditions. Though it had seemed auspicious to her less than a decade earlier, by 1973 Julia Child was actually complaining that food was too "in," getting too much publicity, too much status, too much snobbery. But gourmet food and cooking did not suffer from overexposure, and though its intensity and trends have come and gone, its basic popularity has not let up since.

Child had an impact not only on eating, shopping, and cooking behavior but on the cooking profession, even though she wasn't a true chef. "The professional chefs were not threatened by her," said Russ Morash. "They worshipped her. They sat at her knee and learned lessons because she was so wonderful to them. It wasn't that she was teaching directly. She cared about and gave respect to their profession."

"You look at Boston in the sixties," said Morash.

Chefs were beat up characters in the workforce who could barely be trusted to poach an egg. They had checkered careers, very little academic training, no respect. All of that was to come later. There were a handful of distinguished chefs at the time. They had come up the hard way, scullery guys, no women. Into this comes Julia Child who says, "We have to celebrate the chefs, they actually know something." Whether they did or not, that kind of respect had never been given before. The French took a while to warm up to it, particularly the French professionals, but by the time she finished she even had them on her side which is extraordinary.

Jacques Pépin was a member of that one-time beat up profession, and French at that. "It was considered a low, uninspired, ordinary type of work," he said. He continued with bemusement:

So it has changed a great deal on the social scale. I worked at Le Pavillon when I first came [to the U.S.]. Le Pavillon was considered the greatest French restaurant in America, and we were part of Local 89, which were the dishwashers, the cooks—everyone was together. There was no distinction. We were pretty low on the social scale. And it's now totally different. Now we are geniuses.

It would be facile to pin the shift in attitudes on *The French Chef*, either the one in the White House or the one on TV, as there were myriad contributing factors. "It had started before television," said Pépin, listing some of them:

> [w]omen's liberation, organic gardening, people were questioning the TV dinner and so forth, starting into health and organic gardening and stuff like this, so there was a social change at that time. So cooking became respectable. Movies and articles started coming out, and we had a food editor of the *New York Times* with Craig [Claiborne] and others.

As food writer and friend of Julia, Molly O'Neill, said, "Julia was not the beginning of an era. She was the tipping point."

Though short-lived, a 1967 Los Angeles show called *Everybody Cook* hosted by a perky and appealing young Irish woman named Sally Ogle did its fair share of promoting at least local chefs. Ogle, like fellow Angelino Monty Margetts before her, did not know how to cook and so was not a teacher-host. As an imperfect participant-observer, she showcased prominent chefs in Southern California, asking questions and acting as a stand-in for the viewer and novice cook. This show format foreshadowed what is now commonplace, most notably on daily morning news and talk shows. The interest in chefs—real and incipient—was beginning to catch on. Later in her career, Julia Child continued on her mission. Geoffrey Drummond sees Child's *Master Chefs* phase as her "act three" that "brought chefs to center stage. Then the Food Network took them on tour around the country so it became like *Cats*. That's really noteworthy."

Though her aim was to guide the home cook, Child's influence organically moved back into the professional realm. Antithetical though it is to say about her, Julia Child became a brand by virtue of her presence and absolutely no marketing strategy. While before there were too many to count, nearly every television cook after (or concurrent with) Child was deemed "the Chinese Julia Child," "the Cajun Julia Child," "the Jewish Julia Child," and so on. She was a mold not to be broken but to be recast and referred to in some aspect of any culinary career. Dan Barber, young and esteemed chef and owner of the Blue Hill restaurant in New York said, "Julia Child gave rise to the Wolfgang Pucks of the world." Molly O'Neill said, "[T]he irony is that she took fine food from the professional class and brought it into the middle-class household and made it part of daily vernacular, but she also created a generation of Dan Barbers."

"Unfortunately, Julia was probably the first and last self-effacing celebrity chef," wrote Lehrman. "She wasn't in it for the money as so many people are," said Morash. "She wasn't in it for the fame. She was in it because she truly believed people should know how to eat well, and for those who had what it takes, they should know how to cook it."

Public Broadcasting Ghetto

The French Chef did not have much company—and no threat of competition—in the genre in 1963. As far as cooking shows on national networks, it was still virtually tumbleweeds. Consumer cable television was but a glimmer in the eyes of a few entrepreneurs, and, with only three major networks, airtime was at a premium. By the time the 1960s were in full formation and nearly all the Joneses had television sets, programming had increased, and commercial stations simply did not have the room—or the need—to carry filler home ec–style programs. Cooking shows started to fall off local television schedules when stations started to receive more programming from their parent networks, something that was made more accessible when videotape debuted in the late 1950s. After most local cooking shows had disappeared, PBS—originally National Educational Television—began producing and airing them. The passage of the Public Broadcasting Act in 1967 opened a flow of funding to "pubcasting" and consequently its cooking shows developed a much wider audience. In the 1970s PBS developed a strong niche for shows about food and cooking.

The most salient difference between public and commercial television cooking shows was that PBS stations did not have to bother with "peddling food items," to use Morash's phrase. Secondly, PBS had an educational mission. To this day public broadcasting cooking shows have an inherent gravitas not found on cable or network shows. *The French Chef* launched the reputation of WGBH as the major PBS producer of "how-to" shows, a phrase that smacks of practicality and one that irks Russ Morash.

"That awful word 'how-to,'" said Morash, the virtually undisputed "father of." (He was also responsible for *The Victory Garden* and *This Old House* in the 1970s.) "I just can't bear it. It pigeonholes us." Though he balks at the label, Morash has no choice but to live with the legacy, and of course, most others find it an admirable achievement. The fact remains, according to public broadcasting critic Laurence Jarvik, that "how-to's on PBS are examples of the power and profitability of educational programming, public TV's raison d'etre." Cultural studies scholar Toby Miller referred to PBS as a "crypto-commodified, quasi-bake-drive-funded, kindness-of-strangers ghetto." There was peddling, of course, but it was carried out behind the scenes with underwriters and on screen with viewers all at once during fund drives.

"[Julia] and I were always happy to work for PBS. We don't have to kowtow to the sponsor," said Pépin, who is still hosting shows on PBS as of the writing of this book and gratefully acknowledges that it is an effective marketing venue for his books (cooking shows, whether on public or commercial television, are naturally tied to such commercial offshoots). Child often took pains to conceal product labels on her show. Her no-endorsements policy is now legendary and would be exceptional (and nearly impossible) in today's climate. Even though Julia never worked for commercial broadcasting, she recognized the value of her forum. "The thing I want to do is teach," Child told *Newsweek* in 1972. "And on public television I am free to do what I want."

"It was not teaching," said Morash adamantly. Some may argue semantics, but to Morash, it is an important point.

> It was inspiration, perhaps. We never tried to teach. We deliberately make the distinction between teaching and informing and inspiring. Claiming to be a teacher, there are probably better methods. The time just isn't there to teach well. You can get [viewers] to go back to the books and try it all over again, but with a half-hour television show you just can't do it. You can lift the lid on a subject but you can't do much with the teaching part.

Though their statements seem contradictory, Morash's and Child's goals were always in line. It's just that Child had the idealistic perspective of a democratic gastronome, and Morash had the practical point of view of a television producer.

Once it became apparent that cooking television could actually be entertaining, negotiating the instruction-entertainment dichotomy became a primary charge of every food television programmer. It is an issue about which there can be vehement disagreement, but in the end, each must reconcile the other's existence. "It could be both," said Pépin. "Julia would say that it should be both. She helped me in the sense—you have to lighten up. I know you're teaching, too, [she'd say] but that's important, because it's a visual thing. . . . Julia never had those qualms about anything," Pépin said of her in relation to the instruction-entertainment polemic. "She taught food the way she wanted. She was a very secure and solid person. She had a vision, and said that's what I teach." She would be the first to admit if she didn't know something, he said. "But she felt very comfortable in her skills." As Morash said,

> The other distinction [from today's TV chefs] is that she was a true scholar. She really knew the stuff. . . . I have literally seen people jump out of a cooking school and walk over to the TV station and say, "I'm ready." It's more than that, it requires a lifetime. As it was Julia was brought along pretty quickly. But she never stopped learning.

Child was the main attraction on public television in the 1960s. She was public broadcasting's first national star and the first public TV personality to win an Emmy. "Many people discovered not just food but the world of educational television through Julia," wrote Lehrman. Her accessibility made public TV accessible to a mass audience.

It might seem like a misnomer to refer to the PBS audience as "mass," but PBS audience demographics mirror the U.S. population in race, ethnicity, education, and income. While it may have been a more specialized, wealthier, more educated audience drawn to *The French Chef*—informally evidenced by the exceptionally literate fan mail sent to the station—Child appealed to a relatively diverse cross section, given the typical viewer of other types of cooking shows (i.e., housewives). The beneficiaries included:

Men: On October 22, 1963, Richard Murray wrote, "Dear Mrs. Child. This is not a fan letter, but I would like to tell you, by way of introduction, how much my wife and I enjoy your program. This does not mean much coming from me, but it is high praise indeed from my wife who is both French and an excellent French cook."

A male attorney from Gloucester, Massachusetts, wrote, "It's a rare Monday evening that you are not in our living room. I anticipate your coming by playing your theme music on the piano and in a few seconds there you are—The French Chef, from whom we learn so much!"

In September 1964, Peter from Chicago, wrote to Child that she

[m]ight be interested in the male viewpoint. . . . [T]here goes my Tuesday nights. Any social functions in the future will have to be before or after your show. If they coincide, they're just out of luck. . . . [Y]our sense of humor and down-to-earth approach held my interest, even though I was embarrassed a few times to find myself sitting with open mouth at all the details you were packing into that half-hour.

The young: "Dear Mrs. Childs [sic]," wrote Kate of Berwyn, Pennsylvania in reference to one of the pilots, "My mother and I watched you on t.v. when you made a charlotte russe. We made one and it came out just perfect. I have not tasted it yet because we are having if for desert [sic] tonite [sic]. You have a very good show. I like it very much. PS. I hope your show does not go of [sic] the air."

The old: A Scituate, Massachusetts, woman wrote, "I made a tremendous impression with the Coq Au Vin. It was very satisfying because I am 76 and must struggle a bit for a tiny spot in the sun."

While she had a large following in the WGBH New England viewing area, Child's show reached out into the middle of America, too. A Tulsa woman avowed that "[t]he Oklahoma culture needs such a refreshing infusion—and cooking is one thing everyone can use to improve their quality of life."

Child not only put public TV on the map and ushered in a new standard of cooking show, but she dressed up television altogether: "Really and truly one of the most surprisingly entertaining half hours I have spent before the TV in many a moon," wrote Irene from Cambridge. "In all of television there is nothing more engrossing to listen to and to watch," sang Paul and Hannah in their letter. "Your excellent descriptions are so sprightly and lucid, packed with subtle humor and your movements are as artistic as Da Vinci. . . . We enjoy your talk more than anything to which we listen. It is ALIVE, VITAL, TRUE." In 1972, when Polaroid threatened to remove its funding of *The French Chef*, CBS News producer Jerry Liddell wrote to WGBH president David Ives: "If there's anything I can do, personally, to keep Julia Child on the air . . . please let me know. Without our 'French Chef,' television wouldn't be nearly as palatable." In large part due to such letters, Polaroid reconsidered its withdrawal and continued to back the show.

Child's already solid legacy at times even seems to take on renewed strength. In 1991 Jean Stapleton played Julia in a musical entitled *Bon Appetit!* Smack in the middle of the celebrity chef and foodie wave of the 1990s, the September 1997 cover of *US News & World Report* read "How Julia Invented Modern Life" (carrying Karen Lehrman's article "What Julia Started"). And indeed, Child's cultural contributions have attracted more attention since. Julie Powell's 2005 book *Julie & Julia: 365 Days, 524 Recipes, 1 Tiny Apartment Kitchen* wherein a twenty-nine-year-old office worker sets out to make every recipe in *Mastering the Art of French Cooking*, was a bestseller, and a movie based on the book—Meryl Streep playing Julia—was scheduled for release in 2009. "Her influence in creating today's pop-culture milieu bears comparison to that of Alfred Kinsey and Elvis Presley in their respective fields," noted Karen Lehrman. "If Julia Child's contribution has attracted less notice than that of the Kinsey Report or *Hound Dog* . . . that's because food is less controversial than sex or rock-and-roll." Food had, of course, never been a stranger to controversy, but within just a few years after Lehrman's article, genetic modification, trans fats, and food miles were making headlines on a regular basis—and Child's contribution continues to attract notice.

As a popular culture icon Child could not be expected to escape the sincerest form of flattery. In 1978, she was the inspiration for Dan

Aykroyd's parody on *Saturday Night Live*. Affectionate mockery, perhaps, but unlike most pop culture icons Child was almost never the object of vitriol. As Russ Morash said, "The professionals, the French, men and women—all were universal in their love of this woman. Now tell me another human being. . . . Take your icon and I'll tell you that they don't have that kind of support."

Nevertheless any personage on television, especially a popular one, is a potential target for some kind of backlash. Child had a contentious relationship with French culinary instructor and fellow cooking show host Madeleine Kamman. Among Kamman's resentments toward Child, as she was not alone in noting, was that Julia was neither French nor a chef (as Kamman herself was). Food historian Karen Hess also took issue with the show's title. Julia felt *The French Chef* was justified (though it was not even her idea, it was Morash's) as she didn't call *herself* a French chef—she proudly referred to herself as a home cook. She liked the title because it imparted seriousness, as Laura Shapiro detailed in her biography of Child. "It is short, to the point, dignified, glamorous, and appeals to men as well as women," as Shapiro quoted Child. "Something like *Looking at Cooking*, or variations, sounds cheesy, little-womanish, cute, amateurish." We "called it *French Chef*," said Julia, "because I always hoped we would have a French Chef. . . . Also had to fit it in *TV Guide* on one line."

With regard to the show's content, the adulation was overwhelming, though some did register their disapproval. A well-intentioned Harvard dining hall dietician sent good wishes for the show and pledged to keep watching but did take issue with Child's cavalier attitude. "Had she used a separate spoon for tasting the sauce it would have created a better impression, rather than tasting from the spoon she was using for stirring," wrote the hygiene police representative who continued:

> Had she used paper towels to dry the mushrooms, instead of what I presume was a hand towel and pot lifter which was attached at her waistline, it would have created a better

impression. These are details that the average homemaker might not notice, but as demonstration techniques for such a large audience they left something to be desired.

Another wrote in condemning Child's wine drinking on the air. "Aren't you able to entertain without a crutch? I'm thinking of my grandchildren and I abhor this behavior." A handwritten note on the letter indicated Child's intention of responding with information on a U.S. government finding that "wine is good for you."

The bulk of the negative feedback, however, was directed at the torment the viewer had to endure in not being able to be fully involved with the food. "Our sole cavil," wrote one man, "is that we cannot walk through the TV screen and sit down to CONSUME your magnificent dishes." Another wrote that not being able to eat the food Child prepared was a brand of torture for which Dante would have "created a special circle in the Inferno" if he had seen the show himself.

Changing Face of TV Cooking

Though Julia Child was incontrovertibly synonymous with television cooking at the time, she wasn't completely alone in doing it. In fact she shared *The French Chef* set at WGBH with *Joyce Chen Cooks* in 1966. Chen, of significantly shorter stature than Child, had to wear high heels to use the raised countertops constructed for the towering Child.

The Chen family emigrated to the U.S. from China in 1949, settling in Cambridge, Massachusetts. Joyce Chen had sold insurance in China, but as her son Stephen said, "Cooking was her hobby and her passion." In the spring of 1956, there was a bake sale at her children's school. She made two items: cookies and egg rolls. When Chen came to the school later and saw some cookies but no egg rolls, she assumed that the staff didn't know what they were and didn't put them out. Then she was told that they had sold out immediately, and she was asked to make more. Chinese food was still relatively unknown to most Americans at the time, but there was clearly an interest, at least among intellectually curious Cantabrigians and Bostonians.

Chen began to teach Chinese cooking classes in her small duplex as well as area adult education centers. In 1958, she opened a restaurant in Cambridge that bore her name. In order to draw diners to the exotic items on the buffet line, she had to initially include a few American standards like cold cuts as well as French bread. But the tastes of China became popular in short order, and Chen was credited with introducing Americans to the esoteric recipes and techniques of Chinese cooking. She wrote a cookbook in 1964 and, at first, published it herself because commercial houses refused to include color photos. Craig Claiborne praised her food not just for its

Joyce Chen shared the same set as Julia Child but introduced audiences to a very different cuisine.

good taste but for its healthy attributes. This, too, was a relatively new element in thinking about food. When Chen was approached at her restaurant by another *French Chef* producer, Ruth Lockwood, to do television, Chen was ready. *Joyce Chen Cooks* became the first nationally televised cooking show with a person of color as host.

Though she used the same physical space as Julia Child, for *Joyce Chen Cooks* the set was outfitted with bamboo latticework and wind chimes. On occasion, a Chinese language lesson would appear on the screen, such as the characters and translation for "how are you?" Chen assured viewers they could make the dishes she was demonstrating with ingredients found at local supermarkets and equipment already on hand. As she cooked, she often gave the history of recipes along with anecdotes and personal comments on the similarities and differences between the U.S. and Chinese cultures. Though literally worlds apart, like Julia Child, Chen had a charming personality, and her program included some memorable, unorthodox techniques. Quick on her high-heeled feet, her son Stephen recalled the time when she had removed a pan from the oven but forgot to use a pot holder. Though the dish was cold, it was supposed to give the impression of being hot, so Chen had to pretend she burned her hand. When making Peking duck, she used a foot-operated bicycle pump on the studio floor to separate the skin from the flesh. On the same episode, she displayed a drawing of a duck in a cage to illustrate the process of force feeding, all with a pleasant smile on her face. Along the way, she would acknowledge the complexity and difficulty of the recipe, in vivid contrast to the "so easy!" mantra of most other cooking shows. Like Dione Lucas, the appeal may have been more in watching a skilled performer than in filing away everyday recipe ideas.

Even before *Joyce Chen Cooks* was available, eighty stations inquired about carrying it. Though there were only twenty-six episodes in total, her show was a crucial element in making her a major influence on Americans' interest in Chinese cooking. Her kitchenware and food products—including frozen Peking ravioli, a term she coined—are still sold around the U.S.

Taking It Personally

Cultural differences between the 1950s and the 1960s were not always as stark as the blunt retrospective media brush often paints them, though the social girdle was gradually loosening. By the end of the 1960s the prevailing rebel spirit saw Americans pushing boundaries in every arena, leaving behind the ideals of conformity and security in favor of diversity and exploration. Cooking was becoming for many a casual hobby and for others a link with a personal sense of self. Both were radical changes.

Just as James Beard's *I Love to Eat* might not have been the phrase du jour in 1946, "I hate to cook" might only pass a housewife's lips via a whispered confession, or, more likely, murmured to herself as she assembled casseroles and Jell-O salads for her family in the 1950s. Signaling a sea change, Peg Bracken slapped these provocative words on the cover of her cookbook in 1960. It was as if *The I Hate to Cook Book* was a direct rejoinder to *The Joy of Cooking*, first published in 1931. Bracken understood that women were doing almost all of the cooking, but she didn't believe they had to turn cartwheels about it. "Some women, it is said, like to cook. This book is not for them," Bracken began her introduction. "This book is for those of us who want to fold our big dishwater hands around a dry martini instead of a wet flounder, come the end of a long day." With her clever wit interspersed throughout the book, Bracken provided quick, easy, "untested" recipes collected from friends and acquaintances. Most had a short ingredient list, often including the requisite canned items and onion soup mix, but the majority called for basic whole foods. Bracken saw the recipes as valuable because "experts in their sunny spotless test kitchens can make anything taste good. But even *we* can make these taste good." Though it was still a book intended for women, a demythologizing of the feminine role was beginning.

Julia Child, too, understood that not everyone loved to cook. But she felt strongly that it could be fun and satisfying and wanted to get that message across. In an ironic, though unintended feminist twist on gender roles, learning gourmet cooking afforded home cooks an opportunity to expand their horizons, not in superficially and figuratively consorting with the glittery lifestyle of the in-crowd but to stretch themselves in a more meaningful way. Moving food and cooking to a more central place in Americans' lives was also facilitated by the fact that family incomes tripled between 1950 and 1970, so we had more to spend on ingredients and accoutrements in the quest for meaning.

Like a poem, Julia Child and *The French Chef* were open to interpretation. They served as blank slates on which to project whatever psychic needs presented themselves among viewers. Child generously and instinctively (though not deliberately) gave wide berth to the needs of the populace. She didn't label herself. She liked good food and was open to storebought, canned—anything that she considered *good*—thereby giving the viewer the courage to do the same. It may have been merely coincidental that her seminal show began in 1963, the same year that Betty Friedan's *The Feminine Mystique* was published. But these two events both presented outlets for women—in particular middle-class white women—many of whom had been feeling oppressed by their domestic circumstances. She did not declare herself a feminist, but Child wanted both women—and men—to feel empowered around cooking.

Though she did not make a point of it, Child changed the way Americans related to food *and* to women. "In her books and on her television shows Child injected a revolutionary sense of humor," wrote Martha Smilgis in *Ms.* "Her approach to cooking was a marked departure from an earlier era when a woman's sense of worth was connected way too closely with her abilities in the kitchen." Her salient success allowed women to consider culinary careers. "Betty Friedan may have identified the feminine mystique, but Julia Child—with her . . . meteoric rise in the traditionally male preserve of professional cooking—showed that women could turn the mystique on its head," Karen Lehrman observed. "More important, she did so without declaring herself a victim of men, society, or the more pleasurable aspects of traditional femininity."

In 1972 a woman from Petersburg, Pennsylvania, heard the increasingly widespread message that women did not need to rely solely on their feminine wiles to reinforce their identity. Food could be a road to improved self-esteem. She wrote to WGBH: "Every woman cooks, but every woman *wants to better herself*. Julia Child is the answer. . . . A good cook is needed in every home, after all, a way to a man's heart *is* through his stomach. I know it, I tried sex. They get tired of it [sic] the same variety, not food! . . . Carry on Julia," and then, oddly, "Women's Lib is on your side." Though the viewer did not seem to realize her actions were still aimed at man-pleasing, it was a small step in the progressive direction, inspired by Child.

The Mrs. from Petersburg knew of what she spoke. The kitchen may have been a woman's domain, but it was still a man's dining room. A 1965 *Chicago Tribune* article—written by a woman—bemoaned the attention given to convenience and routine over a man's desires: "Perhaps it's time for the wife to take a closer look at the man in her life and his food needs for a fresh approach in planning daily menus." The times were a changin', but it was slow going.

Despite *Creative Cookery* host Francois Pope's belief that women prefer men as cooking teachers (and a 1964 *New York Times* article written by a woman broadcaster claiming that women don't like to watch other women on TV), male cooking show hosts were still a relative rarity in the mid-1960s. But the decade did see some glimpses of men taking part in the job of cooking. A woman need not worry too much about ceding control of her small but fundamental fiefdom, however, since it was mostly in the realm of the grill where her husband and his peers found their niche. Food historian Harvey Levenstein described a barbecue boom in the U.S in the late fifties and early sixties, partly spurred by vigorous promotion on the part of beef producers and other food manufacturers.

It was no doubt refreshing, at any rate, to see, demonstrating cooking on television, a woman whose monologue was unpeppered with reminders of how much the dish would please a bored husband or finicky children. Unlike her immediate predecessors in cooking instruction, Child had no implicit or explicit agenda to advise housewives (a word that, according to Laura Shapiro, made Child wince) on how to please their families. She wanted people to learn to cook and to enjoy themselves. And her bottom line message was clear: "If I can do this, you can."

It was a confusing and sometimes contradictory time, this swell just prior to feminism's second wave, as the Petersburg, Pennsylvania, letter writer illustrated. On the one hand, feminists of the day were telling women to get out of the kitchen. On the other, Julia Child was welcoming women *and* men into an "enlightened" kitchen as Lehrman called it, much as Dione Lucas had attempted to get people into the kitchen for art's sake but without any personal choice activists to back her up. Many women (as Karen Lehrman wrote, "many an overeducated housewife") leapt at the idea of empowering themselves via cooking, even if they were unaware of the motivation for their actions.

Times a Changin'

The cultural repositionings of the 1960s were reflected most notably in a surge of message and protest songs but also on television shows such as *The Smothers Brothers Comedy Hour* and *The Monkees* and in movies like *The Graduate* and *Easy Rider*. Changes were also reflected in the foods we ate—or did not eat. Rather than gleefully glomming on to the next big thing, Americans, especially the younger generation, regarded the establishment with an element of suspicion. The questioning of authority extended to the food industry, too. Part of the interest in and concern about health came from youthful rebellion against mass-produced and artificial foods in favor of natural products. Monosodium glutamate (MSG) was just one bellwether. At the beginning of the decade the chemical flavor enhancer was still being touted as a welcome food additive and para-convenience item, and by the end of the decade its safety was widely questioned and several food manufacturers banned it from their products.

Rachel Carson's *Silent Spring* published in 1961 and Francis Moore Lappé's *Diet for a Small Planet* in 1971 bookended a decade where Americans became more cognizant of and concerned about the health and safety of their food supply. Interest in health food and vegetarianism increased dramatically as part of the consciousness raised about what we ate, how it affected us, and what it meant. Hunger became a political issue, and a pilot food stamp program began in 1961. Awareness was raised considerably by a 1968 CBS documentary that showed graphic portrayals of some of the millions dying of hunger in America. At the same time, in the continuing parade of paradoxes, television and movie actresses and advertising models portrayed thinness as a beauty ideal. Fashion model Twiggy was a pop icon, and her name is still associated with sporting a gamine physique.

Increased self-awareness, both on the societal and individual levels, seemed to express itself in a global sense as well. In addition to a more pronounced and objective interest in American culture and society—coupled with increased international travel—Americans also looked beyond their backyard fences and national borders with more curiosity. The insularity of the 1950s began to dissipate. As Americans returned from abroad, they brought back a taste for international cuisines. Immigration patterns piqued an interest in the foods of regions beyond France, such as Southeast Asia, Africa, and the Caribbean.

According to food historian Michael Symons, there were changes taking place in cuisines of other nations in the 1960s, too. New Zealand, Australia, and Great Britain—Elizabeth David's books about nonfussy British food were extremely popular in the 1950s and 1960s in the United Kingdom—were experiencing shifts of their own toward an improved culinary scene. While "improved" was a subjective matter, they were generally headed in a more self-aware, sophisticated direction. So as Americans traveled, they may have been exposed not just to new and different foods but to new and different attitudes about food. Though these changes didn't manifest themselves in a flurry of ethnic food programs, they likely made people more receptive to new foods and new ways of cooking. With the exception of Joyce Chen, however, the face of the TV chefs did not begin to reflect any more diversity until the 1980s and then (and still now) mostly on public television.

Television is relatively slow to reflect cultural shifts, and some are more readily accepted than others. National networks did not and still do not take big creative risks given the financial stakes. Public broadcasting was a place where programmers could innovate without fear of losing advertiser support or large audiences. (It took a chance on Julia Child, after all.) As the *Chicago Tribune* put it in 1968, "Educational TV stations, on the whole, are sensitive to the cultural and informational needs of the people. They are filling a gap too often ignored by commercial TV stations."

Without public television, it is conceivable that Julia Child would never have made it onto television and into the venerated spot she claims in American culture. She stumbled into the gap and unwittingly filled a need that is still a challenge to describe explicitly. Because Child was not a manufactured television star, it would be impossible to replicate her trajectory. "No one's come up with anything new since this woman," said Molly O'Neill. "The next great thing hasn't happened yet."

CHAPTER 4

The Me Decade
and the Galloping Gourmet

People who love to talk food and theater are never at a loss
for conversation.

—James Beard

Selfhood through Food

Over the course of the sixties, Julia Child gave home cooks the
nerve to become adventurers in their kitchens and, like her astronaut contemporaries, ushered in a new era of exploration. The spark
that Child ignited set off fires that she could not have envisioned.
"In contrast to the fifties, I think what we were seeing in the sixties
was the beginning of the shadows of the adolescence of a nation,"
said "Galloping Gourmet" Graham Kerr. "We were beginning to
come into adulthood." Child's proper French fare was the learning
sphere as well as a gateway. Americans soon became enterprising in
their newfound confidence and began to branch out. Much of it was
misguided—canned Welsh rarebit quiche comes to mind—but what
youth is blemish-free?

Growing up is always hard to do. While the country had already
lost its innocence in blatant ways, people were trying to hold on to
it by more subtle and subconscious measures. In 1970, we could flip

the radio dial and hear pop happy Jackson 5's "ABC" on one station and Neil Young's hot-off-the-press lyrics of "Ohio" on the next. Countervailing emotions might have fostered reluctance to face an undeniably harsh reality, but there was no getting around the seductive power of newness and change.

I had the good fortune of growing up in an era when real cooking at home was experiencing a renaissance. Women like my mother, who previously did not know from noncanned vegetables, gained creative courage from watching *The French Chef*. Those were the heady days when anything beyond potatoes and well-done meat qualified as "gourmet." While I maintain a sizeable collection of childhood memories, there are few as vivid as a series from circa 1971 to 1972. This period was probably the nascence of my culinary awareness, and I think my mother could say the same about herself. Granted, she and I were engaged in the discovery mission on different levels. She felt the excitement of trying new foods and techniques as well as the social pressure to get with it, while I was the mere willing recipient of her efforts.

On a given Saturday night, my mom's paisley maxi skirt and my dad cueing up Creedence Clearwater Revival on the record player were the first sensory cues to an evening that typified the era like nothing else. My parents invited another paisley-clad, sideburn-and-doubleknit-sporting couple over, and I was allowed to join them as we all sat around the coffee table on the autumn-toned shag carpeting in our Crayola-orange-and-yellow living room. Thereupon stood an avocado green fondue pot and ceramic lotus-shaped bowls filled with sauces like hot mustard, horseradish and soy sauce. Our interactive dinner involved sticking cubes of raw beef impaled on skinny color-coded forks into simmering oil (everyone has their madeleine, and the smell of Sterno and hot oil is mine), and the gestalt allowed every one of us to feel exceptionally grown-up. It wasn't just that I was in first grade and my mother was a young wife and we were both ripe for learning. And it wasn't just happening to us. It was likely happening in kitchens, dining nooks, and living rooms all over the United States.

In the pre-cable 1970s, national television was our communal living room. It brought us together to watch *All in the Family* and *Roots*, see President Richard Nixon deliver his resignation speech, catch the peace-sign brandishing streaker at the Academy Awards ceremony, and understand that we were expected to sport hip-hugging bell bottoms. Eponymous sitcom stars Mary, Maude, Rhoda, and Phyllis made a show of their independence and the gender role renovation underway. TV pushed the hot buttons of race, sexuality, and the peace movement and took risks that are rarely if ever seen in today's cookie cutter programming. It was arguably—inarguably, in my opinion—the medium's golden age.

That same desire for novelty, discovery, and exhibitionism was in the air everywhere. As Americans gathered to debate about the Vietnam War or vituperate about Watergate, it was often over dinner. Home cooks began to pay attention to differences in olive oils, try heretofore unrecognizable fish, and become rendered helpless and deprived without their Cuisinarts, pasta machines, woks, copper bowls, and crepe pans. As Graham Kerr recalled, "The word gourmet became part of the common lexicon. It would be applied to a saucepan that had a wooden handle. And if you set fire to a dish in a restaurant, it would be gourmet." Even in an era of rising inflation rates and a stagnant economy, Americans continued to cultivate an interest in food and cooking, and spend money on the pursuit. They put their knowledge into action by organizing informal gourmet clubs where they could flaunt their stylish taste and engage in one-upmanship. Kerr referred to such behavior—which he encouraged—as the "Society for the Propagation of Delicious Eating."

"The weekend kitchen, where the man has increasingly intruded," wrote Jacques Pépin in a 1978 *Los Angeles Times* article, ". . . has become a social gathering place where arguments over recipes and techniques are settled over a few bottles of wine, culminating in a subjective type of cooking in which each of the cooks participates competitively." While at one time the very notion of *Iron Chef* or *Top Chef* would have seemed as ridiculous as competitive napping, the idea was not born in the 1990s (though the Cirque du Soleil feel might have been). The seeds were planted long before.

Aftereffects of the revolutionary zeal of the 1960s seeped into some of the most staid kitchens, and even formerly square meal mavens were turned on to new cooking trends. Unlike freakishly ambitious author and amateur cook Julie Powell whose 2005 *Julie & Julia* chronicled her attempt at every recipe in Julia Child's *Mastering the Art of French Cooking*, intimidated home cooks thirty odd years earlier might have only attempted a few of the recipes in their treasured and proudly displayed copies. Julia's populist battle cry may have manifested itself in simply questioning tradition. In the 1970s Americans consciously took hold of the ideas spawned in the 1960s and incorporated an antiauthoritarian sensibility into many of their cultural and leisure activities—categories to which cooking now belonged. Many became bolder about the clothes they wore, the books they read, even the way they related to their bosses at work. Women realized they didn't have to cook what their mothers cooked or be the only spouse in the kitchen. They were welcomed to envision cooking as a mode of self-expression. A 1974 Burger King TV ad lured customers with the promise that you could "have it your way," a slogan that could be applied in myriad circumstances in the "me decade." In *Food for Thought: Philosophy and Food*, philosophy scholar Elizabeth Telfer posed a big question and a simple (yet as we will see, ultimately complex) answer:

> Why are eating and drinking held to be so important? Why do so many newspapers and magazines which are basically not domestic nevertheless carry a weekly recipe or restaurant review? . . . If eating and drinking are not necessary to survival but merely one method of feeding and watering ourselves, why do we not save a lot of time and trouble by being intravenously fed and watered during our sleep? The answer is that we think that eating and drinking have a value which

goes beyond feeding and watering . . . we view them as possible leisure pursuits.

A five-thousand word *Forbes* magazine article published in 1976 titled *The Kitchen: America's Playroom* declared, "Cooking, once a demeaning activity fit only for servants, sissies and overweight mothers-in-law, has begun taking on glamour." A bit blunt, but the kernel of truth is there. The ability to cook, entertain, and discuss food with ease was taking on ever-mounting social value. Food had become an accessory and a way to conspicuously exhibit personal taste. As food studies scholar Pauline Adema observed, "Knowing and using the language of cuisine, including exercising one's educated palate, separates those with cultural capital from ordinary eaters." This was the decade in which legendary epicure Jean Anthelme Brillat-Savarin's famously paraphrased line "You are what you eat" was revitalized on a mass scale, implicitly expanded to "You are what you buy, cook, and serve."

Cultural studies scholar Toby Miller, who has spent a good deal of his scholarly energy on food television, described the hierarchies that order, for instance, vegetarians and gourmets. Such categorizations "map a self-styling of cultural politics and personal display onto diet," he wrote. "In each case, the implication is that particular class fractions signify powerfully through what they put in their mouths." Such categorizations, of course, are illusory and fluid. In my family we continued to subsist on Hamburger Helper and tuna noodle casserole during the week, but the weekends called for visits to specialty food stores forty-five minutes away by car to hunt for won ton skins or short grain Italian rice. The goal was cooking for company, and I suspect our pattern was not unusual. All over the country, people began to display food the way they displayed their LPs or coffee-table books. With these casually calculated arrangements—don't we all do it?—we meant to say, "I know what's hip, and I am part of the elite culture. This is who I am." (Insofar as it was the era of expressive individualism, we were still social, consumerist beings with a drive to acquire the same or better things than our neighbors.) More accurately, such exhibits bespoke not necessarily who we were, but who we wished to be. The miraculous thing about food is that it lets us be that avatar for a brief moment.

Galloping Gourmet

The 1960s had Julia Child as its emblematic television cook, and the early 1970s had Graham Kerr. *The Galloping Gourmet* was the first cooking show to aggressively capitalize on the entertainment potential of the medium and to come at the genre from this angle.

It would be easy to say that Kerr leapt on Childs's coattails. After all, *The Galloping Gourmet* appeared on U.S. television in 1969, six years after *The French Chef*. But it would be glib and plain wrong to say so. Not only had Graham Kerr been cooking since he was a wee one in the English hotel kitchens owned by his parents (compared to Julia who began at a doddering thirty-six), but his first televised cooking demo aired back in 1960 in New Zealand ("That doesn't count," Child teased him). True enough, Child was a pioneer in the United States and unquestionably deserves her iconic status as queen of small screen cuisine, but Kerr set a few firsts himself.

Viewers in the U.S. had been well prepped, of course, by *The French Chef*, but the style of *The Galloping Gourmet* was a world apart. The show opened with the snappily-dressed, British dandy of a ball of energy leaping over a tall kitchen chair while holding a full glass of wine, setting the tone for the rest of the episode and raising the bar for almost every cooking show that followed.

Where Child's studio was quiet except for the splat of, say, a sole filet hitting a hot skillet, cracking of chicken bones, or her pleasant chirruping, Kerr's set was home to the first in-studio audience for a syndicated cooking program and the first to have a "hidden camera" trained on the audience. "We could go into the people's faces as they were licking their lips and going 'mmmm,'" said Kerr's producer-wife

Treena. No minor convention that—consider where Emeril would be without his conditioned oohing-and-aahing audience.

As home cooks on the whole became more self-possessed in their kitchens and dining rooms, cooking shows were ostensibly relieved of some of the burden of actual teaching. Kerr heeded the how-to format to a good degree, demonstrating cooking techniques with recipes for dishes like shoulder of lamb Wellington, veiled country lass (Danish applesauce cake), spaghetti con salsa di vognole, and hot cracker crab, but unlike his predecessors, teaching was not the primary rationale. Graham—or more accurately, Treena—thought of his major occupation as comedian.

"*The Galloping Gourmet* is a new phenomenon on TV," wrote Margaret Ness in the *Christian Science Monitor* in 1969, "a cooking entertainer." Imagine—there was a time not so long ago when cooking shows were neither mandated nor expected to amuse. Variety shows, like cooking shows, were older than the medium of TV itself. Injected with 1970s inventiveness and irreverence, the form continued to hold our attention for the entire decade from *Laugh-In* and *Carol Burnett* to *Sonny and Cher, Donny and Marie,* and the indelible *Saturday Night Live.* Rather than a drama and plot to keep us glued to the set, the variety show was a mindless, indulgent entertainment format cut into small, bite-size chunks that hooked us. It was ideal for boomers trying to combat any sobriety—just as it had always intended—brought on by hostages, terrorism, or stagflation. Kerr's spectacle fit this model, too. Each moment held the chance for the unexpected, and whatever ensued would dependably be good for a laugh.

According to his family, Kerr was not the drinker his dipsomaniacal shtick implied. (To wit, "I think I'll have a short slurp whilst doing this. . . .") But his intimate contact with the famous glass of wine made him an ipso facto authority on the grape. Along with an interest in exotic foods, Americans were becoming more curious about wines as part of the package. (To conjure up the conventional wine culture du jour, recall the TV ad "Riunite on ice—so nice.") Kerr would occasionally talk about some of the wines that he drank on the show. "I'd say, 'This is young and fresh and somewhat acidic,'" Kerr said, self-mockingly. "People would talk about the oaky, fruity, butterscotch hint of raspberry because they'd heard other people do it." Personal manager Harry Miller has said he believes Kerr was the first person on earth to talk about pairing particular wines with food. A hyperbolic comment—certainly oenophile Thomas Jefferson must have paid this some notice—but it may well be true that Kerr was the first person widely heard or seen spouting such stuff. People who never had a glass of wine in their lives, Kerr said, credited him with their embrace of the basic tenet of red wine with meat and white wine with fish. In today's uber-sophisticated food culture that rule sounds so elementary (and in some cases faulty), but one has to start somewhere.

"Inevitably you get someone who does something unique," said Kerr obliquely and ever-humbly referring to *The Galloping Gourmet* as such a maverick. "In order to get noticed and come up through the pack, like Emeril did, you have to somehow have something, a slant, or a word or two, a defined persona in order to make it within the genre. It's like Liberace with his clothes and the candelabra."

Emeril Lagasse's "Bam!" and madcap habit of adding ump- teen extra garlic cloves as an afterthought are well known among Food Network devotees and perhaps anyone with func- tional ears and eyes. In the days before TV hit the viewing audi- ence repeatedly with blunt, high- concept ideas, Kerr's trademark

Mostly fun but still instructional, Graham Kerr showed that quick and gourmet were not mutually exclusive.

Everett Collection

was simply his comedic persona. Whereas Julia won untold numbers of fans despite, as her biographer wrote, her being "'all wrong' for television," Kerr was endowed with a made-for-TV personality. The show's title presumably referred to his recipe-hunting visits to various countries shown in taped segments (another convention now taken for granted). But it's fair to say he also galloped about the studio kitchen, flirting, hamming, and performing a veritable slapstick routine. In a half-hour show, he'd take off his suit jacket to cook and gallop then replace it when the time came to dine by candlelight and classical music. He once cooked in a suit of armor and another time in boxer shorts and swim flippers.

Kerr often addressed the audience as a single companion, referring to them as "darling" and "sweetheart." Compared in physicality to both Dick Van Dyke and Gary Cooper, Kerr was both goofy and handsome. Traditionally manly and virile, he was not. This, however, did not detract from his attractiveness, as scores of blushing female fans have suggested. I recall having a bit of a secret May-December crush on him myself (TV is a powerful beast, especially when sitting mere inches from its electrically crackling screen). In fact, his metrosexuality—a term yet to be coined but fully embodied in his being—was an essential part of his charm. As Joan Bowling from Santa Monica, California, wrote to the *Los Angeles Times* in 1969, "This program is a delight. Graham Kerr is witty, gay, light as one of his own soufflés and a trifle bawdy."

In a disapproving review of *The Galloping Gourmet*, longtime *New York Times* television critic Jack Gould wrote: "Whether his recipes are delectable defies electronic analysis." Excellent point, Mr. Gould, and one that is often ignored in discussing cooking shows since there's nothing we can do but believe Kerr and Child when they seem pleased with what they taste test along the way. We can't ourselves judge anything we see prepared on TV, and, for all we know, the marvelous-looking dishes could taste like library paste. But of course, that fact is of little consequence. We imbue our hosts with trustworthiness and rely on visual cues to project delectability. And when a host is handsome and charming, one might be less likely to find fault with the fact that the time for cooking the rice was omitted or that he used directions like "slosh some liquid into the mixture" in place of actual measurements. Part of the cachet of cooking—then and now—is knowing or pretending to know how to use your intuition and not having to always bother with silly old garden-variety measurements like "cup" or "tablespoon." A "glurg" or a "ching" ought to get the point across, no? And besides, who is really watching with pen and paper in hand? Like a soufflé, Kerr was irresistible, and those clamoring to criticize his lack of formality or jot down specific recipes were unfortunately missing the point.

Like Julia Child, Graham Kerr also got his TV career jumpstarted somewhat by accident—and also with an omelet. On Battle of Britain Day in New Zealand in1960, the local news was prepared to show a segment with a representative from the Royal New Zealand Air Force. The physical training instructor was designated but had sprained his ankle and couldn't go on. Air Force Chief Catering Officer Graham Kerr was called in as a last-minute substitute. "I went on, made an omelet and made people laugh," he said, amazed. Kerr became a regular on the evening news, sitting at the end of the lineup, where the weatherman and the sportscaster perch. A television critic, who Kerr jokingly noted had been appointed the previous day, declared him a natural for television. Just three months later, his made-for-TV personality led to his own half-hour television program, *Entertaining with Kerr*, and then there was no turning back. "So I was it. I was a twenty-six-year-old who was alarmed by the fact that he was on national television between *Peyton Place* and *The Avengers* at eight o'clock on a Tuesday night."

Kerr considers New Zealand his training ground, and modestly attributes the show's popularity to the fact that "there was no other television channel, and there were only fifty television sets in the whole country. I would have never made it had I just wandered onto television in the United States." But in the U.S. there were three networks and 95 percent television saturation, and the Kerrs had no problems capturing that market either. After madly successful runs in Australia and New Zealand through 1968, the Kerrs began broadcasting in thirty-eight other countries. The first episode aired in the U.S. in December 1968 and started regularly in February 1969. They taped as many as five episodes a day.

"On a daily basis, five days a week," Kerr said. "We were put on CBS at noon between *As the World Turns* and *Secret Storm*. Lathered between two soaps. And then I think it was within four or five months we were literally in every major market in the United States." The show was on 102 stations in the U.S., and they had one hundred million viewers worldwide by the end of 1969.

Though he had been cooking in a professional environment since the age of ten, Kerr was overwhelmed by the sudden success and felt ill at ease in the role of expert in his mere thirties. (How quaint the gentility—it's inconceivable that even a twenty-year-old today would fear she wasn't worthy of the title of *American Idol*.) "But if a tiger rushes past you and you grab its tail, you can't really let go," he explained. And besides, Treena wouldn't pay his worries any mind. Her main concern was that he be entertaining.

"I am the food person and Treena is completely disinterested in food," said Kerr. "Treena's focus was the audience. She thought that I was the most unutterably boring man in the entire world. 'Appalling,' she said." So Kerr challenged her: "If you're so clever then why don't you produce it?" She readily accepted the challenge.

Treena and Graham have both worn the pants throughout their fifty-plus-year marriage, but when it came to the television shows, Treena chose exactly which pants Graham would wear. "I even made sure his tie matched the candles," she said. "And gave him stories that he didn't really want to tell." Treena would grade his shows based on the comedy. Her ratings likely mattered far more, both to her husband and to the show itself, than any Nielsens. But Treena understood that those viewers attached to the external ratings were the bottom line. "The audience are the money," she said.

They have to be entertained. I said to Graham, "There's a lady sitting there in Des Moines, in a pink dressing gown, curlers in her hair and smoking a cigarette, and you've got to knock that ash off her cigarette." You know, people have worries, but to make them laugh for a little so they can forget, that's what I felt Graham needed to do. Especially with such a boring subject.

"The first absolute rule of television is 'thou shalt not bore,'" echoed Graham, in the tone of an impish student who learned his lesson well.

And so in actuality it was Treena's lack of interest in food that allowed for the show's robust success. She had a background in theater and was the mastermind behind the inclusion of a live audience and the jumping over the chair with the wine. Treena, who has known Graham since childhood, always knew that he was funniest when he was acting naturally. "He has this sense of humor you cannot catch, tie up, and make into a laugh," she said. She would booby-trap the set when she felt Graham was getting tired, creating a situation he had to solve on the spot, on camera, like finding the inside of a cupboard walled off where he was supposed to find one of his ingredients. When the inevitable production battles with network mucketymucks ensued, Treena, with her hands on her six-months-pregnant belly, argued about keeping the comedy in the program and won, boldly telling the suits what was what.

As testament to the comedic virtue of the show, funny people Lucille Ball and Danny Kaye were reportedly avid fans. In June 1969 Wayne Warga of the *Los Angeles Times* wrote, "*Galloping Gourmet* . . .

is probably the most amusing and entertaining show to come on ABC since *The Avengers*, my favorite show." As befalls those in the limelight, however, not everyone was so enamored. Kerr said that a New York TV critic said the show wouldn't last. "This man wouldn't know how to find a saucepan in broad daylight," Kerr recalled from her review. "And his humor just fills in the cracks of what he doesn't know about food." (Two days later, according to Kerr, she issued a mea culpa which he summarized: "This is a sleeper. I got it wrong. Watch this.") The fact that he was entertaining was apparently off-putting to some, as if being funny precluded the possibility of being a skilled cook. Dione Lucas found *The Galloping Gourmet* distressing, saying that "there is no need to introduce buffoonery into cooking."

Members of the food establishment, including James Beard, *New York Times* restaurant critic Craig Claiborne, and the White House chef Henry Haller dismissed him and disparaged his skills. Beard said Kerr was "vulgar and only appeals to a group of menopausic ladies." The *Times* TV critic Jack Gould wrote,

> Apparently, his ambition is to aspire to the informality of the Automat with food brought over from the Four Seasons . . . [Kerr has a] suffocating demeanor of haughty cuteness. Of late he has been gripped with anatomical humor of the most depressing sort. One morning an entire sequence was blipped out.. . . The level of his wit invites misgiving over his standards of taste.

Kerr was, in fact, warned by the Canadian Broadcasting System not to refer to peeling a cucumber as "circumcising" it. When he demonstrated putting walnuts into a "dimpled bottom" (of dough), he raised his eyebrows like a naughty lad inviting reprimand. The atmosphere created by the sexual revolution made the audience—including that lady in Des Moines—more receptive to the flirty innuendos that were an integral part of his style. A "trifle bawdy," yes. While the adage "sex sells" had perhaps not yet become the accepted ruling force of the media, it was already working its magic.

"Standards of taste," in effect, were the coattails upon which Kerr rode. "Culture is going one way, you're going the other and the two of you cross," said Kerr, remarking on the fortuity of the show's timing, tapping into the cultural climate of the late sixties and early seventies. "It's interesting to see where you cross and why you cross. One is only that successful because you happened to have arrived at the right place at the right time with the right thing."

"And with the right producer," Treena added.

Besides the most fitting producer and front man, why did *The Galloping Gourmet* hit it so well? Kerr himself, despite hailing from off the continent, has a keen sense of what was churning in the souls of Americans at the time. In addition to his adolescence metaphor, he described the men who may have seen Europe and Asia for the first time while serving in WWII, and later Korea and Vietnam, who brought back new tastes and a desire for more. "We literally went all around the world," said Kerr, "searching out the classic dishes, to bring them back, to modify them, to make them available to the American public and then the world. It was the world's food for the world, made consumable and entertainable.

"People were beginning to acquire experiences as well as stuff," he said. "Eating wasn't just eating. You could actually experience something and have a story to tell. It was a culture shift from the norm, from the steak and potatoes. And I think we arrived at exactly that time."

Julia Child had already begun to affect and reflect this sea change, and the Kerrs extended and widened it. Like Child, but with greater intent, Kerr allowed an average viewer to witness his flops—a cake stuck in the pan, forgetting to add the egg whites, dolloping his shirt with whipped cream—and take courage, mustering the "If he can do it, I can do it" attitude. One major difference with Kerr was his presence on commercial, not public, television.

When *The Galloping Gourmet* came on the air in the U.S., the only real "competition" was *The French Chef*. But Kerr did not see it that way. He described Julia Child, whom he greatly admired and with whom he shared a fond mutual respect (despite her reported dismay at his use of canned asparagus and packaged ham), as catering to the "viewing intelligentsia," a specific PBS-watching audience. Julia Child's primary focus was teaching, and entertainment was a by-product. Popular though she was, she still only reached the PBS slice of the TV pie. "She appealed to people who could afford to travel and who had dinner parties," Kerr said. "The rest of the great unwashed public watched the programs on the other channels with commercials in them." The great unwashed were the Kerrs's target, which they hit spot on.

When Treena had first floated the chair-jumping idea to her husband, however, he was agape. "What would Julia say?" he asked, horrified. Treena's response: "Bless her heart, but I don't think Julia's going to be a substantial part of your audience."

The other obvious difference between Julia and Graham was gender. As feminism urged both men and women to let go of antiquated, prescribed roles, women were theoretically no longer the sole domestic agents. Though they were entering the labor force in unprecedented numbers in the early 1970s, women were by no means leaving—either by choice or social expectations—their household role entirely. The kitchen, therefore, was getting crowded. But because food and cooking were increasingly intertwined with lifestyle—a gender-blind concept of increasing importance—men became conversant, if not actively engaged, in the goings-on, too. Dad in an apron may have been a far cry from David Bowie's androgynous alter ego Ziggy Stardust, but they were perhaps a product of the same creative momentum.

As Jacques Pépin wrote in that 1978 *Los Angeles Times* article, "No longer afraid of being emasculated upon donning an apron or wielding a whisk, the male is invading this once-sacrosanct bastion of womankind in ever-growing numbers, and with mounting aplomb." Fairly and accurately pointing out that men's domestic dabbling paled in comparison to the time-management and multitasking skills implicitly demanded of the lady of the house, Pépin nevertheless identified an important change in the culture of the kitchen and society.

Though men had previously hosted cooking shows (James Beard, the Mystery Chef, Francois Pope, Chef Milani and men on various local programs), most hosts had been women. Men in authoritative roles were nothing new, however, on the subject of women's domain, and according to several of those interviewed in a *New York Times* article in the 1960s, many men *and* women believed that women preferred to watch male hosts. Kerr, however, didn't simply show women how to cook; he proved that cooking wasn't just a woman's job, espousing the increasingly widely accepted mindset. As Kerr said of the cultural shift and his show's part in it, "It allowed for a man to cut up a bit and enjoy himself thoroughly while cooking. I think it got a few men away from barbecue only and brought him into the kitchen as well."

One boy's club endeavor was *The Gourmet*, hosted by cookbook author and food writer David Wade. The show was a popular daily half-hour broadcast in several major cities in 1969 and the early 1970s, and it boasted celebrity guests and their favorite recipes, including Charlton Heston (cheese tuna puff), Jerry Lewis (Bavarian cream), James Garner (maverick steak) and Mickey Mantle (Mickey Mantle salad). Gregory Peck wrote the introduction to Wade's 1967 cookbook *Dining with David Wade*. Peck's broiled coffee ham recipe read: "Select ham slices the desired thickness. Score around the edges, place onto a hot broiler and broil until some of the ham juice comes to the surface and the ham starts to brown. Brush on the ham a little instant coffee and continue to broil until coffee grains dissolve."

The trend of men-as-equals in the kitchen was even reflected in 1970s talk shows where male hosts like Mike Douglas and Phil Donahue would tie on aprons and participate in cooking demonstrations. The heightened social status of cooking (men's involvement, of course, helped to elevate the status of the hobby as well as helping to increase the spirit of competition) was further evidenced by shows like *Celebrity Cooks*. Produced in Vancouver starting in 1976, the show featured actor-host Bruno Gerussi chatting and cooking with the likes of David Letterman and Margaret Trudeau, as well as Julia Child. If famous people of all stripes were getting in on the act, it was surely something to pay attention to and emulate.

In addition to the breakneck pace and the logistical hurdles—traveling and doing commercials between show tapings—Kerr believes that in gaining international success he also lost something. He had to emotionally wrestle with the notion of becoming an entertainer when what he really wanted was to be a teacher. "With anything that happens in this world that breaks the mold, there has to be a great tension line there somewhere," he said. He always harbored a twinge of anxiety that "because of the methodology" he was never taken seriously as a teacher. "And part of me died in doing that." He was a genuine professional who took great care in doing the research, testing, and development of user-friendly recipes. He worried that people wouldn't believe that every single recipe was important to him. But he did find a motivation to reconcile the dissonance. "Treena explained to me, if you don't do this, you will not have the opportunity to be an influence to other people."

Despite high-flying popularity, however, *The Galloping Gourmet* stopped production in 1971. A serious car accident that injured both Graham and Treena derailed the Kerrs, compelling them to reprioritize and slow down. The show continued in reruns through 1974. In many ways, *The Galloping Gourmet* was as revolutionary as *The French Chef.* Julia made gourmet cooking feasible and Graham made it fun. The Kerrs fashioned a new breed of cooking show, capturing the youthful and the nonserious cooks. Though not a deliberate partnership, Julia and Graham together lassoed virtually the entire (it was possible in those days) TV-watching public. That had an irrevocable effect on the way Americans thought about and behaved toward their grocery stores, their kitchens, their spouses, and their leisure time.

Though the show had a relatively short run, *The Galloping Gourmet* has endured in our collective memory precisely because it came along just at the right time. Kerr had shaped his career in the 1960s but exerted his influence on American culture in the 1970s. That influence is evidenced on a modest scale by the professional chefs who tell Kerr that watching his show when they were tykes inspired them to choose cooking as their career. On a larger scale, the plethora of entertainment-food-cooking-travel shows have Treena Kerr to thank for thinking food is boring and Graham Kerr to thank for teaching us that it's not.

Though gourmet cooking was coming into its own, after *The Galloping Gourmet* went off the air there was little in the way of wide-appeal nationally syndicated cooking shows for the remainder of the decade. Viewers continued to get their cooking instruction from local stations, as they had for decades, and from reruns of Julia Child (and her subsequent *Julia Child and Company* and *Julia Child and More Company* in the late 1970s) and Graham Kerr.

Most national content related to cooking was found in short filler pieces such as Merle Ellis's *The Butcher*, Burt Wolf's *What's Cookin'* ("He's 20 times quicker than the 'Galloping Gourmet'" boasted a *People* headline) that were woven into network magazine or talk shows. The highly mimicked ("very simple, very easy"), mustachioed *PM Magazine*'s Chef Tell Erhardt, for instance, gave viewers ninety-second cooking demos. The dearth of popular, national *Galloping Gourmet*-like shows did not mean people weren't interested. In fact, they may have been practicing in their own kitchens. These accessible segments meant wider exposure and a continued weaving of cooking into the fabric of our lives, as opposed to a segregated, gendered domain.

Food on the Nightly News

Just as the *Galloping Gourmet* piqued the public's interest initially from the broadcast news desk, so did the *Eyewitness Gourmet*. In 1970, New York's ABC *Eyewitness News* investigative and political reporter, Bob Lape, was tapped for a new assignment. "Somebody conjured up the notion," recalled Lape, "that the news department should send someone to a restaurant to film the preparation of one of the signature dishes of the restaurant and we would put it on the air as the kicker, the last thing on the six o' clock news on Fridays." Lape recognized that the plentitude of restaurants in the city and the concurrent interest surely was worthy of some coverage that was otherwise lacking. After reporting on a murder in Brooklyn, he was that "someone" and was sent to a Manhattan restaurant called L'Aiglon. He was told by the owner that they would be preparing veal chop L'Aiglon.

It's veal chop in sorrel sauce, and I thought to myself, "what's a sorrel?" They prepared it on a gueridon in the dining room next to the table where I was seated, and at the end of this three minute preparation, I had to sign off, and somehow I had to say, "Bob Lape Eyewitness News." I thought, well, I guess I have to taste it on camera to indicate that it is good—else why would we be doing this foolish thing in a newscast? So I took a bite of it, chewing desperately because I didn't want to talk with my mouth full and I said "Mm mm," to cover the swallowing. And I pronounced it good and signed off and I was sent out the next week to do it again in another restaurant. And the next week again.

Lape worried when the *Eyewitness* crew went to another French restaurant in Manhattan where the dish was going to be rognons à la moutarde (kidneys in mustard sauce). Not only did he suddenly question the wisdom of the gourmet feature, but he thought the audience would be repelled. To show his editors a thing or two, he told the cameraman to zoom in on the plate of raw kidneys. "I said, 'Kidney lovers, attention! This one is just for you,'" he remembered. "We got five hundred requests for it. And I thought, uh oh, we're in trouble here. This feature has legs." But after the kidney episode—which he said tasted fine since any organ flavor was masked by the sauce—he demanded that he get to choose the restaurant and the dish.

Bob Lape, the "Eyewitness Gourmet," was a newsman caught up in the public's appetite for fine dining.

Courtesy Bob Lape

Lape's father had sold dry goods and staples to grocery stores and institutional kitchens. "I think I brought a plebian palate to the case, a Midwestern meat and potatoes sort." Though he was mindful of choosing restaurants and recipes with an eye to cost and complexity, he said that even difficult dishes like a chocolate gateau New York from Le Perigord garnered 8,000 requests. "I found the audience taught me a lot. Don't ever underestimate it."

Eyewitness Gourmet started once per week, then increased to thrice, always the kicker on Friday, Saturday, and Sunday. The feature aired on ABC stations in the suburbs, the tri-state area, and into Pennsylvania. Lape did the feature a thousand times over the next twelve years.

It pulled between one and a half and two million recipe requests, as many as 26,000 for a single recipe—Junior's cheesecake in Brooklyn. It became a juggernaut. It became a feature so powerful that to my great surprise it would literally pull the ratings up in the last quarter hour of the newscast. . . . People were tuning in from other stations to watch *this*. . . . The feature just became such a vital thing and such a viable thing and such a commercial thing that they were selling adjacencies to it, packages for a quarter million dollars in 1981. It worked like gangbusters. It was a tremendous popular and commercial success.

Lape said the head of the ABC-owned and -operated stations across the country deemed the feature "the hottest thing in the country, not weather, not sports, this eating thing, this gourmet thing." ABC established similar features in owned and operated stations in Chicago, Los Angeles, and Boston.

"The thing became red hot," said Lape. Rather than damage his hard-nosed image as a news reporter as his crew half-jokingly warned, "I found it gave me pleasant egress to most people." He found he got a plum seat from a clerk in a courtroom, for example, in exchange for a simple recommendation for a good Swiss restaurant.

During a press conference, a governor said to him (while other reporters became a bit impatient), "Lape, that sole couldn't possibly have been as good as you said it was last night." On location on the docks, he had longshoremen recognize him and call out, "Hey, it's the guy who eats!"

"It tracked the tremendous period of growth in both interest and sophistication in American dining," said Lape.

I think it was the wealth of food information out there that hadn't been tapped. When I started interviewing these guys and getting them to talk on camera, in those days you would find very few chefs who could do the explanation part. But as years passed the more television generation American chefs that you ran into, the better they were at explanation if not inspiration. We were just showing them how things are made by other people. People like [restaurateur] Drew Nieporent said this was the harbinger of the Food Television Network.

Going with the Flow

The cultural changes taking place during the late sixties and the seventies were surely daunting for some old-timers and social conservatives. TV dramas like *The Waltons* and *Little House on the Prairie* may have quelled the romantic nostalgia many of these folks probably had for the days of butter-churning, general stores, homesteading, and Depression pluckiness. For those who still favored a traditional role model, stalwart TV personality Dinah Shore had a kitchen on her *Dinah's Place* talk show set in the early 1970s. Along with celebrity interviews, her show embraced the traditional womanly arts of sewing, dieting, and decorating, and generally touted the joys of making a happy home.

While the trials and tribulations of single girls was a running theme of many TV sitcoms in the 1960s and 1970s (with Marlo Thomas as "That Girl" and Mary Tyler Moore leading the pack), mixing such shenanigans with cooking might have seemed too bold a move for some. Though Jinx Kragen produced two pilot episodes in the late 1960s based on *Saucepans and the Single Girl*, the cookbook she cowrote with Judy Perry in 1965, the show was never picked up by a network. The book was a light-hearted recipe collection for young "career girls" who were inexperienced cooks. The TV show starred actress Joann Pflug as the single girl, and on the first of the pilots she was preparing for a date with comedian Tommy Smothers. There was a little cooking—mostly dumping quick bread ingredients into a bowl and Smothers wowing Pflug with his peanut butter and jelly sandwich making skills—and a lot of flirting and comedy. Jinx (now Morgan) said, "I don't think any of the suits at the networks understood the concept of the show. To them a cooking show was some frumpy lady with an apron demonstrating boring food made with the advertisers' ingredients. . . . I suspect they just didn't see the potential for the show." Pflug's hiphuggers and frosty eyeshadow apparently did not advertise "home service."

While vestiges of the old guard were still kicking, social progress marched on. Even Dinah had good old boys Frank Sinatra and Spiro Agnew making pasta (though not together). But at the same time, on *Mary Tyler Moore*, Betty White played Sue Ann Nivens, the chirpy, man-serving host of *The Happy Homemaker*, a show produced by the fictional WJM-TV station where Mary worked. Such parody surely signaled that the genus of the Stepford wife homemaker was becoming a relic.

Despite the widespread reverence of Julia Child and her positive influence on international food awareness, the trend in the 1970s, even on PBS, was increasingly an almost un-Julia approach. As Graham Kerr explained, Julia Child was the master teacher for a certain segment of the population but the rest of the viewing public opened up the market to any number of cooking show hosts who may not have been professionally trained cooks, actors, or self-described gourmets.

As the TV industry eventually caught on to the success of the entertainment potential of the genre, "fun" cooking shows—especially those with captivating hosts—saw a brighter future. Disguising common sense and practical advice in an informal, barrel-of-fun format was part of the new charge of television cooking shows. There was also—and still is—an undeniable whole grain dryness associated with PBS programming. Wishing to dissociate themselves from the desiccated, dour home ec image traditionally linked to cooking instruction, producers on both commercial and public television adapted to the trend posthaste.

LaDeva Davis, a junior high school teacher from Philadelphia, was recruited to host *What's Cooking?* on PBS in 1975. As a performing arts teacher, she and her students had gained some recognition for their African dance performance, and after appearing on a local

WHYY program, Davis caught the attention of producers there. "They liked me for my personality," she said. The producers asked her if she was interested (she said yes), *then* they asked if she could cook. "Well yeah, my mother's from the South. All black women from the South teach their daughters to cook. . . . When they found out I could cook, they said, ok we can make this work." (With a touch more rigor and much higher stakes, this may not be so different from how cooking show hosts are born today.)

Like the homemaking radio shows from the Depression and World War II, *What's Cooking* was created during a recession, and its theme, too, was low-cost, high-nutrition. Each show's theme—grains, snacks and appetizers, eggs, pasta—included Davis's spontaneous self, plus nutrition and budget tips. "Eat well save money," said Davis. "That was the whole deal." She worked with a nutritionist on the menus and occasionally used some of her own family's recipes (e.g. corn pudding). "They had other things they wanted to bring in that I knew nothing about," she said. "I wasn't privy to everything that riboflavin is in and what it does or what foods carry vitamin A, C, D, E, etcetera." She learned about Liptauer cheese (a soft cheese spread of Eastern European origin). One memorable theme was the BLT show—brains, liver, and tongue. Hard times call for desperate measures.

When the show premiered in 1975, the *Chicago Tribune's* Dorothy Collin referred to Davis as "a down-home version of Julia Child. . . . Aimed at teaching viewers how to eat on a low budget, [*What's Cooking?*] will focus on persons whose time and income are limited. To get the message across, LaDeva gets right folksy." Collin also quoted a spokesman for the producers who said, "She is speaking to people who might be intimidated by Julia Child." Indeed, one of the show's producers at Philadelphia's WHYY-TV referred to *What's Cooking?* as "a sort of televised 'recession cookbook'" thereby catering to the particular concerns of the era and certainly not, as Davis said, "to Mrs. Gotrocks."

"We're going to make an egg pie," said LaDeva on one episode, "that's quiche Lorraine if you want to be fancy about it. And then we'll try a cheese soufflé. But don't be scared. If I can do it you can do it." This was the same message delivered by Julia Child and Graham Kerr, but with them the "fancy" results often contradicted the intention—sometimes in complexity, sometimes in cost.

"They felt that as a schoolteacher I was eloquent enough to be able to pull off the jargon without being boring," Davis remembered. "And I was black. And there was no black woman cooking [on TV]. There were no black cooks period. I looked black but I didn't look like Aunt Jemima. I didn't look like the woman from *Gone with the Wind*. So I was sellable. To everybody."

Though she was a talented nightclub singer and comfortable performing for audiences, as a result of the TV show, Davis got a taste of what it was like to be an actual celebrity. After the successful pilot, she taped thirteen episodes, then another thirteen. "I was in every newspaper from the *Philadelphia Inquirer* to the *New York Times*, to the *Post-Gazette*, it was amazing. A guy said he turned on the TV and saw me in Arizona." The show was carried by dozens of PBS stations around the country. The *New York Times*'s Shawn Kennedy wrote, "Miss Davis's personality lends a sugar-coating to this Public Broadcasting service series on low-cost, high-nutrition cookery."

The Mike Douglas Show was shooting in Philadelphia during the 1970s, and Douglas came over to meet Davis at WHYY. She became his go-to guest when we wanted to do a cooking segment. She got the chance to meet and cook with Danny Thomas, Alan King, Jamie Farr, Billy Dee Williams, Natalie Cole, comedian Tom Dreesen, Rich Little, singer Maxine Nightingale, and Jimmy "Dynomite!" Walker (they made potato chips, a Walker favorite). All the guests donned identical *What's Cooking?* aprons and were given bowls and spoons to cook along with Davis. Davis was funny and charming and comfortable with the stars. The stars themselves, out of their element (Alan King held onto his cigar while stirring falafel mix) and no longer alone in the spotlight, appeared uncomfortable and poked fun at the endeavor.

Davis said her *What's Cooking?* producer, Lynn Lonker, told her she was to "chit chat and give nutritional information when you're not stirring something. And we want you to be your same funny self

Courtesy LaDeva Davis

Producers discovered LaDeva Davis's sense of humor and personality, which she used to impart practical nutritional and economical tips during the 1970s recession.

so that when you're not saying something you can say something educational where nutrition is concerned and then you can go back and be funny again." She would, for example, talk to her meatballs before eating them, leaving the cameramen and producers doubled over in laughter. Her trademarks originated from her natural sense of humor, not pasted-on promotional strategies: she liked to pose holding a pan over the long hair she piled on top of her head, and on each episode she wore a different apron from her personal collection. Every one had a saying, like "this piggy went to market and ate all the way home," or "I'd rather be playing tennis."

Davis explained:

> So here I was this black woman in this kitchen with all these modern appliances. Every black woman in America is going to feel like, yeah, you go for it, girl, you got it all. And then the white women would certainly go for what I was saying because every white woman in America thought every black woman could cook anyhow, soon as they came out of the womb. Back in those days, they did. So I came round at the right time, I guess.

Courtesy of her skin color and her spunky humor, she was likened to full-time show biz stars Pearl Bailey, Bill Cosby, and Flip Wilson. "Why are they calling me a cross between Julia Child and Flip Wilson?" Davis said to the *Inquirer*. "Because I'm black, I can cook, and they never know what I'm gonna say next."

Looking beyond the Mirror

At the same time that all the fondueing, pasta primavera and quiche making, gender role changing, and cultural getting-to-know-me was going on, TV cooking was warming up to more varied cuisines. Husband and wife team Margaret and Franco Romagnoli demonstrated that Italian cooking was more than just pizza and spaghetti on *The Romagnoli's Table*, an Italian cooking show that started in 1974 on PBS. Italian food was gaining chicdom (*The Godfather* release in 1972 probably didn't hurt) and was found to be more forgiving and malleable than French. For the Romagnolis, meal preparation was a shared experience equal in pleasure to the eating—a concept that became more integral to cooking programs. The gender-boundary blurring dovetailed with the burgeoning atmosphere of ethnic revival and cultural diversity that had been generated in the 1960s. The latter fueled a stronger interest in international and regional foods, and shows like Justin Wilson's *Cookin' Cajun* cropped up in the middle of the decade.

Husband and wife hosts, Franco and Margaret Romagnoli work in tandem, cooking and teaching in perfect harmony.

PBS/NET Programming Files, National Public Broadcasting Archives, Special Collections, University of Maryland Libraries/WGBH Educational Foundation. Copyright © 1974 WGBH/Boston

International Cookbook featured home economist Joan Hood preparing dishes from different countries, geographical regions, and groups such as Native and African Americans. Host Titus Chan taught Chinese cooking aimed at a non-Chinese audience on another staple, *The Chan-ese Way*. The word "bounce" regularly appeared in descriptions of Chan, who earned himself the nickname "Chinese Galloping Gourmet."

There was another earnest movement taking place as well. After the 1950s, when serving canned spinach indicated the height of urbanity, a natural cooking movement began in the 1960s as an offshoot of the counterculture lifestyle. Americans were awakening to the vulnerability of the environment and the provenance of their food. Notions about food commingled with the camp and hedonism of disco to the fully antiestablishment outlet of punk rock. A large segment of youth culture—those still mentally at Woodstock as well as those metabolically embracing punk—placed high value on living a simpler life outside of the market economy. Just as it was for middle-class suburban families, cooking was a mode of self-expression and for many young people an opportunity to be in charge and do as they pleased without any authoritative interference. In places like Berkeley, California, where restaurateur Alice Waters and company (she opened her restaurant Chez Panisse in 1971) were making a religion out of consuming locally grown foods from small farms, the movement had taken off earlier. Francis Moore Lappé's *Diet for a Small Planet* was published that same year wherein the author advocated eating "as low on the food chain" as possible and had a significant impact on the increase of vegetarianism in the U.S.

While far from a hippies' medium, television offered a tempered, less politicized version of the quasi economic-political "countercuisine," as American Studies professor Warren Belasco coined it. Just as public broadcasting stations in the 1970s pioneered many international- and regional-themed cooking shows, they were also a breeding ground for cooking shows that focused on the environment and morally aware eating. On *Natural Foods*, Beatrice Trum Hunter, a food and environment expert, taught viewers how to use yogurt, grow bean sprouts, and make baby food. On *Cooking Naturally* Kathy Dinaburg's primary objective was "to raise people's consciousness about what they eat, to make them aware of the nutritional information that will help them eat more wisely." In the early 1980s, cookbook author Kathy Hoshijo hosted a vegetarian cooking program, *Kathy's Kitchen*. Hoshijo, whose family moved to Hawaii when she was a young child, became interested in natural and local cooking and started writing newspaper cooking columns. As happened with Dione Lucas, Joyce Chen, and even Julia Child, Hoshijo taught small-scale cooking classes, found them to be popular, and was able to move to a wider audience via television.

These shows also highlighted an interest in personal health and well-being and concerns about food safety. The butter-and-cream-pushing Galloping Gourmet even returned to commercial TV with a three-minute filler in 1975 called *Take Kerr* (his surname, handily, is pronounced "care") in which he promoted repentantly healthy cooking tips. In contrast to *The Galloping Gourmet* where nutrition was a virtual nonissue, *Take Kerr* was about taste first and nutrition a close second. "After all, our body can't be traded in, and spare parts are hard to come by," Kerr told a *Chicago Tribune* reporter in 1975. "We're basing *Take Kerr* on the premise that the further the cook's family has to sit away from the table because of stomach bulge, the worse the cook's job has been done." This statement could have easily been uttered thirty years hence, and Kerr's prescience has led him to more zeal and books on the topic in recent years. The Kathys, Beas, and remade Grahams were once a small minority whose voices were barely heard above the decade's decadent din, but their ilk is in power today. The punks and hippies grew up to be "bourgeois bohemians" (to use journalist David Brooks's phrase) and keep revenues for places like Whole Foods in the growing billions. In fact, the philosophies of associating food with societal change that took hold in the late 1960s and into the 1970s set the stage for sweeping changes in food politics and consumer behavior in the 1990s. But first, the 1980s intervened.

CHAPTER 5

Cultural Capital and the Frugal Gourmet

Money changes everything.

—Tom Gray

Earning a Living

At the bus stop on the morning after Reagan defeated Carter in the 1980 presidential election, my best friend and I shared precocious, melodramatic tears. Though at the age of fifteen I was too naive to fully know why, perhaps a part of me mourned the loss of my beloved goldenrod-toned, sandalwood-scented, "Free to Be You and Me," Helen Reddy–tinted decade and sensed that I'd be confronted with unbidden demons. Prescient emotions they were: ABBA was replaced by Wang Chung, beanbags tossed out to accommodate sectional sofas, ponchos pushed out by blazers, and Rush Limbaugh's voice rose above Maude's.

That day was the beginning of an era of dramatic highs and lows—politically, economically, and culturally. On the upside, the U.S. economy experienced an unprecedented bull market, and the end of the decade saw the fall of the Berlin Wall, followed in short order by the end of the Cold War. As they were in the 1950s, many Americans were brimming with confidence about their bulging

wallets and superpower status. Like most decades, depicted in cari-
cature posthumously, the 1980s are best remembered by conspicuous
wealth and ambition, illustrated by the likes of TV shows *Dynasty*
and *Lifestyles of the Rich and Famous*. But on the downside there was a
devastating stock market crash, chronic national debt, and the emergence of the AIDS and crack cocaine epidemics. Despite the lows,
American spirit—either preternaturally plucky or fueled by denial—
could not be dampened. And just as the 1950s had its sparkle-smiling
TV families, Bobby McFerrin's hit song, "Don't Worry, Be Happy," was
a prescription many followed without resistance in the 1980s. The me
generation that had found itself in the 1960s and 1970s was asserting
itself, now with spending power and a virile desire to grab the bull by
the horns. Values that focused on inner happiness were still there, but
many found that the satisfaction of material cravings was an important and justified aspect of maintaining psychological contentment.

Professional ambition dominated the lives of the newly minted
yuppies and led to a widespread trend of longer work hours. According
to research by sociologists Juliet Schor and Laura Leete-Guy, in 1989
a fully employed American was working 149 hours more per year
than his or her counterpart had been twenty years prior—an increase
of 56 percent. (This figure includes "non-market" hours engaged in
work such as home maintenance and childcare.) It was not only the
desire to acquire and to accumulate capital that drove people to work
more, but it was the ostensible enjoyment of work itself. In a seeming
shift in priorities, for many, work was not a leisure-time killer—it was
pleasurable in and of itself. Work (or money-earning activity), rather
than play, was the new mode of self-expression.

Women—now composing about half of the workforce—made
especially big strides, continuing to stream into the labor market
in ever-higher numbers in their power suits and shoulder pads and
on up the ladder toward the glass ceiling. Despite a still cavernous
pay gap, desegregation of gender roles was progressing. Even Betty
Crocker had to acknowledge that times were changing, albeit on a
slanted playing field. A Random House press release for her 1985

Betty Crocker's Working Woman's Cookbook assured us that "[e]fficiency at home and on the job is *not* incompatible" and painted a forbidding portrait of the target audience:

> A woman who works 9–5 and has a home-cooked dinner on her family's table by 7 must be as efficient in her kitchen as she is at the office. Today's working woman requires timesaving recipes that she can trust to be nutritious as well as appetizing. Combining a 40-hour-a-week job with the production of nearly 1,000 meals a year demands maximum use of minimum time.

The full description, studded with figures, is likely meant to appeal to the serious career woman and the international-esque recipes— "quick-and-easy" skillet Stroganoff, "do-ahead" tamale pie—to the enlightened homemaker. Acknowledging the "two-career woman," Betty appeared to have her fictional finger on the pulse; she knew all too well what time it was. Schor and Leete-Guy calculated that fully employed women increased the number of work hours in the market alone (therefore *not* including the domestic work they still engaged in—usually the lion's share of it) by 287 hours, representing a 204 percent increase or the equivalent of seven forty-hour workweeks per year.

I was a blissfully oblivious college student in the 1980s, existing in that work-leisure bubble that had no relation to the external world. My relationship with food consisted of effortlessly donning the freshman fifteen, engaging in sophomoric dieting, and spending a restorative junior year in Paris, feasting on fromage and patisseries. I don't recall watching a cooking show, following a recipe, or having much intellectual interest at all in what I ingested. Certainly it was due in part to my age and circumstances, but I think many Americans could say that they, too, dropped out of the world of home cooking, turning to boil-in-a-bag Lean Cuisine, whatever could go in the microwave and, for a significant segment, dining out. (While the leisure class had expanded in the 1980s, it was still an exclusive membership and dining out was still a luxury to many.) According to research cited by the market research firm NPD Group, in 1987, 2,000 representative households reported that 56 percent of the foods and beverages consumed at home required no heating appliance. The same research group showed that completely homemade food was the most rapidly declining food type.

Cultural historians have noted that preparation of food has predictably been minimized at times of leisure and times of crisis. While the 1980s would be better categorized as the former, it was not exactly the belle époque. Work and leisure were one and the same, and home cooking was one of the casualties of the time reallocation. Men and women were equally disinterested in spending too much time toiling in their own kitchens, but they were equally interested in food and its attending cultural capital. "Aesthetics had displaced functionality," wrote cultural studies scholar Toby Miller. The new values paradigm simultaneously increased the market for convenience foods and haute cuisine, another example in the long list of contrasts that exemplified food in American culture and a host of cultural phenomena in the 1980s.

Though we were introduced to the likes of McDonald's McPizza and Hamburger Helper taco mix, it would be unfair to characterize the decade as another dark age of gastronomy (the 1950s being a relatively recent and more apt example). In the produce realm alone, we opened our culinary world to kiwi, passion fruit, mango, star fruit, radicchio, blood oranges, wild mushrooms, blue and Yukon gold potatoes, jicama, mesclun, arugula, and lemongrass. Though we take them for granted now, before the 1980s we didn't know from flavored vinegars, tricolore pastas, pesto, risotto, polenta, or gelato. Southwest cooking—Cal-Mex and Tex-Mex—became a regular part of our gastro-vocabulary. The "foodie" persona was introduced in Ann Barr and Paul Levy's 1983 *Official Foodie Handbook*, the subtitle of which commanded readers to "be modern—worship food." The word "foodie," commonly believed to have been coined in a 1982

Harpers & Queen magazine article cowritten by Barr and edited by Levy, is defined in the *Handbook* as "a person who is very very very interested in food. Foodies are the ones talking about food in any gathering—salivating over restaurants, recipes, radicchio." Movies like the Japanese *Tampopo* and the Danish *Babette's Feast* depicted stories wherein the joys of food were central to the plot and, while not made in the U.S., were popular among elite American filmgoers. Though food had already achieved cultural capital in the previous decade, the 1980s burnished it and encrusted it with pink peppercorns and diamonds.

Rise of the Chef

But most importantly, this was the era of the ascendance of restaurants and the celebrity chef. Those Americans who benefited from the economic boom were eating in high-end restaurants as a way to showily spend their money or to conduct business. Power breakfasts and power lunches conflated business and eating. Instead of entertaining at home on the floor with a fondue pot, people were entertaining themselves and others at restaurants. If the 1970s were a burgeoning testament to the expansive notions about living and eating well, the 1980s were the peak. Already-rich Americans had the ability to indulge their whims to the showiest of degrees, which then paved the way for haute cuisine. The restaurant business flourished. Rather than learning to cook at home from the likes of Julia Child on the small screen, a chef's work was admired and tasted up close and in person.

Though the abandonment of the kitchen could be seen as a distancing from an interest in food itself, dining in restaurants allowed us to become more aware of food and receptive to novelty. We were in actuality indulging ourselves and taking part in what food writer Molly O'Neill called an "epicurean revival." As Edward Engoron, host of Los Angeles radio show *Perspectives on Food*, told the *New York Times* in 1989, "When they've just seen Julia Child do paella, they feel more comfortable when they go to a restaurant. They know what's in it. It helps them know how to order." And as cultural scholar Phebe Shih Chao wrote, "Restaurants with inventive menus teach more people about eating, help create a demand to learn about food; consumers knowing more about food then become more demanding customers. The message is that acquiring sophistication means as much as money in the move up the social ladder."

The 1970s had seen a countercultural trend away from traditional meat and potatoes fare, ushering in an interest in regional and international restaurants and illustrating middle-class America's desire for more adventurous and exotic foods. By the 1980s, many chefs whose names became known beyond the walls of their restaurants and the limits of their cities—Mark Miller, Susan Spicer, Anne Rosenzweig, Dean Fearing, Lydia Shire, Stephen Pyles, Jeremiah Tower, Jonathan Waxman, Paul Prudhomme, and Michael McCarty, to name a few—were creating New American, American Regional, and California cuisine using fresh ingredients and grilling with mesquite wood.

Wolfgang Puck, an Austrian chef-restaurateur working in Los Angeles, found himself a well-appointed home in this climate (and later on TV). Arguably the iconic celebrity chef of the 1980s, Puck made a name for himself as a pioneer of "fusion cuisine," a blend of ethnic or regional cooking styles—in his case it was often fresh California and classical French cuisines—that underscored Americans' openness to new eating experiences. Though they had been served at Alice Waters's Chez Panisse in the 1970s, Puck made "designer" pizzas common in the 1980s.

Puck had an enormous impact on Americans' eating habits as well as on the industry. His ambition was to "reposition the entire profession of chef." As he told the *Los Angeles Times* in 1978, "I am very happy with what is happening to chefs. I am very happy that chefs can drive Rolls-Royces." Now represented by entertainment management agencies, chefs and their restaurants, wrote sociologists Priscilla Ferguson and Sharon Zukin, have become "investment objects in their own right." Molly O'Neill observed the trend in her 1992 *New York Times* series "Resetting the Table: The Changing American Meal." The 1980s, she wrote, were a "boom decade when chefs went from earning low hourly wages to six-figure incomes and climbed the social ladder from servant to social savant." In 1985, the PBS program *Great Chefs of . . .* (San Francisco, New Orleans, Chicago, etc.) presented master classes with noted chefs. Unlike previous cooking shows, this series expected a certain level of viewer proficiency, implying that audiences were more sophisticated and ready to take cooking—or at least food—more seriously. *Cooking at the Academy*, which aired on PBS in 1991, was another case of the serious food show. Such programs were revolutionary in their own way in that they were filmed in cooking academies and restaurants, and they brought professional level skills to the television. Instead of emphasizing particular recipes these shows—host-less and star-free (at least by current standards)—put the spotlight on technique demonstrated by academy instructors or veteran chefs.

Watching Instead of Cooking

Cooking shows were on the rise by the end of the decade. "For a growing number of Americans, cooking, an activity that was once an obligation, has become a spectator sport," reported the *New York Times* in 1989. "They consume information about food the way baseball fans hoard statistics on their favorite players, because it is easier than ever to eat without cooking." Reflecting the calorie consciousness of the day, a *New York Times* television roundup included a similar article called "When It's Better to Watch Food Than Gorge On It." That this point was being made by such reportage signaled the emergence of the most persistent paradox of them all, which still puzzles us to the present day: people love to watch cooking, but it does not mean they love to cook or that they even do it at all.

Other than *Mama Malone*, a sitcom about an Italian widow who hosted a cooking show from her Brooklyn apartment, which ran for one season in 1984, there was still little in the way of syndicated cooking shows on commercial television for much of the decade. Commercial cooking shows, never considered especially sexy or exciting—except by Kerr's blushing audience—were lost in the bacchanal of real life, as well as the rampant proliferation of cable television. Instead of watching the same shows at the same time, Americans were tempted in myriad directions. The veteran broadcast networks had to compete with the likes of upstarts TBS, USA, ESPN, CNN, MTV, HBO, and Fox.

While regional cooking shows continued to be produced in some markets, most of what was shown nationally continued in the form of short "five-minute filler" pieces like those hosted by *PM Magazine*'s Chef Tell. Tell Erhardt told the *Christian Science Monitor* in 1987,

> Everybody is very busy today. They want to learn shortcuts. Preparing a complete recipe in ninety seconds? No—the audience knows I'm only showing the important steps. I chop the onion or garlic, julienne the carrots, season the chicken or meat, arrange everything in a casserole for the oven, then—by the magic of television—voila! There is the finished product, golden brown and bubbling.

And as another testament to Americans' interest in food and chefs, as Tell professed on his website: "The show [Philadelphia's *Evening Magazine*] was so bland, I think the only thing that stood out were these segments. All of a sudden, everybody knows me. Everybody's my friend."

Tell's awe at his unlikely celebrity echoes that of Jacques Pépin, who finds the profession's shift in status ironic: "Now we are geniuses!" Not incidentally, the fact that several of the most popular cooking show hosts of the 1980s were men was indicative of both the increased status of cooking and the fading out of traditional gender roles. Pépin began his television career appearing in his chef role on the game show *What's My Line?* and *To Tell the Truth* and talk shows like *The Merv Griffin Show* and *The Mike Douglas Show* before he began his cooking show. In 1982 Pépin began hosting *Everyday Cooking*, repurposing the gold standard professional French techniques for simple home cooking. Completely at ease on television, he has always simply performed the same expert moves on camera that he executes as naturally as breathing. He doesn't need to rehearse, he said, because he has the timing worked out in his head, just as he has always had to do in a restaurant kitchen.

The venue for Pépin's *Everyday Cooking* happened to be the place where all those fans were doing their spectating—public broadcasting. A 1989 *Washington Post* article entitled "PBS' Feeding Frenzy: A Raging Appetite for Cooking Shows" featured sixteen shows, a mixture of newcomers and mainstays. On one Saturday afternoon, reporter Eve Zibart observed, one could watch nine different cooking shows among her three local PBS stations (a number that evokes a mere shrug these days). On the one hand, this was an indication of the seriousness that food and cooking had assumed, while on the other it could be seen as the consignment of cooking shows to the confines of the quiet and learned how-to, limited audience environment that kept cooking in the teaching rather than entertainment camp—that "crypto-commodified, quasi-bake-drive-funded, kindness-of-strangers ghetto," as Toby Miller described it.

In fact, in a paradoxical twist, even though people were not doing so at home as much, cooking had taken on a gravitas and a newfound respectability. While it's true that women were working more, many essentially carrying the load of two jobs, historian Sidney Mintz referred to the ". . . continuing success of the mythology of 'not enough time'" as a feature of contemporary American life. It can always be argued that you make time for what's important to you, and cooking continued to be important to many people.

It made sense that PBS was where the action was at the time, given the earnest attitude around food. Various PBS affiliates boasted accomplished host-chefs with engaging personalities who became celebrities in their own right, though some clearly stood out above others. Julia Child was still in the mix, too. With her reputation solidified to the point that viewers could trust her on any culinary topic, Child was able to afford a departure from her bailiwick, French cuisine. She hosted *Julia Child & More Company* and *Dinner at Julia's* in the early part of the decade wherein she covered cuisines outside the borders of France. The viewing public got to know Pierre Franey, Madeleine Kamman, Kathy Hoshijo, Keith Floyd, Martin Yan, Jane Brody, Nathalie Dupree, Ken Han, Carl Oshinsky, Franco Polumbo, Mary Metzger, and Earl Peyroux, all of whom had a theme, be it healthy, Asian, French, or some underrepresented slice of American ethnic heritage. Homemaking guru Martha Stewart made her TV debut in 1986 on PBS with *Holiday Entertaining with Martha Stewart.*

The PBS crop of shows in total did more than a fair job of representing the varied and sometimes competing interests—including health, speed, simplicity, and foreignness—of Americans. While Americans were keen on new eating experiences and living the high life, there was a countervailing trend that, while it had been a regular conundrum of the human condition, was a particularly marked paradox in the era of having it all. We wanted to not only eat like, but also *look* like the rich and famous, and so in the days of the *Jane Fonda Workout* (former antiwar activist turned exercise maven), Olivia Newton John's "Let's Get Physical," and ubiquitous aerobics classes, we forced ourselves to feel the burn as well as watch the calorie count. "The lighter the food, the higher the status," wrote William Woys Weaver, the author of *America Eats: Forms of Edible Folk Art.*

Eating light was popular not only for reasons of vanity. Those who came of age in the 1960s had incorporated morality into their food choices, treated their bodies like temples, and found it untenable to relinquish a mantra of treading lightly on the earth. Their inevitable ageing now compelled them to pay heed to their health for prosaic physical reasons. Foods like oat bran, fish oil supplements as a source for omega-3 fatty acids, and olive and canola oils became popular for their reported health benefits. The media demonized red meat. A 1988 Surgeon General's report on Nutrition and Health stated that ". . . the relative magnitude of the associated health concerns [of nutrition] is comparable [to that of smoking cigarettes], with dietary factors playing a prominent role in five of the ten leading causes of death for Americans." This indulgence-fear dichotomy was a typical symptom of the decade's extremes.

With a nation in a heightened sense of awareness and trepidation about food, public television cooking shows quietly delivered. But this time around, unlike when President Franklin Roosevelt took on the nation's nutrition standards, and radio announcements and cooking programs broadcasted stern injunctions, TV hosts simply incorporated helpful tips within palatable packages. Instead of direct sanctions, the idea was more "you asked for it," since citizens were genuinely interested, whatever their reasons, in eating healthier.

New-age earth mother host Kathy Hoshijo was truly an offspring of the 1970s. In 1980 PBS premiered *Kathy's Kitchen*, which focused on vegetarian food and achieving a healthy weight. In 1986, PBS aired both *Good Health with Jane Brody* hosted by the *New York Times* health columnist and *Floyd on Fish*, hosted by British cookbook author and restaurateur Keith Floyd.

In seeming contrast to the style and glamour but perfectly in line with the workaholic lifestyle of the 1980s, prepared, frozen, and microwaveable foods experienced sizeable gains in sales over the span of the decade. "For a moment in the mid-1980s, it seemed that the millions of time-starved family cooks would let industry provide dinner," wrote Molly O'Neill. By the mid-1970s microwave ovens were more popular than gas ranges, so that by the late 1980s, 80 percent of homes had one. Over 760 microwaveable products were introduced in 1987 alone. Compared with the other, more anxiety-provoking use of the word "nuke," Americans were pressing the button on their microwave without thinking, which was exactly the point. Sure enough, Donovan Jon Fandre hosted a PBS cooking show just for this very massive demographic, too. The show's title, *Microwaves Are for Cooking*, implied that their use was commonly limited to simply reheating or making born-microwavable grocery items.

With its breadth and quantity of shows, public broadcasting was essentially the decade's Food Network.

Beyond French

Though same old same old was out, French cuisine—which had comprised a solid slice of the American pie for over two decades—hadn't completely lost its grip on the national psyche. Having been the province of the elite in the earlier half of the twentieth century, the French sensibility slowly trickled down. As Duke professor Alice Yaeger Kaplan observed,

> It's in the 1970s that snippets of French begin to be heard on American network television: In the genre, a late 70s commercial for yo-plait [sic] yoghurt is a veritable allegory of class mobility slogans in the French invasion. Jack Klugman, the most American of American character actors, ingests a spoon of yo-plait [sic] and suddenly comes forth with a torrent of fluent French inviting viewers to get "la culture francaise."

In the 1980s, French food was still considered by many to be the pinnacle of refinement, particularly among a good swath of the middle class wishing to trade up. French or haute is, even now, often considered a signifier of sophistication.

The desire for French cuisine coexisted with a quintessentially and increasingly common American desire for even classical gourmet food to be quick and easy. "One could even speak of a 'croissantization' of the French cultural icon," noted Kaplan. Fast-food chains (Burger King introduced the Croissanwich in the early 1980s) and TV chefs catered to this desire. Sometimes the latter were hosted by actual French chefs, other times by ambassadors. From 1984 to 1991 French chef-instructor Madeleine Kamman hosted *Madeleine Cooks*, a forum for her demonstrations of French cooking techniques using American ingredients. Pierre Salinger, former press secretary to President Kennedy, hosted *Dining in France* in 1986, a combination chef showcase, travelogue, winemaking, history, and French lifestyle program.

Given the prominence of food in the 1980s cultural tableau, however, there was room for more than French. The American palate was broadening to include the cuisines of a variety of foreign cultures

as well as previously overlooked pockets within its own boundaries. Asian foods, with their inherent emphasis on seafood, fresh vegetables, and light sauces, became especially popular in the health-conscious era. Chinese-born American chef Martin Yan was the popular host of the James Beard Award–winning *Yan Can Cook*, starting in 1978, exemplifying the need for speed combined with an interest in international trappings. *Yan Can Cook* illustrated the typical "foreign" kind of cooking show, but given the wealth of cultures in the U.S., the term could be applied to anything from outside one's region or one's usual habits. Regional, down-home, "comfort" cooking could even be considered "foreign" in a certain light. Nathalie Dupree, chef and cookbook author, featured southern Americana fare on her Atlanta-produced *New Southern Cooking* starting in 1987. Even culturally aware Connecticut Yankees were open to new cuisines, making shows like this popular right out of the gate.

As more Americans became interested in non-Western cuisines, Martin Yan filled a gap.

Cajun and creole cooking had started to become popular outside Louisiana in the 1970s but reached a peak in the 1980s. Well-respected chef Paul Prudhomme created a watershed blackened redfish at his now legendary K-Paul's restaurant in 1980, creating not only a potential threat to the fish species, but the start of a powerful Cajun

Photofest

cooking trend. All manner of foods were subject to being blackened or etoufèed, and gumbo and jambalaya became household words nationwide. Cajun spices found their way into fast food, too—Cajun Spice Ruffles potato chips, for example. Justin Wilson was perhaps one of the most recognizable cooking show hosts of the past thirty years (and the Cajun Spice Ruffles spokesman) even if his name wasn't always easily forthcoming. His longtime day job as a safety engineer was the first forum for his storytelling. "He would do safety talks and he didn't want people going to sleep," said his daughter, Sara Wilson Easterly. "You know, be careful, be safe, big deal. So he started throwing these stories into them, and the men loved them. So he was asked to do speeches all over the world. And then you throw this cooking into it, and it was a very well rounded balance."

Wilson had a proclivity for cooking well before he began entertaining crowds. His father, Harry Wilson, who was Louisiana's commissioner of agriculture for over thirty years, owned a large farm when Justin was growing up. Easterly related her father's story: "So one day grandpa came to him and said 'okay, Justin you gotta go out in the fields and you've got to help your brothers and sisters or else you got to stay in here and help your mother in the kitchen.'" "And [Justin] said, 'that was a no-brainer to me. I'll stay and help mama.'" He got his cooking-for-an-audience chops, as many of his predecessors had, doing cooking demonstrations for a gas company. Though he was on local public television at the start of the 1970s, the following decade was his moment in the sun, thanks to the popularity of Louisiana's culinary offerings. His shows on Louisiana cooking showcased his quirky Cajun storytelling, though he was sometimes criticized for not being a true Cajun and for reinforcing unfavorable stereotypes with his hyperbolic speaking manner. Wilson's trademark down-home southern manner, red suspenders, and "I gar-on-tee" became a weekend fixture on public television stations across the U.S.

In the introduction of *Looking Back: A Cajun Cookbook*, Wilson gives a typically Wilsonian storytelling version of his start on television in 1971 (at the age of fifty-seven):

I was sitting in a little restaurant in Denham Springs, Louisiana, right outside of Baton Rouge, when a young man walked up to me and said, "Mr. Wilson, my name is Bob Rowland. I am with Mississippi ETV."

I said, "Bob, that doesn't spell a damn thing."

He said, "No, but it stands for Mississippi Educational Television and we would like for you to do a cooking show for us."

. . . I told him, "You must be crazy to think I can cook on television." He said, "I might be, but I believe we could have a good show."

Justin Wilson was instrumental in the Cajun cooking trend.

Easterly said, "It's amazing that you turn on the television now, and we have a whole network devoted to different types of cooking. To be one of the pioneers of that is really incredible." Easterly helped her father and a small crew prepare food for his shows. They had to make two full recipes for every dish, the "ready" one and the one Wilson prepared on camera. "I told him there weren't too many eighty-year-old men who could wear out forty-year-old women but he was doing a damn good job of it," said Easterly. "He had determination. It didn't matter if he felt bad or not. When he walked out and the cameras were rolling, he was something. He loved performing, and he loved people. And after each show we would serve the food, and he would sit down and visit with people and sign autographs and cookbooks."

Easterly describes her father's mission as helping people understand that cooking was *fun*. When people would ask him, as they often did, with great earnestness what type of wine he cooked with, he was nonplussed. "He said, 'Whatever kind of wine you like to drink. This is not rocket science.' . . . As he would say, 'You pass a good time' while you're cooking." Part of the secret to his success was quite likely that it was an antidote to the overly serious and often haughty attitude taken on by many chefs and diners alike under the new foodie-ism.

Wilson's shows are still aired occasionally around the country, and his fans still wax nostalgic about him on the Internet. It's the shows from the 1970s and 1980s that tell a story for Easterly. "I look at those old shows and see the green refrigerators and the harvest gold formica countertops, and it's not beautiful and granite and stainless steel. I love [the current kitchen styles], but it's not from whence we came. It's very interesting that people are so attuned to those things now." Easterly said that when a Memphis television station began airing some of the old shows a few years ago, "You cannot imagine the people that would watch that and the emails and the letters, thank you thank you thank you for this. . . . There are a lot of people cooking today that might not be cooking today whether it's professionally or recreationally had it not been for him."

Frugal Does Not Mean Cheap

The recognition factor and minor celebrity status achieved by some of the aforementioned cooking show hosts of the decade was negligible in comparison to one in particular. If PBS was the decade's Food Network, Jeff Smith was its Emeril.

As a faculty member and chaplain at the University of Puget Sound in Washington in the 1960s and 1970s, Smith developed and taught cooking courses, one of which was called "Food as Sacrament and Celebration," a seminar combining cooking and theology. He eventually decided to leave the university and delve into a life in food, opening a restaurant and cooking school called the Chaplain's Pantry in Tacoma. He began his TV career in the 1970s, taking a first stab with *Cooking Fish Creatively* on the local Tacoma public broadcasting station. Despite the show's inauspicious beginnings—"just awful," as Smith described it—changing the name seemed to help. *The Frugal Gourmet* caught on, moved into other regions, and was eventually picked up by WTTW in Chicago. By 1983 the show had gained national exposure and quickly became one of the most widely watched cooking shows of all time.

Given the lavish backdrop of the 1980s in which the *The Frugal Gourmet* was set, the title might have implied that Smith was offering a taste of the good life to the millions of Americans who harbored champagne wishes and caviar dreams but couldn't afford them. On some level he was doing that—bringing gourmet, esoteric food to regular folk, to allow people who didn't make a killing on Wall Street and didn't have the money to travel to be able to enjoy the riches of the decade and vicariously visit other countries—but overall, the dishes he presented were not the trendy foods of the day. He cooked traditional African stews, Filipino adobo, Italian peasant food, and a fair amount of nonelegant meats like ribs and gizzards. Geoffrey Drummond produced many of Smith's shows in the 1990s. "Whereas Julia tended to have a very mid and upscale audience—what you think of as your classic PBS audience, more educated, more affluent— her reference was France and traveling to Europe," Drummond said. "Jeff was mainstream American, taking his audience on an adventure when he traveled to Rome or Greece. It was about our ancient ancestors. It was much more cross-cultural."

In many respects, Smith was anachronistic and not representative of the 1980s except perhaps in tantalizing opposition to the prevailing fashions. He certainly capitalized on the pervasive interest in food, but from a fundamentally different vantage point than many other fine dining advocates of the moment. As Robin Leach highlighted the lifestyles of the rich—who seemed to dine out exclusively—on screen and Wolfgang Puck twirled us around the world of the celebrity chef offscreen, Smith gave us benediction to enjoy our riches, be they monetary, cultural, or spiritual. In the midst of the revelry and immoderation, he was another symbol of the perennial conflict of opposing forces in our collective psyche. On one hand we were living greedily, as though these were our last days, and on the other we needed a salve and a sanctuary, even if a barely noticeable nondenominational, nonspecific religious or spiritual one.

Smith adamantly denied any connotation of either stinginess or vanity suggested by the show's title. He intended, in fact, to send the opposite message. He encouraged viewers not to waste anything and to pay attention to every detail, and, in essence, to live richly. In the introduction of his 1984 cookbook *The Frugal Gourmet*, he wrote: "The term 'frugal' does not necessarily mean 'cheap.' It means that you use everything and are careful with your time as well as with your food products. Fresh foods, prepared with a bit of care and concern, will result in terrific meals with lower costs. And the term 'gourmet' does not mean 'food snob.' It means a lover of good food and wine and, as far as I am concerned, of people."

Therein lies the heart, or at least a couple of chambers, of his appeal. Making people feel good—even virtuous—while watching him because they were learning (public television's bailiwick) about other cultures and taking part in rituals that knit family, history, and global togetherness. With "the Frug," as he was affectionately known, eating and cooking became something much more than its surface manifestations; not just techniques and dinner on a plate, but a philosophy. "*The Frugal Gourmet* is committed to trying to understand other peoples and trying to educate your own children to understand other people," he said on one episode. "A cuisine, a style of cooking is a way of thinking more than it is a way of eating. . . . We do things [with certain food products] because of the way we think about ourselves."

Practiced at rousing a crowd, Smith parlayed his skills as a Methodist minister into preaching to a television audience. Though he embodied the learned qualities of many a cooking show host on PBS, he departed from the usual sedate nature by injecting visceral passion into every word and grain of salt. He left no quiet reflective moments to let the camera do the work. He talked constantly and rapidly, without a script. Smith was *on* every minute of the show. "As a TV personality, he was absolutely terrific," said Drummond. In 1995, *Interview* magazine's food columnist Hal Rubenstein wrote, "Sometimes he grandstands like a forgotten center fielder in need of an ego boost . . . but Jeff Smith cooks at a pace an audience with little patience can understand."

Like Arthur Godfrey, whose legendary radio broadcast style made a listener feel as though he was talking to him alone, Smith might begin with, "When I'm on the air, when we're together . . ." His casual, intimate mannerisms could make a viewer swear the Frug could see through his screen into her home. He conversed with his audience in no uncertain terms, weaving in assumed utterings of his viewers. He didn't rely on simple polite conventions, but treated you playfully, as if you were a good old friend. While demonstrating a Japanese dish that called for fresh ginger, Smith admonished the viewer for even *thinking* of using the powdered ginger in her spice rack. "It's been there since 1936, don't lie to me," he said. While chopping the ginger he said, with mock exasperation, "Keep those fingers bent under. I don't have to tell you again." When he brought out the miso: "I know it looks strange. Calm down." Or, "I know you're pushing your friend in the ribs saying, that isn't how so and so made it."

Jeff Smith managed to combine anthropology, psychology, and spirituality with rapid-fire monologue and cooking instruction in every *Frugal Gourmet* episode.

PBS/Photofest © PBS

When concocting a somewhat laborious Italian gravy, he said, "I know it's hard work!" With Smith, we didn't hear "look how easy!" which we had seen with the home economists and which we see everywhere today, but rather, it's hard and it's worth it because look at what you get—not just a rich gravy but a connection to your ancestors. He was preaching—in a barely noticeable, nondenominational, nonspecific religious or spiritual sort of way—the righteousness of hard work and the importance of appreciating everyone and everything.

Since he was not a trained chef, Smith's goal was not to impart the intricacies of technique. "He was smart, although his knowledge was challenged by a lot of people," said Drummond.

> The avid people in the food community, at that time a much smaller group—the foodies before they were called foodies—really disliked him because they felt he didn't have real cooking school or chef skills. I guess he was a bit of a charlatan in some ways, though I hate to call him that because he connected people with food and culture a lot. But his actual culinary knowledge and skills weren't up to where a lot these formalistic peoples' were.

Graham Kerr had been criticized similarly, as are many television chefs today. There is an expectation, perhaps, that if someone is teaching us to cook, they ought to be a master. Obviously, however, it has little bearing, if any, on the success or popularity of a cooking show. The criticism stems less from a concern about home cooks not learning precise culinary technique (does it matter anyway?) than from these hosts' popularity. Anyone who is well-received and successful will be found lacking by those whose turf he dares to step onto. "The food people are jealous," Smith's editor, Maria Guarnaschelli, told the *New York Times* in 1988. "It's a small world, and they all know each other and snipe at each other, and Jeff suddenly appears and transcends all that."

Smith could expose viewers to numerous dishes in thirty minutes, partially because he talked and moved rapidly but also *because* his focus was not on technique. His goal was to expound on the

origins of whatever he was chopping or braising. Phebe Shih Chao
commented on his unorthodox m.o.:

> As the food becomes more intricate and "foreign," paradoxi-
> cally there is less attention than ever paid to recipes, ingre-
> dients, precise amounts . . . in an April 1997 episode of the
> "Frugal Gourmet," he displayed, he did not prepare, kasha,
> not difficult but "foreign" to a large part of America, chatting
> the whole time about things that had little to do with kasha.
> Supposing you had never tasted kasha, would you know the
> proportion of water or stock to grain to get the texture you
> want, and in what form the egg is supposed to be (whole?
> lightly beaten? hard-boiled?) The chef did not expect his tele-
> vision audience to learn from watching.

He *did* want them to learn, maybe not so much about how to
make kasha, but about the people who eat kasha, or at least what he
thought about the people who eat kasha.

As much as the Frug was beloved, he was also reviled. Besides
the discrediting of his abilities by formally trained chefs, his manner and his mission—the same manner and mission that made him
so popular—were also targets for attack. Smith continually brought
his viewers into non-American worlds, often places where the concept of gourmet, let alone a full belly, were incomprehensible—a bit
like the irreverent and self-centered character in the British comedy
Absolutely Fabulous boasting of her bowls from Ethiopia, where the
indigent native population, after all, has "got nothing to put in them."
Smith talked so fast—and remember, without a script—that sometimes his mini-lectures came across as glib and overly generalized.
While making a stew from the former Nigerian state of Biafra he
said, "The people of Biafra," who he had seconds before described as
being wiped out in a terrible war, "were neat people."

In 1992, journalist Barbara Grizzuti Harrison wrote a detailed
and contemptuous essay on Smith—several years before a disgraceful

scandal involving him was made public—for *Harper's* magazine called "P.C. on the Grill." It seemed that in Harrison's view, Smith was a poster child for a culture too full of cloying messages of "Self- and Universal Love." She lumped him in with Gloria Steinem, Marianne Williamson, Oprah Winfrey, Leo Buscaglia, John Bradshaw, and Sam Keen, all of whom were popular proselytizers of sorts—"gurus," Harrison called them—in the school of the inner child and making good money doing so. She ridiculed him for making statements, I presume, like "When you eat from a common pot, you remember who you are." Comparing Smith to Julia Child, she wrote, "Julia felt no obligation to fill our minds with pure and lofty thoughts while we were filling our stomachs with sauce veloute."

In reference to those who bought his cookbooks (of which he already had over a dozen), Harrison said, "The Frug's fans are not purchasing recipes, they are buying comfy-cozy liberal pieties and beatitudes." She found him by turns condescending, "coy," "smarmy," and "unctuous." The Frugal Gourmet, wrote Harrison, "clothes consumption in piety. Americans are distancing themselves from the greedy eighties."

Perhaps like James Beard and Dione Lucas, Smith was a little ahead of his time. To discuss food as a topic beyond nutrition, cooking techniques, and restaurants is now commonplace but might have seemed overkill to some just a couple of decades ago. Though it wasn't new—writers, artists, and academics have been using food as a window to society and human nature for centuries—to see such a thing on TV was novel. Few would argue against the notion that food indeed does reveal our identity not just via anthropology, but also psychology and sociology. As food and restaurant consultant Clark Wolf contends,

> Everything is about food. Everything. I firmly believe that if we gave our young people an education, the way we used to talk about liberal arts, a general education in history, culture, economics, sensory evaluation, politics, biology, chemistry,

anthropology, sociology through the eyes of food, we would
be a better educated happier society.

The words could have been taken right from the mouth of The Frug.
However, while Smith may have been a minister, he was no monk.
While he was endowing food and the watching of his show with piety,
Smith also had endorsement deals with several major brands. "It was
very much a business, and he made a lot of money doing it," said
Drummond. He continued:

> Julia had million dollar endorsement offers from places like
> McDonald's, and she wouldn't touch it. It was so against her
> ethos. She never did a commercial. [Smith] appeared in mag-
> azines and trade shows with different companies. He had a
> line of knives, something with KitchenAid and others who
> were in business with him as a celebrity.

Though Dione Lucas had her soups, Graham Kerr had his Bash
n' Chop, and Justin Wilson shilled for Ruffles, Smith was the first
cooking show host to realize the empire potential. As the *New York
Times*'s Bryan Miller wrote in 1993, Smith "is to television cooking
what McDonald's is to hamburgers." Indeed millions were served
via his numerous hotcake-selling cookbooks and TV program. "The
Frugal Gourmet was a mass market chef," said Drummond. "Frugal
Gourmet's shows were *hugely* popular, way more popular than Julia's.
His books sold more than a million copies, which was huge for cookbooks then. Julia's books never came close to that. . . . Julia used to
say that when she went to get gas in her car everyone would ask her,
do you know Frugal?"

There is an argument to be made, as some have, that Smith's
immense popularity was due to the sheer ubiquity of shows. In
explaining one of the keys to the success of *The French Chef*, producer
Russ Morash had credited series—and repeated airings of series—as
"the way you get into the soup, into the American television psyche."

But if people don't like you at the outset, a larger dose is not going to help.

Successful distribution surely didn't hurt, but Smith—like Child and Kerr before him and Emeril Lagasse later—had a fortunate combination of assets that propelled him to fame. Any of the markedly successful TV chefs did not come to the table with just a great personality or a clever marketing plan or good timing. Child—unwittingly—had the personality and the timing but certainly no masterful scheme. Boston's WGBH simply built it, and they came. As television audiences grew savvier and more demanding, and competition for viewers became fiercer, producers had to craft a complete package to ensure that they would come, as *The Frugal Gourmet* did. "In many ways he was the model of what you see with Emeril and Rachael [Ray] because he had this huge and loyal following, a personal following that was about him," said Drummond. "With Julia it was really about the food, and people loved her as the messenger. With Jeff it was about *The Frugal Gourmet* and food came second. If he had been interested in paintings he might have been able to do the same thing."

Despite his remarkable professional success, Smith's private life was riddled with misery. "He had an alcohol disease and in private tended to be very aggressive—often nasty and belligerent with people—whereas on screen he was Mr. Peace and Goodwill and hugely popular," said Drummond. In 1997, seven men accused Smith of sexual abuse when they had been teenagers. Though he settled the lawsuits, his career was effectively ended. Smith, who died in 2004, is still primarily associated with the allegations and remembered in the smog of scandal. The lawsuits nearly obliterated his professional legacy. "Jeff crashed and burned because of accusations of being a pedophile," said Drummond. He continued:

Books were pulled off shelves, shows were pulled off the air. He died solitary, never convicted of anything, but it killed him. He had been so not nice to so many people, and that's an easy way of saying it, being an asshole to so many people, mistreated so many. There was no reservoir of good will except for those he'd made big donations to and they just sort of kept quiet about it.

As host of one of the highest-rated cooking programs in history and virtually the best-known cooking show host of the decade— aired on public television, no less—Smith's significance cannot be ignored. His prescience in crafting a show that was more about food and people than strictly about cooking made him a pioneer. Even though his program was a forerunner in significant ways, he was not to be credited with such. "It's amazing how quickly he became forgotten," said Drummond.

Though PBS might have looked like a quasi Food Network, by the end of the 1980s, creative minds in the cable television industry were already at least one step ahead. Even though PBS had a history of innovation and continued to maintain that reputation, in the qualified opinion of Lynne Rossetto Kasper, it did not go far enough with its food programming. Kasper is a cookbook author and the host of *The Splendid Table*, a public radio show covering a broad range of food and cooking topics that began in 1995. She described a conversation she overheard at a café near New York University in 1993, wherein two young women were both professing their habit of turning on the Food Network as soon as they returned to their dorm rooms.

Lamentably, it's a sign of what public television let slip through its fingers. They never got, until it was too late, what those cable channels could do. They could have owned food on television, and they did for a very long time. And I don't think they appreciated as it was evolving what a channel completely devoted to the house, like HGTV, could deliver to a prospective funder who becomes an advertising entity or what the Food Network could deliver to that prospective person who would pay the money. . . . I have tremendous regard for public television, but I always thought that that would be the place where the great experimentation would be. Imagine the minds that created *Sesame Street* which we take for granted now. *Sesame Street* wasn't like anything that had come before. . . . Imagine if that kind of creativity went into creating food shows.

The imagining is moot. Public television did not have and could never have the resources to build what the creators of the Food Network had in mind. "We like to think we're a really important element in public TV's whole thing, but it doesn't come close to Ken Burns's *Civil War* or *Newshour, Sesame Street, Nova*," said Geoffrey Drummond. "That's really what public TV is about. In comparison food is small, whereas on the Food Network it's everything." Indeed, when the Food Network was born, it took the niche concept to an entirely new level. One might say it was kicked up several notches.

As television critic Charles McGrath wrote in the *New York Times* in a 2008 article called "Is PBS Still Necessary?" just a few months after Kasper uttered her disappointment, "If you're the sort of traditional PBS viewer who likes extended news broadcasts, say, or cooking shows, old movies and shows about animals gnawing each other on the veld, cable now offers channels devoted just to your interest. Cable . . . siphons off the die-hards." The Food Network definitely siphoned from PBS (though as we will see later, it can also be a feeder). In the process, the network had a dramatic impact on the genre—some would say created a new one—and on Americans' relationship to food and cooking.

MODERN PERIOD
(1993–Present)

Bravo/Photofest © Bravo. Photographer: F. Scott Schafer

CHAPTER 6
A Network of Its Own

This is the television business, not the food business.

—Alton Brown

An Idea Takes Flight

If this consideration of TV cooking shows were the equivalent of looking at a friend's family photo album, then moving into the 1990s would see your friend wheeling in a handtruck piled high with albums containing the most recent additions to the family. Was there something in the water, you wonder, that led to this family's sudden fertility explosion? Yes, there *was* something in the water, in the air, or maybe in the Kool-Aid. While that something had been accumulating over time, it needed the right conditions to flourish. It needed an agent.

In 1990, Joe Langhan was a program production manager in the cable television operations of the Providence Journal Company in Rhode Island. The company's new president, Trygve Myhren, had an itch to start some cable networks, and Langhan was one of the people charged with coming up with ideas. The assignment was to seek out niche categories in the print world "which weren't being addressed or weren't properly tended to by cable," as per the new boss's directive.

Langhan went out and scoured the newsstand magazine racks to try to pinpoint trends. The idea of bringing magazines to television was not new. Over thirty years earlier, in a report on NBC's *Home*, a network executive wrote that the program "is dedicated to the proposition what whatever the service magazines can do well in print, we can do better with sight and sound and demonstration on TV." At the time of Langhan's exploratory mission, *Bon Appetit, Food & Wine, Cooking Light, Eating Well, Cook's*, and *Gourmet* were showing healthy subscriber and circulation rates. According to reports brought back to Myhren by Langhan and others, the subjects of food and cooking were obvious rising stars with consumers. Not only were the magazines and cookbooks faring well, but "food and food accessories," as Myhren calls them, were the most advertised category. Ponder the vast ad potential—from I Can't Believe It's Not Butter to McDonald's to Viking appliances. Food was clearly a subject that could especially benefit from the sensory elements that TV could offer (and print could not). But Myhren was obligated to wonder, "Will people actually *watch* food? So they watch some cooking shows. Can you do more than that?"

Maybe back in the day it was possible to be at the right place at the right time, a piece of luck from which Julia Child and Graham Kerr modestly claimed to have benefited. But twenty and thirty years on, no one is going to throw money at an idea without testing it silly. The Providence Journal Company business development team conducted what felt to Langhan like "millions of focus groups," and while he determined that only about half the people who watch cooking shows actually cook, the interest in the topic was incontrovertible. Those findings, along with the encouraging market data, gave the company the audacity to pursue the idea of a network focused solely on food and cooking.

Early on, it was understood that content had to include more than mere cooking instruction. Fortunately cooking involves food, and food is a topic of great elasticity. (Curiously, most of us continue to refer to the genre as "cooking shows" by force of history and habit, the way we say "you guys" to a group of women or "come over to my house" even if we live in an apartment—it's not accurate, but the nomenclature goes unquestioned since the point is always clear.) Myhren could easily envision "the Julia Child sort of thing" but needed help with the rest. When the channel was first being developed, Myhren got calls from friends in the business and read the same sentiment in trade magazines saying, he paraphrased, "These guys were off their heads. There's no way you can make that into a twenty-four hour channel." With cooking shows still perceived as educational, and featuring only an occasional wacky character, it was indeed a bold move. "The idea, the guts it took in the early 90s. 24/7?" said *Splendid Table* host Lynne Rossetto Kasper. "That's incredible." But the 1980 introduction of a twenty-four-hour news channel had managed to challenge the long-held convention of an hour-long nightly news hole. So Myhren naturally turned to Reese Schonfeld, who, along with Ted Turner, had founded CNN, to head up the project. Schonfeld "had a great talent for conceptualizing shows," said Myhren. "How do you fill up the schedule with things that people really find valuable? I believed that Reese could do that. His talent for running a very efficient, lean operation on the one side and his creativity on the other side, I thought would be very important."

Schonfeld was solidly situated among that half of the projected populace who didn't cook. "I didn't know anything about food," he said. "But I understood even before the Providence Journal called that it was an attractive business proposition. It costs very little to produce television cooking shows in comparison to other kinds of programs, and there's an enormous amount of advertising available." Similarly, Joe Langhan told producer Geoffrey Drummond, "I'm a TV guy. I'd be just as happy putting bowling on as cooking." The decisions being made at this level admittedly take the romance out of the budding entity. Yes, Americans had a passion for food, but the fact that they seemed to put their money where there mouths were is what sealed the deal. "This is half business and half food really," said

Schonfeld, a statement that encapsulates everything about how cooking shows have grown over the past two decades. So, the agent that was needed to activate the popular interest in food was not just Joe Langhan, Trygve Myhren, or Reese Schonfeld and their colleagues. It was all of them understanding and putting into action the fundamental ingredients of food television.

The program lineup in the early days of the Television Food Network (TVFN)—a name given to the enterprise by Jack Clifford, chairman of Providence Journal Company subsidiary Colony Communications, which became the Food Network after Schonfeld left—was something quite different from what we see these days. For the most part, ideas emerged from a 1980s mindset, reflecting the notion that interest in food equates with haute cuisine and dining out. Overall, the network featured "serious chefs," notable restaurants and luminaries of the food establishment. California chef John Ash, then *New York Times* restaurant critic Ruth Reichl, renowned cookbook author Marion Cunningham, *GQ* restaurant critic Alan Richman, and socialite and tastemaker Nina Griscom together granted a weightiness and credence to a subject that many felt was finally being given its due. In the early days, to inexpensively fill airtime, the network gave an incidental nod to the genre itself by showing old programs, including those hosted by Dione Lucas, Jacques Pépin, and Julia Child. The network had its critics from before day one, of course, but one hasn't made it until one gets a bad review. In a letter to Dione Lucas's grown sons, Lucas collaborator Marion Gorman wrote, "The new TV Food Network cable channel . . . has started. Overall it is pretty awful. Most people agree that the Dione Lucas shows are by far the best programming on it."

One of the first original shows on TVFN was the remedial *How to Boil Water*, hosted by the dauphin of the network, Emeril Lagasse. Knowing that many viewers didn't cook, it was as if the network was easing into the topic not only for themselves but for a large percentage of their viewers. The show didn't come off well, mostly because Lagasse was stiltedly reading from a script, the commercial benefits of his natural ebullience having not yet been revealed and encouraged. Some of the other early shows on the network betrayed the shaky legs of a fledgling operation unsure of its mission. They weren't bad ideas, but they understandably lacked courage. To poke things along, Schonfeld said, "We wanted one name star that people would recognize." So *Robin Leach Talking Food* had the *Lifestyles of the Rich and Famous* host taking viewers' calls to a celebrity guest, while the guest's recipe was prepared by a chef on screen. *Food News and Views* (later revamped and called *In Food Today*) was hosted by a minor celebrity, Donna Hanover, who was simultaneously donning the mantle of first lady of New York City as her then-husband Rudy Giuliani became mayor in 1994. Her cohost was food and wine writer and cookbook author David Rosengarten. The news-style program, in the vein of *MTV News*, was a logical attempt at interesting a niche audience and a potential outlet for content that went beyond just cooking to include anything related to food. The show included a range of features from the informational and earnest—news segments on food additives, FDA regulations, oxygen bars, Julia Child's birthday, interviews with cookbook authors and top restaurant chefs—to the frivolous and fluffy—TV cooking demo bloopers, bad beers, and how the cast of *Friends* would look if they were fat.

Cookie maven Debbie Fields (as in Mrs.) hosted her own show. "She had very long fingernails," said Schonfeld. "We got letters all the time, how can she cook with those fingernails?" There was a diet show with Lou Aroni, "the most important diet doctor in NY, had Fergie [the duchess] as a client," said Schonfeld. David Rosengarten's critically acclaimed culinary expedition *Taste*, wherein he prepared dishes from Buffalo chicken wings to spaghetti with clam sauce to madeleines, lasted seven years. Most of the shows' sets were crude and relatively bare, embellished with frilly and classical music. They were excessively talky and noticeably lacking in action. Rosengarten would soliloquize for several minutes about the differences between red sauce in Italy and America without ever using his hands for anything but gesticulation. Griscom and Richman traded gentle jibes while discussing a restaurant in Vail, Colorado—they could have been Siskel and Ebert—while a congealed, untouched sample of a Vail meal inexplicably sat on the table before them. Two shows in particular foreshadowed the network's potential to offer trained chefs with colorful themes and affable personalities. *Too Hot Tamales,* hosted by Mary Sue Milliken and Susan Feniger, emphasized Latin flavors, and *Chillin' and Grillin'* featured the distinct barbecue styles of Food Network fixture Bobby Flay and "haute country" cuisine chef Jack McDavid.

The Prince of the Network

Despite its inconsistent content in the early days, the Food Network had an audience. While viewership, ratings, and subscribers steadily increased during the first few years on the air (Nielsen started reporting its ratings in 1995), it was not until 1996 that the network began to come into its own and resemble its current incarnation.

Before he was Emeril with an exclamation point and even before his ill-fated *How to Boil Water,* Lagasse appeared on a 1993 episode of the Julia Child–hosted *Cooking with Master Chefs* on PBS. "[The show] was very content integrity oriented. It was not a casting call," said producer Geoffrey Drummond. "It was a different kind of food show." It was also the first cooking series to earn a nomination for a national Primetime Emmy award. "Unlike any other," said Drummond, "these shows were the first to put chefs out there on a pedestal and say these people are culinary artists." The program highlighted distinguished chefs like Jeremiah Tower, Alice Waters, Lidia Bastianich, Charles Palmer, Michel Richard, Nancy Silverton, and Lagasse, a relative unknown outside his New Orleans restaurant parish.

"People didn't know him," said Drummond. "He ended up being the lead show in the series and was the one we sent out to reviewers because there was a way he interacted with Julia, a charm and an ease, along with food that was good." On the episode, Lagasse did a crab and crawfish boil, in the backyard of a New Orleans Garden District home. "There was a little bit of bawdiness with Julia where he taught her how to pinch the tail and suck the head," said Drummond. "They just delighted in each other." The camera trained on Julia and Emeril sucking crawfish heads, both of them characteristically hunched over the task and relishing every bit.

The episode would now likely seem humdrum to many and wouldn't stand up to the sophisticated production showpieces on the Food Network today. Drummond knew Emeril had exceptional talent, but *Master Chefs* could only take him so far. Even though *How to Boil Water* was not Lagasse's best vehicle, it got him far more exposure than an appearance on one episode of a PBS series.

A new Food Network show, *The Essence of Emeril* was doing well in early 1995, and, according to Langhan, focus group participants said they liked who they thought was "the Italian guy from Brooklyn." Lagasse, however, is not a New Yorker. Coincidentally, he grew up in Fall River, Massachusetts, just across the bay from the Providence Journal Company. Fortuitously, he was also a graduate of the prestigious Johnson & Wales culinary arts college located minutes away from the company in Providence. "We went to [Johnson & Wales] and said we're looking for people who could be TV personalities," said Myhren, recalling the start-up days. "Reese knew what he was looking for. They gave us some names, one of which was Emeril." Lagasse had already made a name for himself as the executive chef of Commander's Palace in New Orleans (replacing Paul Prudhomme) and at the time of TVFN's talent search had recently opened his own restaurant there. Joe Langhan and Schonfeld's assistant "spent three days in a room watching every cooking tape in existence at the time and we saw the [*Cooking with Master Chefs* episode] and a few others with Emeril as a guest," said Langhan, "and we agreed that Emeril had potential."

While focus group results proved favorable for Lagasse, they were not as strong for *The Essence of Emeril* itself, so Schonfeld and the team began to think of other ways to feature him. "After a while," said Langhan,

I began to think that Emeril was at his best when I let people who were Emeril fans into the studio and he began to react to them in a fun way. Emeril would do from six to sometimes eight half-hour shows a day at that time, and it would be tough to get excited after a while. That's when it occurred to me that if we filled a studio with fans it might be even better.

Lagasse agreed to try it. "The plan was developed," said Langhan, "including a great suggestion by the promotion writer to make it like *MTV Unplugged*, where the audience would be all around him and eliminate the separation of audience and talent."

Around the same time, the network was facing a characteristically complicated media company financial situation that was, of course, largely dependent upon the success of the programming. Media consultant Erica Gruen had been working with Schonfeld and the network on advertising and marketing issues since TVFN's embryonic stages. "Reese Schonfeld—who was a really great guy and a tremendous powerhouse in terms of energy—came out of the news business, and his concept of the Food Network was a news network," said Gruen.

So you basically take out anchor desk, put in stove, take out anchorperson put in chef and that was the Food Network. And it was just talking head, talking head, dump and stir programming all day long with a break in the evening for a news show about food. So the quality of the programming was terrible because there was not enough money there to support that kind of idea.

According to Gruen, when she was hired as President and CEO of the network in 1996, it was on shaky ground. Because of business decisions that were made before her arrival—most importantly that the Food Network was being given away free to cable operators, which was an unprecedented move in basic cable television—Gruen found herself in a tight spot. "I stepped into a job where I was the only CEO of a cable television network that had only one revenue stream—advertising." She was also only the second woman to run a cable television network as CEO; the first was USA Network's Kay Koplovitz. "There were a number of problems with the business plan," she said. In February 1997, the Providence Journal Company was sold to A.H. Belo, a large Dallas broadcaster, who had no interest in the albatross Food Network that was bundled with the other profitable stations that Providence Journal had owned, and, in turn, Belo wanted to keep the doors open just to be able to set it free to another buyer. "Belo owners never understood the value of the programming they'd bought," said Myhren. (Belo's acquisition took place the month after *Emeril Live* aired.) It struck Gruen that this was a fulcrum moment, and the network could either blast off into outer space or crash to the ground. She and her new management team intentionally turned a blind eye to the corporate meshugas and went about transforming the content.

Gruen's strategy was to shift the programming emphasis from people who like to cook to people who love to eat. "I'd worked in television long enough to understand that people don't watch television to learn things," said Gruen.

They watch television to have fun. It's an entertainment medium. And if they learn something while they're having fun, that's good too, that's a plus. But if you want to learn how to cook there are tons of cookbooks and magazines you can read. You're not going to watch television to learn how to cook. . . . So we can provide an entertaining experience but we don't have to give every little detail.

Emeril Live, which Gruen referred to as "the lynchpin of the whole strategy," was on the air within eight months of her taking the

CEO job, though it had been in development prior to her arrival. Said Langhan, "We developed a budget that was four times our normal cost and the programming committee agreed to stick our neck out on spending the money and cutting other things out." With 15 to 20 percent of the programming budget behind the show, it was a risk, but one that paid off in no uncertain terms.

"He was popular immediately. [*Emeril Live*] was our number one rated show from the beginning," said Schonfeld whose instincts had been spot on.

"It was Reese [Schonfeld] who recognized [the potential] in Emeril and fostered it, but Emeril was the magnet," said Geoffrey Drummond. "It was Emeril who was the driving force that built the Food Network." Whereas the Food Network started out, in Drummond's view, as a place to where people bounced back and forth with their remotes, it became a destination channel because of Lagasse. "He was the first to begin to get audiences, and that's why the network became Emeril all the time."

AP IMAGES/Richard Drew

Emeril Live was the foundation for the continued success of the Food Network, dramatically changing the tone of the genre.

Emeril Live was a critical ingredient in helping the network flourish. Its immediate success brought a wave of positive publicity and with it the ability to attract more and bigger advertisers. "We put on the *Two Fat Ladies* [hosted by British cooks Jennifer Paterson and Clarissa Wright Dickson, trolling around on their motorcycle with sidecar and cooking stick-to-your-ribs meat-centric dishes] shortly after Emeril and created a whole new brand for the network," said Gruen, emphasizing that both shows were innovations, significant departures from what had preceded. So the door that looked as if it might close on the whole operation, opened up wide when the popular programming proved to a new buyer that there was the potential for a profitable business there. And who bought it but Scripps, one of the cable operators who had sold its shares back to the Food Network when it looked like the network was going south. Scripps, who launched the Home and Garden Network in 1994, owns the Food Network as of this writing.

Communications scholars Gary Edgerton and Brian Rose likened *Emeril Live!* to a talk show. Like David Letterman or Jay Leno, Emeril performed in front of a live audience, had a band, tells jokes, stood behind a "desk," interacted with the audience and band and was the main element of the show's appeal. The major difference, they said, is that Emeril talked *about* tuna tartare instead of *to* Christy Turlington. A hybrid talk show/cooking show was exactly the kind of change Gruen was going for—she envisioned Emeril as the Johnny Carson of food, she said. In fact, in early episodes, Emeril came out and did his opening monologue in street clothes before changing into his chef whites to cook.

Emeril Live became the emblem for the new style of cooking show—the live audience, the in-studio band, and the high energy host who comes out to cheering crowds like a rock star. Lagasse is comfortable in both his chef whites and his TV role, commanding the in-studio audience, face-diving the camera, exclaiming orgasmically over the results of his food preparation. Caricatures notwithstanding, television critic James Poniewozik made a crucial point about the dawn of the Emeril/Food Network era in a 1997 piece in *Salon*:

> *Emeril Live* isn't about cooking. It is, first, about how much the slavish posse loves Emeril (and therefore how big a star he must be) and, second, about the audience's gratification. It wants to taste the andouille; it wants to scream its way onto national TV; it wants Emeril to yell "Bam!" "Pork fat rules!" "Kick it up a notch!" "Makes ya happy happy!" and "Weah LIVE, bay-BEE!" about 50 times apiece. It gets what it wants, and the results can be plain embarrassing. Still, in a genre

once dominated by prissy Francophiles preaching to elites between pledge drives, Emeril is probably the most effective evangelist for serious cooking America has ever had.

As different in execution as *Cooking with Master Chefs* and *Emeril Live* were, Geoffrey Drummond sees Lagasse as a direct extension of the popularizing tradition started by Julia Child.

He has a combination of being a really hard, diligent worker and a charismatic personality. There is integrity around his food and his person that relates to the audience, and it really works. In a way he's very much a protégé of Julia's even though he didn't work with her. . . . I've always felt from the beginning that he was definitely the next stage in Julia's mode of reaching an audience in the same way that Julia brought a generation of people [into cooking] who were my parents' age.

Child, who appeared semi-regularly on the Food Network in its early days, said of the operation in its more mature stages, "[We're] lucky to have it. Emeril put it on the map, gas station attendants slap their thighs—they just love him. *Iron Chef, Two Fat Ladies*—marvelous they have shows like that. They have to be entertaining. In public TV you don't have to be so entertaining." Generous and self-effacing words from the woman who put PBS on the map herself, galvanized a genre, entertained a generation, and whose influence is evoked relentlessly.

In early 2008, as Lagasse's contract with the Food Network came to an end (somewhat mysteriously, though likely a typical changing-of-the-guard strategy to focus on attracting new and younger viewers), so did his decade-long prime-time reign. (Shortly thereafter, Martha Stewart Living Omnimedia acquired a good chunk of his culinary franchise, including rights to his television shows.) Nevertheless, his longevity is remarkable. "If you went back through cable television history," said Gruen,

> [T]here may be a handful of shows like *Sports Center* on ESPN that had that kind of tenure in prime time. There are really very few shows that survive ten years anywhere and certainly in prime time and certainly as much of the franchise that Emeril still is today. They've developed Rachael Ray and Paula Deen and so on, but nobody has the kind of breadth of audience and longevity that Emeril has.

A Network Mainstay

Sara Moulton, the executive chef at *Gourmet* magazine, became a Food Network stronghold starting in 1996, when she began hosting *Cooking Live*. Unlike most of the people we see on TV today, Moulton never aspired to be there. A Culinary Institute of America-trained chef, she had been working with Julia Child on her 1979 *Julia Child and More Company* and then again with Child at *Good Morning America* helping her prep for on-air demos. Eventually she was invited to go on air and found it pretty breezy simply explaining how to do something and never having to look at the camera. When Reese Schonfeld approached her about doing her own show on the budding Food Network, she thought, why not?

"I was absolutely awful," she said, remembering her stint at *How to Boil Water* after it had been deemed it wasn't Emeril's best showcase. Being alone in front of the camera, she found, was a completely difference experience from talking to Charlie Gibson, et al. on *Good Morning America*. "So while I said everything I wanted to—you know I was very educational—I never once smiled, and my hands never stopped shaking," said Moulton. "I held up the asparagus to show what it should look like and it was waving around in the air because my hands were shaking so much. So I walked out of there, said that's it, I didn't want to do TV anyway. That's ridiculous." But the Food Network didn't give up on her and set her up with media training because they wanted her to host *Chef du Jour*, a program that Langhan described as "the first look that we had for almost all of the people that eventually got on the network." Moulton recalled the trainer (Lou Ekus, who has since coached numerous TV cooks) saying to her, "We have to think of some reason that *you* should be on TV. And I said, 'That's exactly it. I should not be on TV.'" During the process, however, remembering that she was a good teacher ("that's the one thing I can say and brag about and pound my fists on my chest and say, 'I'm a great teacher,'" she says) made a critical difference, allowing her to proceed with confidence. "So I said, okay, that's my mission."

After *Chef du Jour*, Moulton was asked to sub for Michèle Urvater, the host of *How to Feed Your Family on $99 a Week*. One of those weekday shows, it used a live call-in format, and unbeknownst to Moulton, this proved to be her shining arena. Because she could talk to someone on the phone—and at the same time exploit her teaching skills—she was no longer alone in the kitchen. Moulton's own show, *Cooking Live*, began in April 1996. Moulton wanted it to be called *The Kitchen Shrink* but the TVFN was keen on using the word, "Live," which it truly was, not taped before a live audience. "What you saw was what was really happening," said Moulton. "I dropped it, I burned it, sometimes I never cooked it."

Joe Langhan recalled Moulton asking him for advice if she didn't know the answer to a caller's question. "I told her to repeat the question in order to buy time and make sure that the audience understood it, then tell people what you do know about the general topic, and, if in fact you do know the answer, tell them that too, but, if not, tell viewers to tune in tomorrow and you will give it to them," he said. "Within minutes of the first show someone asked about swapping Greek oregano—which they had—for Italian oregano—which they did not—in a recipe they were going to make. Sara handled the question just as she was told, telling viewers about oregano, how and why it was used, and there were over forty varieties, et cetera, and I knew she was the right choice for that show."

Wednesdays were cook-along nights wherein home cooks were invited to literally cook along with Moulton in real time. Get-ahead ingredients were shown on the screen at commercial breaks. In a pre–Super Bowl "chili cook along" episode Moulton took a call from Richard in Port Washington who wanted to know if he should remove the seeds from the jalapeno. Debbie from Green Bay asked how many chipotles she should use if she had the canned variety. Though Moulton was a bit breathless and rushed at moments in her hour-long show, it was not the choreographed spectacle that Rachael Ray performs in *30 Minute Meals*. Watching *Cooking Live* truly did approximate being in the kitchen with Moulton, watching her go through each motion that it really takes to prepare a meal. She started with a whole head of garlic, not a little glass dish with pre-measured minced garlic. She wore an apron and rolled up her sleeves while she worked. She used a "garbage bowl" (an invention often misattributed to Rachael Ray) for her scraps.

The immediately recognizable charm about Moulton was her naturalness and folksiness. She thought aloud before answering her callers. As she chopped an onion, leaving the root end attached, she reminded viewers that the technique makes for even dicing, saying "you know the routine." The best way to peel garlic "as you've all seen before," she said, is to smash it first. "Let me get my can opener," she said as she fished for it a bit on her crowded countertop, "which you know is always a big undertaking for me." These refrains made the

J. Scafuro

Sara Moulton (center), a Food Network pillar for nearly a decade, on the set of *Cooking Live*.

viewer feel smart, as if Moulton was saying, "I know you know this, but I'm just reminding you." Such a tenor also created intimacy. The implication, as it was with The Frug, was "You watch me all the time, you know me, we're friends, we're cooking together." The benefit of shooting live—other than using Moulton to her fullest potential—was that having real people call in made other viewers feel it was real. And the intimacy, the pseudo-friendship that viewers developed with Moulton, kept them loyally returning. Langhan was intent on the live format because the viewers' questions (and emails) "provided direction to the content in an immediate and emphatic way." If the assistant producer reported a substantial number of viewers asking questions in the same topic area, the producers could instruct Moulton to change her focus mid-stream. "In contrast," explained Langhan, "making a typical taped show meant you had to figure that out months before the actual airing of a show how much was enough to talk about a certain aspect of the topic."

"For someone who never wanted to be on TV, I really came to love it," said Moulton.

> I loved teaching and I loved meeting people. And I learned so much by doing that live show. I had to know everything about everything because people could call in with a question about anything. . . . I also invited on guests with specialties that weren't mine. So it's like I'd get a private cooking lesson on TV while everybody else was getting a cooking lesson. It was like a kid let loose in a candy factory. What do I want to learn how to do today?

In addition to *Cooking Live*, Moulton also hosted *Cooking Live Primetime* where other Food Network personalities would gather and the result was more a variety show, with segments on wine, equipment, and ice sculptures, for example. While the second live show only lasted eight months, the original one lasted until late 2001. Shortly thereafter, a new show, *Sara's Secrets* filled the gap minus the callers, thirty minutes shorter and with the addition of some bland background music perhaps meant to fill the space where the live callers had been. *Sara's Secrets*, shown in reruns in the daytime in 2008, is probably one of the most old school of the Food Network shows simply by virtue of Moulton sporting an apron, tying her hair back, measuring ingredients, and providing actual recipe text. She comes across as engaging and charming as ever, but in some ways she became a wallflower at the dance when compared to the cleavage-baring, highly styled mega-stars who populate the network. In spring 2008, after her Food Network contract ended, Moulton found a new—and more comfortable—home on PBS with *Sara's Weeknight Meals*, based on her cookbook of the same name. "So that's my new brand," said Moulton. "Everybody has to be branded."

Personality Trumps All

What Food Network programmers were discovering, in addition to the half-business and half-food principle, was that the key to commercially successful cooking shows comes down to one thing. As Erica Gruen put it—and the company mantra remains the same over a decade later—"We're really here to put great personalities on the air." They do it exceptionally well. By just one measure, in 2004, the network was rated first "in terms of having well-liked hosts and personalities" among all broadcast, cable, and satellite TV networks.

So oddly enough, on a channel devoted to food, the content almost becomes secondary. Without a scintillating host, everything else falls flat. This is why the host-driven show is truly the hallmark of the modern cooking show. As chef, author, and food show host Anthony Bourdain said, "Experience has shown [the Food Network] that people don't really give a shit what's cooking. They care about *who's* cooking." Though the powers—no matter who they were—would have eventually come around to this, it was the early success of Emeril that brought that tenet to the fore. "It's about the talent," said Bob Tuschman, senior vice president of programming and production, who has been following that rule faithfully and doggedly since his start at the Food Network in 1997. Explaining what makes a good cooking show Tuschman said, "The most important thing is the person at the center of the show. You have to have an expert who is a master at their craft, but on top of that they also have to be a personality who can bring the subject to life and excite people about it." To wit, Emeril, who was not only enormously popular with viewers but universally respected in the food world. His talent and success in both areas is irrefutable.

Joe Langhan thinks it is crucial that the TV talent share the same passion as the viewer. "The viewer thinks [the host is] the luckiest person in the world getting to do what they love on TV and make money at it. Act like it. Share that passion." Invoking pioneering radio and television entertainer Arthur Godfrey, Langhan said, "He was the first to understand that broadcasting is a conversational medium." As Langhan described, Godfrey treated the camera as if it were one person, so viewers felt like they had a special relationship with him. Cooking shows are especially apt examples of what sociologists first described in the 1950s as a para-social relationship—that is, a false sense of intimacy fostered by someone on the TV screen talking to us. Tuschman said the network looks for hosts "who people really can relate to and who people feel like they know intimately. They know everything about them. They want to spend time with them. Everybody in the audience wants to go sit and have a beer with Emeril and talk to him." As Paula Deen told contestants on *The Next Food Network Star* in 2006, "Look into that camera and picture it as if it's one of your dearest friends."

As television industry executives like Langhan have learned, often the hard way, someone you think is going to be good on TV doesn't always get it and it doesn't always work. "Being on TV is not the same as being successful," he said. Culinary historian and editor-in-chief of *The Oxford Encyclopedia of Food and Drink in America* Andrew Smith said, "There are a lot of people in the food world who felt they should have been on the TV. They can make food better than Rachael Ray. There's a part of it that's professional competitiveness and a feeling of 'why is she on there and I'm not?'"

Bob Tuschman is all too familiar with the dilemma. "Some of the chefs I admire most in the world and I think are just brilliant and I love going to their restaurant unfortunately just don't have the personalities that make them suitable for television," he said. "And it's heartbreaking because you know they are the most talented people in the world and you respect them so much and you never want to tell them that you don't have a place for them here."

But plenty of people think they've got it. So many, in fact, that the Food Network even made the audition process into a prime-time show. *The Next Food Network Star*—note the title is not "The Next Food Network *Host*" or "The Next Food Network *Chef*"—is a survival of the fittest competition wherein skilled contestants undergo a series of challenges such as executing a live cooking demo broadcast, making personality-themed pizzas, and creating stadium food for a professional basketball game, until the last one standing gets to host his or her own show. "Our first year of *Next Food Network Star* we got in over 10,000 tapes of people who wanted to be on it," said Tuschman, who is one of the judges on the show. "And we watch every single one of them." The volume of submissions is a testament to the seeming fact that everyone and his sous-chef wants his fifteen minutes. "Our job here is to find the people who have both the food chops and personalities to bring it to life," said Tuschman. "So finding them both in the same body is the biggest challenge we have."

None of the finalists are naïve enough to think that just being a good cook is enough to win. Many of them, in fact, have a background in performance or at least believe themselves to be skilled in this area. One of the show's promos features contestants getting ready for their close-ups and strutting out into the glare of the limelight. The judges' comments to the contestants explicitly state what it takes to be on the Food Network, but if they don't have star quality coming in, they're not going to acquire it in the six to seven weeks it takes to shoot a season. As Tuschman asked contestants on the 2006 *Next Food Network Star*, "Is your personality big enough, strong enough, distinctive enough to command a nation of viewers?" Guy Fieri, the tattooed, spiky-haired jester who won the 2006 contest, got props for his chops and, as of 2008, is still riding the crest of his *Next Food Network Star* victory. He has commanded the nation of viewers as host of *Diners, Drive-Ins and Dives* and *Guy's Big Bite* and appeared on network specials *Ultimate Recipe Showdown* and *Gotta Get It: Gadgetmania*. He is also—ka-ching!—T.G.I. Friday's spokesperson.

In conjuring up the memorable cooking shows on any network, it's not the food or even the theme that quickly comes to mind so much as the host. The United Kingdom, which has perhaps an even more rhapsodic relationship with the genre than the United States,

BBC/Photofest © BBC

Jamie Oliver appeals to the Food Network's coveted young, urban, male demographic while offering British-ness that Americans so eagerly consume.

graciously exported two galvanizing hosts to American television. Jamie Oliver, whose first show, *The Naked Chef*, premiered on the Food Network in 2000, represented the young, male demographic that the network has constantly sought to balance out the genre's traditional viewership. Oliver, who was raised in a professional cooking environment, presents cooking as a pared down (the provenance of the "naked"), simple, casual, social endeavor. With his cockney accent, boyish exuberance, and bed-head hair, he projects casual mastery as he eyeballs measurements. He zips around London on his scooter, visiting his regular shopkeepers and, at the end of every episode, has his attractive young mates around to "tuck in." Sometimes he'll join his band and play drums. Like most hosts of the modern cooking show, Oliver assures us that cooking is loads of fun and "easy peasy." Americans, famously fervent consumers of all things British, ate him up.

A sexy woman who makes breakfast while wearing a silk bathrobe and who utters in a silky British accent, "I'm going to *imbue* these strawberries with a luminescent ruby *glaze*" is not your mother's cooking show host. Nigella Lawson, former journalist turned television personality, hosted *Nigella Bites* on the Style network starting in 2001. It had begun in England the year before. She was hailed as an anti–Martha Stewart (a term applied almost as frequently as the "[insert ethnic background] Julia Child"), stealing bites of her creations and admitting to hangovers and the food binges that cure them. Like Jamie Oliver, she had the irresistible accent, enviable London home, and a collection of inter-

Nigella Lawson's persona and foods exude accessible sensuality.

Channel 4 Television Corporation/Photofest
© Channel 4 Television Corporation

esting friends with whom to enjoy the fruits of her purported nonlabor. Lawson's commonsense demeanor not only encourages home cooks but makes people, especially women, feel that indulgence is as healthy as beta carotenes.

The New Definition of Celebrity Chef

Nothing is new. In her study of celebrity chefs, scholar Signe Hansen outlined three conceptual categories dating back to French chef Marie-Antoine Carême, who catered to the aristocracy in the early nineteenth century with his elaborate haute cuisine feasts. Carême and his ilk were celebrities because they had the means to access and entertain those with wealth and fame themselves. The next category includes those chefs fortunate enough to earn stars in the seminal *Michelin Guide* in the early twentieth century—these chefs were perhaps noted more for their culinary ability than their predecessors. In the late 1970s and 1980s, the term "celebrity chef" referred to the likes of a Wolfgang Puck or an Alice Waters—chefs who were *celebrated* for their innovative cuisine and their well-reviewed restaurants, and gained famed through word of mouth and print media via rave reviews.

The third category includes those whose celebrity was hastened (or invented) by broadcast media. Twenty years ago, a celebrity chef might be an entertainer posing as a chef for a special event or TV show. Florence Henderson, best known for her portrayal as the *The Brady Bunch* matriarch, is just one example of the latter as host of two cooking shows on the Nashville Network in the 1980s and 1990s. TV personality John Davidson and his wife hosted spe-

cial pre-holiday *Holiday Gourmet* shows on the Nashville Network in the early 1990s. But after the Food Network began churning out sparkly personality-centric programming, the term "celebrity chef" acquired a meaning different from any previous. Emeril was the first in a long line of stars *created* by the Food Network. That path to fame is now a well-worn and coveted trajectory.

"Chefs used to fight to be on the [network]," said Reese Schonfeld. "It's so much exposure for them. We really helped to transform Emeril from a local phenomenon to a nationwide phenomenon. More than anything else that established us as a place that everybody wanted to be on. 'Make me Emeril! Please make me Emeril!'"

"Cooking has become the apple of the media's eye," wrote Lee Siegel in the *The New Republic*. "Which means that anyone who performs this most ordinary of functions—that is, just about every adult—is a potential cynosure of electronic attention. A potential star." Drama scholar Martin Esslin described an analogous repositioning-of-the-ordinary event wherein French avant-garde painter Marcel Duchamp submitted a urinal to be displayed in a New York art museum in 1917. "He drew attention to a phenomenon of basic importance," wrote Esslin.

> Once an object, man-made or natural is taken out of its ordinary context and put onto a pedestal or into a frame, it is made to say, "Look at me; I am here to be observed!" and immediately that object acquires some characteristics of a work of art. In its new context the urinal is seen as a form, a three-dimensional shape rather than as an object of daily use. Its significance is transformed by the act of showing it off.... [T]he newscaster who reads the evening news becomes, simply by appearing in the framed square of the television screen, a performer on a stage, an actor.

This dynamic just as well describes both a TV cooking show host as well as the food being prepared. Both have achieved stardom.

Just like any other entertainers, TV chefs have graced magazine covers, written memoirs, and been featured in televised biographies. In 2007 four *Ladies' Home Journal* covers (granted, a very similar audience to the Food Network) featured Food Network hosts—two with Paula Deen, one trio of Emeril, Giada De Laurentiis, and Ina Garten, and one with Sandra Lee. "Chefographies" of popular Food Network stars began airing in 2006, suggesting that Emeril Lagasse's childhood is as interesting to viewers as Tom Hanks's might be to an A&E's *Biography* viewer. A wax likeness of Rachael Ray joined a wax likeness of Wolfgang Puck at Madame Tussaud's New York City outpost in early 2007. Since they are celebrities, fans are not merely interested in their skills as a chef (if they ever were), but in the whole person. What in their childhood led them to this point? How did they become successful? The black and white childhood snapshots and unflattering early video of our heroes are always a draw, too.

It used to be that the success of a cooking show or sudden popularity would catch producers and hosts by surprise. Thanks to the reshaping of the American mind by reality television, many people now expect immediate fame and are bitterly disappointed when it's not forthcoming. But in the age of insta-celebrity, the stars still need to be aligned—personality, zeitgeist, distribution—for good things to happen. There is still the capricious market and the fickle audience that often make success elusive.

Whether genuinely surprised or acting humble, *Paula's Home Cooking* host Paula Deen said of her fame to a reporter in 2007, "Only in America can this happen to a sixty-year-old, overweight, gray-headed woman." Deen is known for those characteristics, her molasses-dipped Georgia drawl and her hearty (or heart attacky) southern comfort food. She balances out the light and health-conscious contingent on the Food Network, a fact that draws critics. Food and restaurant consultant Clark Wolf, for example, said, "Paula Deen should be illegal in most states. It's unhealthy food." However, he adds with significance, "It *is* compelling television."

Backstory counts for an awful lot when you're famous, no matter what you're famous for. Deen's memoir reveals her struggle with agoraphobia, a shattered marriage, and other instances of heartache and joy. Its title, *It Ain't All About the Cooking*, could easily be a descriptor of what it means to be a celebrity chef today. Where Wolf wanted her banned, chef and food writer Molly O'Neill defended Deen and explained her popularity: "Her appeal is her story. And there is real substance there. I hear peers and colleagues denigrating her. I don't think they've watched her enough to understand, the woman's a preacher. She happens to have some food. Her message is about the triumph of a life and triumph of hope over despair. America is looking for that." As our expectations of media—and food television in particular—have changed, the fact that they can find such a message on the Food Network doesn't strike anyone as peculiar.

Even though TV cooking hosts are regarded as celebrities, as Bob Tuschman said, "One of the things that separates us as a nonfiction network from a lot of the other TV possibilities is that nobody on our air is an actor. Everybody is just who they are as people. And in the best way, these people really can't act." Tuschman said they look for hosts

> who are exciting, interesting, quirky, down to earth, relatable, charismatic, fun experts. And when you find those people you are hoping that the audience will develop a long-term love affair with them. When I think about the shows that have lasted the longest on the air, it's always shows that are based in real people and non-actors. It's the Oprahs, the Johnny Carsons, and the Jay Lenos. They tend to be shows that are rooted in real personalities.

An apt analogy, the love affair. Just as in any relationship, the very characteristic that initially draws one in can end up grating. With celebrities, along with the adulation and popularity comes criticism and backlash. TV chefs fall prey to the same negatives as anyone in the public arena (Oprah comes to mind), becoming targets for viewers' projections, wrath, or a host of misdirected emotions and expectations. As much as they have followings that could overstuff the Mall of America, they also have—to put it mildly—their detractors. While there are hundreds of Internet fan sites for the Food Network and its various ambassadors, there are blogs devoted largely to the censure of Rachael Ray, Sandra Lee, Paula Deen, Jamie Oliver, and others. Sometimes it's because their dishes are insulting to purists who believe in fully homemade food, and other times it's simply because they are overexposed. Because they have quirks and catch phrases (unlike a benign newscaster, for example), the very mannerisms that boosted their popularity become the object of ridicule. When these hosts appear day in and out, multiple times per day, familiarity breeds contempt. That contempt is exacerbated when the hosts begin to appear outside their natural habitat, on a Crest or Dunkin Donuts ad, or on the cover of their own magazine. In the U.K., there is a strong sentiment that Jamie Oliver has gotten too big for his britches and overstayed his welcome (the cockney accent more often now described as "mockney") even though—or perhaps because?—he continues to innovate and support charitable and socially conscious causes. In the U.S., given that the Food Network virtually became the Rachael Ray Network as of 2003, she has become a similar target.

At times producers have become overzealous with the popularity of the genre and overshot. In 2001, Emeril starred in an eponymous network sitcom about himself and his cooking show. Just as he had failed to shine in *How to Boil Water*, he flopped in *Emeril*, again because he was reading a script. Rocco Dispirito, chef of a popular and critically acclaimed New York restaurant, starred in a 2003 reality show called *The Restaurant*. "People hated Rocco for that scripted reality show, the product placement," said Geoffrey Drummond. Producers have inevitably bumped up against some of the boundaries of the adaptability of food television.

The veneer of celebrity itself can damage someone's credibility, laying on a thick layer of gloss where some would say it has no place. Simply by appearing on TV, hosts are flattened and become two-dimensional. A host/chef, for instance, by virtue of the power of the medium and Americans' obsession with celebrity, becomes more celebrity than chef. This may raise their standing in the eyes of a general audience while simultaneously lowering their standing in the food world. Trained and talented professionals are guilty by association, devalued by non-TV chefs because they deign to appear on shows that appeal to the masses, alongside the likes of the untrained, girls-next-door, ex-models, or dog biscuit bakers. Criticism was unfairly leveled at Graham Kerr, a dutifully earnest cook, when he appeared on the air in the U.S. in 1969. He was not *serious*, some presumed, because he was getting laughs—on purpose. Differentiating between "serious" food television—PBS programs and perhaps the daytime recipe-oriented shows on the Food Network—and the more intentionally entertainment-oriented shows—prime-time programs like *Iron Chef, Rachael Ray's Tasty Travels,* and *Unwrapped*—was a distinction not considered by many pre–Food Network. But as people began to take food and cooking more seriously (thanks in part to Kerr), cooking paradoxically became both a more popular leisure-time activity and an entertainment opportunity.

CHAPTER 7

Good Television

Should cooking on TV be judged only by the reliability of the recipes and not, say, by its aesthetic potential as drama, melodrama, or even farce?

—Krishnendu Ray

Let Us Entertain You

Over the past two decades the entertainment threshold has climbed to dizzying heights in all manner of media. While the bar has been raised most conspicuously in big studio movies and video games, Americans have also come to expect eye-popping thrills from their TV screens, big and small. People in the biz refer to these dazzling features and feats as "production values" or "television values." Former Food Network president (and former Home and Garden Television [HGTV] president) Judy Girard explained the success of the network to the *New Yorker*'s Bill Buford in 2002, a year after she'd been on the job: "We introduced television values and started running the business like a normal network." Though perhaps it was previously thought of as being run as an "abnormal" network, that, in a way, was what helped generate initial interest. (A whole channel devoted to food? This I gotta see!) But then to keep feeding it, the new creature had to conform to the rules of its environment. The network couldn't be sustained as a mere dump and stir forum. That is why live broadcasts, in-studio bands, viewer call-ins, audience participation, celebrity guests, fetching décolletage, spectacle, and high energy are now regular and anticipated features of such programming. High stakes, high drama cooking shows are now considered "normal."

As Girard said, several years after leaving the Food Network,

> We started getting Bobby [Flay] thinking about how to be more accessible in what he was doing and same thing with Mario [Batali]. And we just kind of took the entertainment side of Emeril and worked harder with that so that people could both understand his food and be entertained by his show at the same time. And that's really the formula we followed forever after. . . . And every time we made a change of adding a band or having a theme to the show or whatever, the ratings would go up.

With regard to the network's initial relative success, Reese Schonfeld said, simply, "You get a fairly large interest group with no [broadcast outlet] alternative." Besides the fact that the Food Network's mounting success opened the doors for other broadcast outlets to try food-related programming resulting in comparable alternatives on other network and cable channels—Discovery, TLC, Bravo, Fox, Style—there is also a lot of TV programming and production know-how that goes into keeping it successful. After Schonfeld left the network in 1995, his successors continued to develop new strategies. Of the resulting programming, he said, "It's lost some of its seriousness, but I think that's what they had to do." Of competition program *Iron Chef* he confessed, "I would never have put that on the air. I would never imagine for a minute it would have worked."

Food Network Senior Vice President of Programming Bob Tuschman explained, "The same way that we need the food chops and the personalities in our hosts, the network needs to have both the food experts and the TV experts. And we work very intimately with each other to make sure that the information is unimpeachable and always has to be one hundred percent accurate." Big picture-wise, he attributed the network's popularity to something less material: "I think when you add in the great personalities, the beauty of the subject matter, and all the sense and sense memories involved in it, it just makes for really great television."

While in-studio commercial cooking shows are still relatively inexpensive to produce (PBS shows cost more), the economics of cooking shows has changed considerably since hosts like Corris Guy and Julia Child had to bring their own ice buckets to keep food cold and their own hotplates to cook it. The work of the TV experts, the sausage-making operation, is lost on the viewer in the same way that a fiction reader is not aware of the writing process when it's done well. "We don't want you to think about what we're doing as professionals," said Tuschman. "Our work should be invisible." All that should be left for the viewer to see is the beautiful finished product. Paradoxically, the content of the cooking shows is supposed to be about revealing how things are made.

Food Porn

Once the network decided it wanted to capture people who love to eat more than those who like to cook, "The marketing message changed dramatically from here's what's coming up next to here's a slow motion shot of beautiful ripe red cherries falling through water into a bowl and visualizing the sensual appeal of food and the fun aspect of food," said Erica Gruen. (Remember Clementine Paddleford's description of cherries in 1941 in *Gourmet*? One could squint and see a pattern of cherries as the symbol of the pursuit of happiness in America.) This is a strategy that many refer to as "food porn." Though the "porn" term had probably been used for years behind the scenes by production teams, it became part of the common jokey lexicon once the Food Network started behaving less like PBS and more like "Skinemax." Today's camera angles, lighting, colors, and sounds are a world away from David Rosengarten's information-filled but unmoist monologues, delivered from a wobbly, faux-kitchen set. Though the recipes might often be the same then as now, presentation trumps content. Add to that the sexy hosts and kitchens, close-ups of food, fingers, lips, Emeril's "oh yeah babe," groans of pleasure from the hosts and the aroused audience, and it's tough to argue against the analogy.

Depending on your predilection, episodes are full of money shots—not just the cascading cherries, but maybe the flipping of the seared tuna steak or the frosting of the cake. And there's something to the watching of someone else cook and manipulate food that is almost as titillating as the thought of eating it. "One of the reasons for the success of cooking shows in general," Jeff "The Frug" Smith explained in the late 1980s, is that "there's a kind of voyeurism going on." Those who claim cooking shows are like porn often contend, as Anthony Bourdain does, that "you're watching others do something that you're not likely to actually do yourself." A twenty-three-year-old male cooking show habitué told a *Fortune* reporter that he could barely boil water. "But it's the same reason I watch sports," he said. "[Cooking] is something that I really can't do, so I like to watch someone who can." This vicarious motivation, however, doesn't completely explain the attraction. I can't yacht or golf, but I have no desire to watch other people do it. There has to be something else at work.

Sensuality is the bailiwick of modern food television. While some viewers are motivated to watch cooking shows by a desire to learn, potentially all of us are motivated by desire itself. As many have said (including Giada De Laurentiis, an object of desire for some herself), "We eat first with our eyes." The visual stimuli of preparing and cooking food are irresistible—the stirring of cream into melted chocolate, the kneading of bread dough, the slicing of rare beef, the mashing of potatoes. And the transformations are mesmerizing—the whipping of egg whites from a gelatinous soup into fluffy peaks, the carmelization of onions, the thickening of pudding, the baking of dough. Even the sounds of cooking—sputtering oil, whisk hitting side of copper bowl—are amplified. When it comes to the big two—taste and smell—we are dependent on the hosts to transmit the sense experiences to us. De Laurentiis (*Everyday Italian*) is particularly good at sharing hers. She gives specifics ("Mmm, peaches are juicy, crunchy from the amaretti cookies . . ."), not just yummy noises. Hosts also use facial expressions, decrees of "delicious," or, like Sandra Lee, "unbelievable" or, in the case of Rachael Ray after tasting her Buffalo chicken chili mac, an ambiguous but persuasive, "that's rockin'!"

One of the challenges for *The Next Food Network Star* contestants was to taste and describe dishes without using such empty words. It proved to be most challenging indeed, and the would-be hosts did not fare well. For the most part, anyway, we're at the mercy of our own imagination. While Julia Child didn't seem to feel the need to describe the taste of her dishes, it didn't matter. Viewers still wanted it. "We are physically unable to taste the meal the host presents to us," wrote Andrew Chan in *Gastronomica*, "thus, for us, the relationship between the chef's exertions on the program and the resulting by-product is never consummated. We are always left wanting more, so there is a reason to tune in again." Above all, food television is like pornography because, just as sex is a part of everyone's life in some way, shape, or form, so is food, and to see it idealized on a screen surely sets off those zingy, colorful pleasure centers in our brains.

The powerful effect of the television medium itself cannot be overestimated. As drama scholar Martin Esslin wrote,

> The appeal of television is, at the most basic level, an erotic appeal. TV brings other human beings into close proximity for detailed inspection. The people we view in close-ups on the television screen appear to be as near to us as our sexual partners during an embrace. And yet they are glimpsed behind a glass screen, through a window that cannot be

opened. . . . The world it shows us on its stage, behind that window through which we can see but cannot grasp or touch, is essentially a world of fantasy.

If a viewer is able to suspend disbelief, the fantasy is left intact. Leaving the messy bits on the cutting room floor helps. The same trick of making it look so easy is used on other reality shows that purport to teach the viewer something useful. As mass communications scholar Ron Becker observed about the real estate–based HGTV programs,

> [T]hey usually ignored the profound anxieties of home inspections and mortgage negotiations [and the] . . . contentious price-negotiations and bidding wars. Here, everyone gets the house they want; everyone—the buyers and the sellers—wins; no one loses. Who wouldn't want to get involved in such exciting stories that always have a happy ending?

As porn photographer Barbara Nitke has pointed out, food TV and porn have something else in common. In both genres, plot is not important and in fact just gets in the way of the action, which is what the viewer is ultimately after. Nevertheless, there *is* an element of narrative structure that plays a part in the appeal of TV cooking. While this has always been true of cooking shows to some extent, it has become an increasingly important part of the seduction in contemporary shows. Rachael Ray coached a group of *The Next Food Network Star* contestants with this advice: "The most important thing is storytelling. You're not just out there to make a burger or a chicken breast, but you're going to share a story with someone and along the way they'll learn a recipe."

Judy Girard insisted that storytelling is an integral element of modern television principles. "All television shows have a beginning, middle, and end. They tell a story and they have drama," she said. "At HGTV the storytelling is the big reveal of what happens.

Does the house sell, does the room get the makeover, what does it look like?" Now that food television deals in reality TV, of course, there's the drama of "who will be eliminated?" But even dump-and-stir shows were always hard to walk away from until you saw the end product. The reveal may not be as dramatic as a life-changing home renovation, but the food result is eagerly anticipated nonetheless. The same questions could be asked of a cooking show. "Does the room get the makeover?" becomes "Did the pie crust turn out right?" and "Does the house sell?" becomes "Does Rachael pronounce it delicious?" even though we know the answers to both will always be yes.

"Way More than Cooking"

In 1993, despite the established success of CNN and MTV (the music channel that started in 1981), the idea of a single-subject channel was still a relative novelty. We now take for granted the existence of dedicated TV networks for just about every segment of American life. Our music, animal, game show, cartoon, travel, health, home repair, shopping, comedy, crime, legal, surgical, historical, sports, and soap opera needs are finally provided for, with new needs and their solutions continually being developed.

In a 2007 *New Yorker* review of a drama on Lifetime (a cable channel self described as focusing on issues "for women and their families"), writer Nancy Franklin noted that "[A] niche channel's job isn't to appeal to everyone; it's to be as obviously niche-y as possible in order to appeal, with relentless specificity, to particular advertisers." Though that truism is what allowed the Providence Journal team to go forward with their idea, the Food Network is nevertheless a quirky exception to the niche-y-ness of niche channels. It *can* appeal to everyone because food is such a broad and pervasive topic. As Schonfeld told a reporter in 1993, "There's almost nothing you can do on television that you can't do with a food angle." Food television's niche, one could argue, is life. Producers and advertisers are able to literally capitalize on the fact that while we don't all cook or even shop, we do all eat. The Food Network is the only cable channel about which one can say with certainty that every viewer shares its content-related characteristic—unless we describe, for instance, all CNN viewers as people who are consumers of information. Since we all eat, we could declare that the target viewing audience for the Food Network is people who are alive. Its advertising niche is anyone who goes to or sends someone else to a grocery store.

Though born as one of the first niche channels, once it started acting like a "normal" network, the Food Network couldn't seem to help but to try to provide something for everyone. What are generally referred to as cooking shows these days actually encompass far more than the traditional cooking show (aka the "recipe show," "dump and stir," or "in the kitchen" daytime programming in Food Network-ese), where there's a chef at a kitchen counter preparing food and explaining what she or he is doing. What people refer to as "cooking shows" are not just the recipe shows, but they are also those unruly offspring that, for lack of a better system, can be categorized along with recipe shows as "food television." Not only has the topic expanded to include anything food-related, but there has been a steady genre-blending that has further altered the scene. While PBS and "in the kitchen" Food Network shows still abide by many of the functional elements of an instructional cooking show, most often in Food Network prime time—therefore in the minds' eyes of most viewers—as the network's press materials state, you're getting "way more than cooking."

The shows in aggregate reflect Americans' myriad desires and multiple personalities. Shows have appealed to the desire for gourmet and sophisticated (*Wolfgang Puck's Cooking Class, Barefoot Contessa*), quick (Curtis Aikens's *Food in a Flash, 30 Minute Meals, Quick Fix Meals with Robin Miller*), easy (*How to Boil Water, Chic and Easy*), dietetic (*Low Carb and Lovin' It, Calorie Commando*), vegetarian (*Meals without Meat, Mollie Katzen's Cooking Show*), home and comfort (*Paula's Home Cooking*), savvy and technical (*Good Eats*), and indulgent (*Death by Chocolate, Sugar Rush*)—though none of these themes are mutually exclusive. Viewers seem ravenous for programs highlighting both the fine (what brand of balsamic vinegar tastes best?) and the bigger picture (follow the life a lemon from tree to lemonade) aspects of food and cooking.

Most hosts blend the need for speed, health, and enthusiasm ("look how easy!") in varying proportions. To lasso the crazy-busy viewer who still tries to find the time to cook at home, hosts like Rachael Ray (*30 Minute Meals*) and Sandra Lee (*Semi-Homemade Cooking*)—our contemporary Poppy Cannons—teach time- and money-saving lessons infused with persuasive encouragement. They show viewers how to appease their multi-faceted, often contradictory appetites in the time it takes to watch their half-hour shows. Cake mixes, Velveeta, frozen spinach, and other store-bought or pre-cooked ingredients mingle on the ingredient list with extra-virgin olive oil and Japanese breadcrumbs.

"Food television has become really important, like sports or anything else," said *America's Test Kitchen* producer Geoffrey Drummond on the subject of food television's metastasis into the mainstream. "The latest incarnation of that is its growth out beyond Food Network." With its genre-bending mix of shows, food television looks like a microcosm of the broadcasting landscape itself. In 1995 on cable channel TBS, actress Annabelle Gurwitch and comedian Paul Gilmartin hosted a combination cooking and movie commentary show, *Dinner and a Movie* wherein they would make, for example, Sean Penne Pasta while watching *Fast Times at Ridgemont High*. Food has also met dating (*Date Plate*, segments of *Queer Eye for the Straight Guy*) and game shows (*Pressure Cooker, Ready, Set, Cook*). An invisibly integrated network of viewing habits—the audience for HGTV's home makeover program *Design on a Dime* are apt to watch Food Network's *Kitchen Accomplished*—parallels the merging of food and cooking into the broad American *lifestyle* swath, a trend which serves viewer-consumers, programmers, and advertisers.

The travel/adventure/food sub-genre has been a particularly winning combination and, other than staid, out-of-state restaurant review segments on *Food News and Views*, was not originally part of the Food Network vision. Out-of-studio shows appeared with increasing frequency in the late 1990s, heralding a way to keep viewers interested as well as another step in the weaving of food and lifestyle. *FoodNation with Bobby Flay, Calling All Cooks, Best of . . .* , *Food Finds*, Alton Brown's *Feasting on Asphalt*, Rachael Ray's *Tasty Travels* and *$40 a Day*, Guy Fieri's *Diners, Drive-Ins and Dives*, and *Road Tasted with the Neelys* take viewers on virtual trips around the U.S. to sample regional restaurants and cultures. Popular prime-time fare though these shows are, the Food Network must continually keep its eye on that fine line between veering too far away from the kitchen—or even too far away from food—so as not to alienate their core viewers.

In 2000, Anthony Bourdain's restaurant industry memoir, *Kitchen Confidential: Adventures in the Culinary Underbelly*, was a bestseller, and it was no surprise to anyone but him that he was approached for television. "I'd been mercilessly slagging the Food Network and their biggest stars at every opportunity in the press," he said. "I thought they would never let me on the premises much less finance, for them, what was a big budget show and definitely something of a departure."

Despite frequent public dispatches infusing descriptions of the Food Network with phrases like "horrors on screen" and "ready-made bobblehead personalities," Bourdain was invited to meet with Food Network executives after his book was released. Going along for the ride and expecting nothing from it, he was stunned that, by the end of a meeting for which he didn't even bother to shave, he had a deal that turned into *A Cook's Tour*, an around-the-world food-discovery adventure series. "I get a definite sense that though their business model was very successful, I think they were sick of their own programming and a little embarrassed by it," explained Bourdain.

I think I appealed to some suppressed perverse streak in them and I think in some ways I was penance to their sins. We broke every barrier that they'd ever set up, you know, they bleeped for language. There was some pretty disturbing stuff by Food Network standards. They took a *huge* chance and were in fact very supportive throughout.

At the time of this stylistic detour, Eileen Opatut was in charge of programming and Judy Girard was president. As Girard said about the different approach of the show, "It was [a departure] and it got too expensive to do over time." Bourdain claimed that another reason the show eventually stopped production was that the network thought his foreign locations were too exotic for their audience. It veered too far, not from food but from the Western world. "It didn't have a huge rating although it had a very passionate following," said Girard. *A Cook's Tour* is still in Food Network syndication, and Bourdain currently has a similar show, *No Reservations*, on the Travel Channel, where he is free to roam Asia and Africa in search of spiky, malodorous, or semi-deadly edibles. Bourdain cohabitates on the Travel Channel with fellow foreign funky food hunter Andrew Zimmern, host of *Bizarre Foods*.

As scholars David Bell and Gill Valentine write in *Consuming Geographies: We Are Where We Eat,*

[K]itchen table tourism and armchair tourism are neatly linked together by the food media; cookery shows, magazines and newspaper columns bring exotic delights into our homes, and encourage us to put the world on our plates (and in our ovens)—the link is made even more explicit in hybrid forms which link travel and cookery. . . . The food media's role is thus absolutely central—even more so, it might be argued, than that of the supermarkets which import the produce.

New York Times restaurant reviewer William Grimes sees another perspective: "The rise of the travelogue food show strongly suggests that most television viewers do not really want to duplicate the efforts of the television chefs. They want to take a very inexpensive trip." Both observations isolate the core of the allure. Eating and traveling is something we can now do vicariously with great success, and together they sink us further into our Barcaloungers.

"Culinary Combat"

Like much of the entertainment industry these days, TV is reluctant to take big chances. With high production costs, profit-seeking investors, and fragmented audiences, it's more prudent to stick with what's proven to work. That approach is why we see chick lit with those whimsical little line drawings of gamines on their covers overpopulating the new fiction table at the mega-bookstore. And that's why we see a chef yelling

Chef Gordon Ramsay—bawling out a contestant on *Hell's Kitchen*—has made a name for himself as a premier chef/restaurateur and as a hot-tempered perfectionist.

demeaning bleeped obscenities and dramatic "eliminations" of military-postured junior chefs (those from hard knock backgrounds or who are just never-quitters) on Fox, Bravo, and the Food Network.

TV not only mirrors society, but it mirrors television. It stands to reason that reality and competition shows, so popular on other network and cable channels (*The Apprentice, Survivor, Amazing Race, American Idol*), have inevitably burrowed their way into the food show genre (*Top Chef, The Next Food Network Star, Iron Chef, Hell's Kitchen, Ultimate Recipe Showdown, Food Network Challenge, Throwdown with Bobby Flay, Dinner: Impossible*) where trained chefs or beloved BBQ-ing pillars of the community compete for top jobs or pure triumph. Until relatively recently in our history, nothing more than a dropped utensil or a curdled sauce would ever threaten a cooking show's predictable, happy end. Now contenders get humiliated and obliterated, dishes get dissed, and food (and maybe even hair) can burn on semi-live TV.

Americans' consumption of competition and elimination shows has become the national pastime. Food and restaurant consultant Clark Wolf believes this appetite reflects inherent facets of our national character. "Americans like winners. And losers," he said. On the Food Network website *Iron Chef America* (adapted from the original Japanese *Iron Chef*) is described as "Ultimate Fighting Champion meets Julia Child" (later changed to ". . . meets Jacques Pépin" after Child's death). The true sweat and signs of concentration on the brows and faces of the master competitors—including Mario Batali, Masaharu Morimoto, Cat Cora, Michael Symon, and Bobby Flay—take earnestness to a new level. With a formal introduction by the chairman, play-by-play commentary by Alton Brown, and clock ticking in the kitchen stadium, the chefs and their assistants must come up with several recipes for one secret ingredient revealed to

them and the audience at the top of the show. It is a nail-biting event to watch, from the adept racing around of the chefs down to the pronouncements made by the sometimes questionably qualified judges. The type of critique issued on Food Network elimination shows like *Iron Chef*

Serious skill meets serious entertainment as chefs Bobby Flay and Rick Bayless face off on *Iron Chef America* in 2005.

and *The Next Food Network Star*—"I would have liked to see a little more heat in this," "I just personally don't care for sweet sauces on my fish"—are *American Idol*'s Paula Abdul compared to the Simon

Cowell-like measured and abusive denunciations on *Top Chef*. Pronouncements about contestants dishes have ranged from *Top Chef* head judge Tom Colicchio's "That's the worst bread salad I've tasted in a long time," to *Hell's Kitchen* Chef Gordon Ramsay's spitting, "Get out of my [expletive] kitchen, you worthless [expletive]." Season after season, however, *The Next Food Network Star* judges have become harsher, gentle constructive criticism proving to be less worth the wait for the viewer. Bleep-infused judgments or not, competition makes for damn good television.

Edutainment

So if the secret to success is the host, and the whole operation is about entertainment, then why not just fill up the air with telegenic chefs juggling plates or swallowing flaming kebabs? Why even bother with the pretense of recipes and teaching technique? The answer is that the instructional element is essential to the Food Network's continued success and is what sets it—and home repair, gardening, design shows—apart from other television entertainment.

Even though, according to the Providence Journal's and perennial unofficial reports, supposedly half of the viewing audience doesn't even cook, the other half presumably does. While audiences may not be learning in the same way that housewives did when they were schooled by home economists back in the day, they're still receiving information that they apply in their own kitchens.

Judy Girard at one time confessed that she and her colleagues "didn't know if you could bring television principles to an information category and make it a successful television program." When asked about walking that wavy line between entertainment and instruction, she said, "It's always a struggle. . . . It's not an exact science." She described cooking show content as "a progression of information." It is successful, she believes, because "there are so many people in the country who do have that core passion about food or cooking or just an interest in learning something." Current

Food Network president Brooke Johnson, too, spoke about finding the balance between inspiration, teaching, and entertainment and described what they do at the network as an art.

> If we had to line things up, the most important thing for the brand is our authority. We are genuine experts in this. So we never want to let go of that in the interest of letting entertainment values take too high a position. But it's both. Part of the reason people watch a Rachael Ray or a Paula Deen or an Emeril Lagasse or whomever is because it's entertaining to people as well as instructional.

As Sara Moulton—who strongly believes it's possible to teach and still entertain—said, "In my mind there was no better entertainer slash educator, equally both, than Julia Child."

There are varying levels of instruction, too. After all, just because one set of viewers may have learned to grill fish on a crosshatch of rosemary sprigs, there's always a new crop of viewers, maybe those reaching adulthood or recently divorced and having to cook for themselves, who still need the recipe for boiling pasta. Other people just become interested in cooking at a certain point in their lives. Some even fit the very profile of those young housewives watching the home economists in the early 1950s and are finding their needs met. On a 2008 episode of *Paula's Home Cooking*, Deen touted the benefits of her chicken Florentine recipe: "All you new brides out there, I hope you're listening, because this is something you'll rely on from the beginning of your marriage to the end of your marriage." Deen can get away with such a retro sexist comment—Emeril or Rachael Ray could not because each personality has his and her own set of values, eccentricities, and loyal viewers. Such an attitude about gender roles—along with recipes like the one for "cheese fry casserole"—are critical to Deen's popularity.

Judy Girard remembered that when she got to the network in 2000, "It was all high-end chefs, and nobody can cook what high-end chefs do. They could get *technique* from them, how to slice and dice and things like that, but the broad appeal of the actual food that they would prepare and the practicality of preparing it for a family of four on a weekday night just wasn't there." Interestingly, half a century after home economists taught housewives how to manage their domestic environment, the directors of the modern-day cooking programs are coming back around to the basic idea of service and providing useful, practical information. "I think [programs have] to be filled with a lot of nuggets of information," said Bob Tuschman. "Tips, techniques, takeaway. Because again, we know a lot of people are watching who may not ever make that recipe, but you want to give them things they're going to remember." But it's no longer sufficient to teach unbuttressed by a highly produced, entertaining format. It's a tough crowd out there, calloused by years of television watching.

Whether a particular viewer perceives food television as instruction or entertainment depends on his or her relationship to cooking—if it's something she'll use, it's instructional, if it's not, but she likes to watch, it's entertainment. They're not mutually exclusive. Entertainment is more powerful a lure than instruction and certainly takes precedence in production. But the ostensible presentation of instruction is a selling point. As Judy Girard said of Food Network viewers, "They veg out by learning instead of vegging out totally." But why would the powers care one whit if we learn, really? There's nothing at stake if we are a nation of stupid cooks. They do care that we watch. Viewers can feel better, however, about spending time watching a cooking show than they might about watching *American Idol* or *CSI* because they at least have the illusion that they are taking in useful information. The subject alone lends virtuosity to the endeavor. Even though many people won't cook, "It's like a self help show in that it makes you feel better about yourself," said Bourdain. "Like buying a diet book and not going on a diet. You got the book." And if you feel good about watching, you're more likely to do it again.

In the 1940s and 1950s, home economist–hosted shows were pedantic, bordering on condescending, assuming that *women*

202 WATCHING WHAT WE EAT

needed to be taught every detail. As food writer Molly O'Neill said, "There was a need for a teacher at that time." Food television is occasionally criticized now for failing to make people better cooks, and indeed showmanship has won out, though the conventional wisdom says that most people simply aren't using it for learning. Maybe we don't need it to teach us anymore. Not only do we have myriad other sources for learning to cook, but food and cooking are so mainstreamed that we have learned a good deal via osmosis. "When I first started doing [Cooking Live] people had no idea what panko breadcrumbs were or a Peltex spatula or a Microplane," said Sara Moulton. "Now that's boring for me to bring up. Everybody knows what that is. I don't think I'd dare to chop an onion again. Everybody knows how to chop an onion."

Nowadays any pedagogy is served with a lighthearted, "cooking-is-fun!" attitude, and instruction is coated with a thick veneer of entertainment. It is not quite education by stealth, since both programmers and viewers claim to have an interest in imparting knowledge and learning. As the New York Times's William Grimes said of the appeal of Julia Child's shows, Americans have a "passion for self-improvement." That passion has only intensified in recent decades. Now we have the opportunity to satisfy our ids and our superegos at the same time, and, in fact, we expect it.

Because it is rather absurd to imagine getting any of these supposed thirty-minute meals that we see on TV actually whipped up in thirty minutes, what contemporary shows offer are really ideas and tips more than actual instructions. In the summer of 2007, cookbook author and New York Times "Minimalist" columnist (and host of The Best Recipes in the World on PBS), Mark Bittman, issued "Summer Express: 101 Simple Meals Ready in 10 Minutes or Less." The list consisted not of recipes but a series of short commands ("Fried egg 'saltimbocca': Lay slices of prosciutto or ham in a buttered skillet. Fry eggs on top of ham; top with grated Parmesan"; "Boil a lobster. Serve with lemon or melted butter"). Why was it such a heavily emailed article? Because that's what we want and need right now. Ideas. We're too busy to think about it, just tell us what to make and we'll do it. We've collectively learned to cook, so we don't need details. But lists like this and "easy peasy" shows perpetuate the notion that we're crazy busy, so it makes us feel even more so, and so on and so on. Watching Rachael Ray talk a mile a minute makes us feel even crazier and breathless. If we have time to watch the show, don't we have some down time? Apparently we choose to watch instead of cook.

For the past two decades especially, there has been the perennial quest for fast, but also delicious and healthy (or at least not too unhealthy) food. The healthiness profile of a dish is almost always mentioned these days. If it's healthy, it's a selling point—"good AND good for you!" If it's fattening, the host—Paula Deen notwithstanding—feels compelled to comment about how it's not exactly diet food, but it's worth it, a (usually female) host will say with a sly smile as she licks sauce off her fingers. In the vein of the health-conscious programs on PBS in the 1980s, the Food Network addressed both weight loss (*Calorie Commando, Weighing In, Low Carb and Loving It*) and overall health with shows like Curtis Aiken's *Meals without Meat* and *Healthy Appetite with Ellie Krieger*. Even with a trend toward "retro" comfort foods such as mashed potatoes and meatloaf, recipes were revamped to reduce the unhealthy aspects while preserving authenticity. There is a welcoming back of butter and cream, not only because one can make the choice to buy high quality, grass-fed dairy products, but because we've learned by now—haven't we?—that what's good for the soul is good for the body.

There is new material for food television to teach us. As we sally forth into the twenty-first century, there is less of an emphasis on dieting (it's so 1980s) and more of an emphasis on food's integrity as a way of approaching health. As a result, there is a leaning toward real, organic, locally grown food—health-promoting but not deprivational. Food is connected to our personal and societal values and, as some might argue, imposing elitist values onto middle and working class circumstances. Jamie Oliver has re-fashioned himself as a savior of both artisanal traditions and the health of British schoolchildren. Occasionally *Top Chef* contestants (are ordered to) channel their cutthroat urges into helping their fellow citizens eat better. In one episode they were challenged to update American classics—meatloaf, chicken à la king, fried chicken, tuna casserole—with lower fat and cholesterol versions to be served to Elks Club members. In another episode, contenders were put to the test of making a five hundred-calorie lunch appealing to overweight kids at Camp Glucose.

As Erica Gruen said, people don't watch to learn, but learning can be a by-product. While people might not focus as they would in a cooking class, it is clear that many do absorb useful information. A 2008 episode of the *Ultimate Recipe Showdown* offered a telling convergence of the elements that compose a modern-day cooking show. The program, sponsored by T.G.I. Friday's, was hosted by Marc Summers (host of *Unwrapped*) and multi-show host Guy Fieri and featured regular-folk contestants pitting their tried-and-true recipes against one another while Fieri and Summers provided ESPN-style color commentary. Rita Linda from Coral Springs, Florida, made her family-famous matzoh balls. As she skillfully shaped them using two spoons, Summers asked her, "Where'd you learn that technique, Rita?" Without hesitation or a pause in her actions, she answered, "The Food Network." In the fourth season of *The Next Food Network Star*, two contestants also credited the Food Network with specific facts and techniques that helped them move ahead in the competition.

As Martha Stewart told *New York Times* food writer Kim Severson in 2008,

> People are watching food as entertainment but there are also people who really want to learn. I have always stuck to my guns and said I want to be the do-it-yourself, how-to, but not cut corners. I want my program to be kind of relaxed but also intense and educational. And a lot of these other shows have . . . the pretty buxom girl sort of leaning over the table and at the

same time opening a can. That's not really my style of cooking, but people like it. I don't care where you get your inspiration as long as you get inspired and get some knowledge.

PBS, the Real Teacher

When it comes to learning, public broadcasting is still the go-to
place. *Sesame Street* has long been teaching preschoolers the basics of
reading and counting, and *Victory Garden*, *This Old House*, and *The
French Chef* taught grown-ups many of the basics of domestic life.
While Julia Child claimed that it wasn't necessary to be entertaining
on PBS, in a lower-stakes fashion, many of the TV values still apply.
While a PBS viewer may, generally speaking, be more likely to turn
on the TV with an eye to absorbing intellectually stimulating information than a Food Network viewer, he still doesn't wish to be bored
while doing it. The Corporation for Public Broadcasting has just as
much interest in "viewers like you" making financial contributions
to local stations as the Food Network's advertisers do in attracting
consumers like you.

In many network and cable food shows, there is a pretense of producing art. As evidenced by beautiful surroundings, the background
music, the flower arrangements and the attention to presentation, it
is made clear that aesthetics are of primary importance. Even though
cooking purports to be something everyone can do, commercial TV
hosts make precise emulation impossible. Whether it's part of their
quirky charm or just the way they cook, many hosts don't even use
measurements, much less share them explicitly with the audience.
When they do, it's often in free-spirited, nonspecific language—a
bunch of this, a dash of that. They might say, "two tablespoons of
olive oil" while they eyeball it, no clunky measuring spoon in sight.

The cult of personality is not the mighty rule of the land on PBS
cooking shows as it is in commercial television. While Julia Child,
Justin Wilson, and Jeff Smith were tremendous boons to stations'
welfare, there is a tacitly different ethos that goes into developing

public TV programs. The whole idea behind televised cooking demonstration is to be able to show the viewer how to work a recipe, but time constraints and entertainment values can get in the way. Where most contemporary commercial cooking shows traffic in enthusiastic encouragement, guilelessly giving the impression that with a little pluck and thirty spare minutes, you, too, can do this, the most-watched cooking show on public television, *America's Test Kitchen*, starts out with underlying pessimism.

"Recipes don't work," said Chris Kimball, the editor of *Cook's Illustrated* magazine, upon which *Test Kitchen* is based. The "you can do it" message is still here, but the raison d'etre of *Test Kitchen* is to supply the tools and confidence needed for the viewer to replicate the recipe. *Test Kitchen's* closest kin on the Food Network is *Good Eats*, where host Alton Brown delves into a layman's science of, for example, egg whites or flour or legumes so that you can avoid potential pitfalls in your own cooking. Where Giada De Laurentiis, "Barefoot Contessa" Ina Garten, and even Emeril are more about inspiration, Kimball and his crew are about pragmatism. Watching *Test Kitchen* is like checking into a cooking clinic.

The show also flagrantly breaks the number one rule of "good television": it doesn't have one central personality as a host. Producer Geoffrey Drummond said *America's Test Kitchen* "is a great example of how you can grow a niche product with a really strong audience and no star." Said Kimball, "The value of the ensemble cast to me is the inclusion of the audience." Everyone in food television talks about inviting the viewer in, but the invitation can obviously vary greatly in its execution. The personalities of *Test Kitchen*, which began airing in 2001, are the real-life editorial staff members of *Cook's Illustrated*—a bible for those who take home cooking seriously and have no use for airbrushed photographs of lavish feasts on private garden patios. *Test Kitchen* is the televised version of the magazine, which is color-free except for the muted tones on the fine art-wrapped cover and includes hand-illustrated recipe demos, taste tests and equipment ratings. It distills into a few minutes the explicit attempts, failures, and successes that serve as prologue to each of the magazine's recipes.

If there is anything close to a host, it's Kimball, who, with his trademark bowtie and no-nonsense demeanor, serves as interlocutor and facilitator. He said that someone once described him as "the simple-minded oaf" who is not the expert but a stand-in for the audience. "So I ask Adam or Jack or Bridget why, and what happens if you do it another way. Occasionally I break out of that and talk directly to the camera but most of the time I'm there just to ask the questions they want me to ask." (Julia Child played a similar role whenever she worked with another chef, gener-

Courtesy of America's Test Kitchen

Chris Kimball (in bowtie) and Geoffrey Drummond (in glasses across from him) on the set of *America's Test Kitchen*, a program whose mission is not to wow viewers, but to make sure their recipes work.

ously asking questions to which she often might have full well known the answer.) When Kimball tastes something he doesn't care for, his facial expressions speak a thousand words, but he doesn't spare the viewer the actual words either. Unlike Rachael Ray, he is just as likely to pronounce something mushy or bland as to give it praise—and he's very unlikely to deem anything "rockin."

That said, "[t]he genuine rapport between us [the staff/cast]," said Adam Ried, *Boston Globe* cooking columnist and *Test Kitchen*'s equipment specialist,

> does help set *America's Test Kitchen* apart. Chris, Bridget, Julia, Jack and I have known each other for years. We've cooked together, eaten together, argued together. I think the

ease that comes from familiarity is evident in the show. No one's a celebrity, for sure, but we are friends. Viewers sense that and seem to enjoy it.

In their large, enviably equipped test kitchen, the on-air *Test Kitchen* staff prepares relatively simple, honest, comfort food: glazed meatloaf, pork chops, buttermilk mashed potatoes, pan-roasted broccoli with gruyere sauce, blueberry scones, lemon layer cake, and the like. The show's aim is as straightforward as Kimball. "Our job is to make sure [recipes] do work and by explaining it—why you cream instead of melt the butter—you add the explanation that people want," said Kimball. "They realize if you listen to anybody else on television and try to make their recipe, it may or may not work. I'm sure it works for [the host], but there, people haven't thought long and hard about what's going to happen to that recipe in somebody else's kitchen." *Cook's Illustrated* recipes—the same ones that appear on *Test Kitchen*—are tested forty to fifty times apiece, sometimes more.

Test Kitchen is a working recipe show. Kimball thinks the notion of cooking as an art is nonsense and he'll have none of it. His approach is to understand the recipe inside and out. It's the same way Julia Child worked. But even this method, too, finds its critics. Referring to modern cooking instruction in general, scholar and food bookstore proprietor Nahum Waxman lamented contemporary Americans' unfortunate recipe dependence. His belief is that the need to follow recipes to a tee distances us from understanding food.

The fact is, we are living in an age of recipe dependency, of cooks who crave (and writers and editors who feed the craving) safe, reliable ways of guaranteed, error-free cooking. Both sides, writers and readers, are participating in a Faustian bargain, grasping success . . . or reasonable success— in exchange for the risky, even treacherous, chance-taking that comes from the exercise of free will. . . . What we are really accepting in exchange for a culinary safety net is ignorance and dependency.

While Waxman's desire for all cooks to fully understand the food with which they are dealing is a noble one, practically speaking, it is impossible for even a curious cook to delve into, given the demands of modern life. Certainly Chris Kimball would not disagree that people should understand the properties of what they're cooking—all that testing they do leads to such discovery—but he and his staff/cast are doing the work and sharing their findings with their readers/viewers who will hopefully absorb and learn more as they go along.

The very bells and whistles that make for good television are also the noises that sometimes distance viewers from the source. Where cooking shows used to entail a quiet, pseudo-one-on-one relationship between host and viewer, the modern day host is a celebrity, and while he may be endowed with authority and expertise, he is also remote and untouchable. Though Tuschman portrays the Food Network hosts as real nonactors, there is so much cultivation of their personalities that they are transformed into commodities. Indeed it is an authentic, no-frills quality that appeals to *Test Kitchen* viewers. "We don't have great Q ratings," said Kimball. "We're not Katie Couric, we're not Rachael Ray. We're just real people in a real kitchen and some people like that feeling that it's not put on, it's not an act. . . . Nobody can come to us and say you should be more entertaining because we wouldn't know how to do it. That's not who we are."

But even kind and gentle PBS cannot resist the powers of the appetite for competition—perhaps more aptly referred to in this context as a strong sense of restorative justice. Of the equipment ratings on *American's Test Kitchen* Kimball said, "I think a lot of people love to see the $200 saucepan lose to the $30 saucepan."

Equipment specialist Ried agreed.

The testing and tasting segments do provide an element of competition, but more than that they reinforce the solid, no-nonsense zeitgeist of [the show]. Determining through first-hand testing the strengths and weaknesses of different electric mixers, food processors, raspberry jams, medium-roast coffee—whatever is under investigation—draws in the maximizers, the researchers, the evidence seekers—the *Consumer Reports* crowd. The curiosity, though, is no conceit. If a hardware store cast iron pan can do a job as well or better than a gourmet shop French enameled pan, for a fifth of the price, I want to know. And so does Chris.

Where cooking and food are the center of the show on *Test Kitchen*, Kimball describes the Food Network as "selling the personality. Food is not that important on the Food Network." Yet, like many Food Network, shall we say, nonpromoters like Anthony Bourdain, Kimball quickly gives the Food Network its due when it comes to promoting the topic in general. "Food Network has done a great service by bringing people into the food world, some of whom will move past that and eventually come to us because they really want to know how to cook," said Kimball. "Emeril and Rachael Ray and all those people have . . . just broadened the market. Rachael Ray is probably responsible for 100,000 of our [magazine] subscribers because over the years she's got enough people interested in the idea of cooking and some of them discover us and say now I really want to know what's going on."

Kimball's vision of *America's Test Kitchen*—"We're about information and along the way if it's also entertaining for people then it is"—is exactly the converse of what Erica Gruen said about the Food Network—"They watch television to have fun. . . . And if they learn something while they're having fun, that's good too." The easy flippability of these maxims demonstrates how food television can satisfy so many.

CHAPTER 8

"Democratainment":
Gender, Class, and the Rachael-Martha Continuum

Food, far more than sex, is the great leveler. Just as every king, prophet, warrior, and saint has a mother, so every Napoleon, every Einstein, every Jesus had to eat. Eating is an in-body experience, a lowest common denominator, by nature funny, like the banana peel or the pie-in-the-face of slapstick. The subversive comedy of food is incremental. Little laughs add up to big ones, big enough to poke a hole in our delusions of star-wars domination and bring us down to earth. The gut, like the bum, makes the whole world one.

—Betty Fussell

Men, Women, and Children

What would have once been unabashedly described as women's programming is now referred to by various industry members as "task-oriented formats," "information categories," or "lifestyle programming." By losing that old-fashioned label, we might assume that such programming—including the cooking, gardening, crafts, and home decorating on the Scripps networks HGTV, DIY Network, Fine Living, and the Food Network—has broken free from gender constraints. After all, *everyone* has tasks to complete and *everyone* needs information. But the content of these shows—especially the daytime lineup—is essentially the same as that of yesteryear's home-making shows; and a mere gander at the number of sponsoring ads that feature a toilet brush- or skillet-wielding housewife belies the idea of an inclusive target audience.

"There still is a gender issue here," said Marsha Cassidy, author of *What Women Watched: Daytime Television in the 1950s.*

> It seems to me these shows try to address younger women and men who enjoy cooking as a means of creative expression, a key element in the inspiring, "fun" shows of today. This is different, however, from the reality of cooking as an everyday chore. It's almost always women who drag themselves home from work and feed their families night after night under difficult circumstances. Hardly the fun, creative fulfillment hyped on the cooking shows.

Various data do show that women spend at least twice as much time as men doing domestic work, a time gap especially marked when it comes to food labor.

Whereas cooking shows used to be explicitly geared toward women homemakers, they have been increasingly marketed to both men and women. Viewership is still skewed toward women, however, and evening out the gender gap by targeting younger and male viewers has been a focus of the Food Network since the mid-1990s. On the whole, professional cooking offscreen is still male-dominated, as the majority of executive chefs and restaurant owners are men. But there has been no shortage of critics decrying sexism in cooking television. There exists an ironic dynamic on the Food Network between a macho, patriarchal vibe vying for real estate and a traditional female preserve of home cooking and cooking instruction. In trying to make the point that cooking shows aren't just for women, it could be argued that the Food Network has gone too far in the other direction.

Prime time has generally been dominated by the more entertainment-heavy shows, many of which happen to be hosted by men—Alton Brown, Emeril Lagasse, Jamie Oliver, Mario Batali, Alton Brown, Bobby Flay, "Ace of Cakes" Duff Goldman, and the chefs from *Iron Chef America*. Programs like Tyler Florence's *Food 911* and Danny Boome's *Rescue Chef* both feature women in culinary distress who call upon a male chef to come and save them, usually from the potential wrath of their husbands and families. It is notable that more men have out-of-studio travel adventures while women cook at home and for parties. A good deal of press was generated after the

first woman, Stephanie Izard, won Bravo's *Top Chef* competition in the show's fourth season in June 2008. It is also barely necessary to mention that women tend to dress in close-fitting, low-cut tops or other sartorially inconvenient items (bell sleeves, dangling hair and jewelry) while the men more often dress practically or professionally (chef's whites). In addition to the bloodsport aspect, the ladies are a draw for the male audience, too. "I've met some young men recently who said they started watching the

Food Network/Photofest © Food Network

Cordon Bleu–trained Giada De Laurentiis knows her craft, but her appeal goes beyond culinary skills.

Food Network because of Giada because she was so pretty," said Sara Moulton. "And likewise Rachael Ray. I mean pretty's not the word they'd use, but . . ." Even before Moulton's contract ended, she saw the writing on the wall and knew that her time was up. "If they decide they want to work with you, they'll reposition you and give you a new show and reinvent you," she said. "I think [the Food Network] saw me in a different category, not for the fifteen- to thirty-five-year-old males. They were looking for younger, really pretty women with cleavage and big personalities. Not that I didn't have all of those things, including cleavage, but they didn't ask."

While the glass half empty sees sexism, the glass half full sees progressive sex role transformation. As Marsha Cassidy conceded, "Cooking shows have allowed women to achieve economic and industry power." But it's the men who have seen the greater change in intangibles. As Reese Schonfeld said, "Sociologically I think the biggest thing we did was Emeril. I think it's Emeril who made it possible for men to cook. [It's] different from guys in the kitchen wearing aprons." And Geoffrey Drummond said, "[Watching cooking shows] was not a manly thing. Even our *Master Chefs* was predominantly watched by women. A few more guys were beginning to get interested because of chefs like Charlie Palmer, Robert Del Grande, big guy guys, but Emeril really made it something guys would like to do." Of Emeril's impact on the demographics of the Food Network audience, *Salon's* James Poniewozik wrote, "The largest segment of his viewership was men over 30—including firehouse crews watching his show en masse—and thus he was TVFN's ticket to not becoming Lifetime Network II."

While shows like Bravo's *Queer Eye for the Straight Guy* and the Food Network's *Date Plate* are evidence that cooking skills and food savvy are prized among men as well as women, on both programs it is often the man who is guided by a lifestyle expert to impress a woman with his cooking prowess. "Do you like to cook?" is a question posed to both men and women these days and an affirmative answer suggests a creative, cultured person, a sensualist (dateable), and, if male, then liberated. At the same time, thanks to changing gender role expectations, women don't have to like it. In fact, for a woman, it is sometimes a postfeminist badge of honor to answer with an emphatic "I keep sweaters in my stove," as *Sex and the City's* Carrie Bradshaw proudly confessed.

The Food Network officially targets adults aged twenty-five to fifty-four—not exactly every breathing human, but a vast swath of the population. As of 2008, the channel reaches over 96 million homes, is watched by nearly 900,000 viewers nightly and prime-time viewership has increased every year. Reese Schonfeld plucked out a few bits of telling ratings information as he flipped through the latest numbers in July 2007: Food Network had twice as many viewers as CNN overall, considerably more than CNN in prime time and more viewers aged eighteen to fifty-four than any news service.

Appealing to the whole family is one way to get around using narrow category definitions. Beta Research Corporation's 2004 "brand identity" survey ranked the Food Network tenth among most "family-oriented" broadcast, cable, and satellite television networks in 2004. Even though it is not explicitly marketed toward them, it's popular among the truly youthful, too. In 2006, two pre-teen sisters were the James Beard Award Best Webcast winners for their cooking video instruction on Spatulatta.com. A well-circulated video in 2008 showed a three-year-old boy mimicking *New York Times*'s columnist Mark Bittman verbatim after watching his dad's podcast of the Minimalist making chocolate ganache. Kids are naturally drawn to the entertainment of food television just as their parents are— often possibly for the same reasons of mesmerizing entertainment. Elementary and secondary school students have the option of taking cooking and gastronomy classes at school and in extracurricular programs where home economics classes may have fizzled out decades ago. Young Chefs Academy, a chain of more than 150 franchised cooking schools for children in the United States and Canada, was established in 2003. Such mainstreaming of food was undoubtedly facilitated by the Food Network.

The Rachael-Martha Continuum

When the Food Network first began, its audience was, as Erica Gruen put it, "fairly old and downscale" (although the network's pioneers strongly disagree with this assessment). With calculated changes in programming, the viewer profile gradually morphed from your great aunt into your law firm associate. "The Food Network sort of became symbiotic," said Gruen. "The network became more fun and lively, and it appealed to a more affluent, more educated group of people who then in turn became more interested in food and watched more Food Network. The Food Network at some point became more of an influencer on popular culture."

Fat wallets are a desired segment of the viewing population, sought after by advertisers. And since popular culture trends affect spending trends, the people with the spending power indirectly affect what's projected on TV. As baby boomers became more willing to spend more of their income on kitchen appliances and high-quality ingredients, food television reflected that. Although many of the network's shows and their upscale trappings are judged to be too unrealistic for the average viewer to relate to, data tells us that those enviable kitchens that we see on screen may actually look like the kitchens of many of those watching. According to Nielsen ratings, in 1998 the Food Network ranked number one among the top thirty cable networks in attracting viewers twenty-five to fifty-four-years-old with an annual income of $100,000 or higher. During Judy Girard's time at the helm, Food Network viewers were among the most affluent viewers nationwide. "We did a show on how to feed your family on ninety-nine dollars a week. I didn't realize, looking back at the changes in American life, that there weren't that many women at home any more worrying about how to feed their family on ninety-nine dollars a week," said Reese Schonfeld. *How to Feed Your Family on $99 a Week* was a daytime show, and the target audience was out of the house earning ever-increasing salaries.

But when there is economic flux in the nation, television programming responds in kind. "The number one way we remain a business and make money is through ratings," said Food Network president Brooke Johnson.

A number of years ago, the network used to be more high end, haute cuisine-oriented, béchamel sauces and whatnot.

Both independent research and Nielsen ratings told us that most of our viewers were home cooks and they want material they can cook at home. When someone like Rachael Ray's ratings explode, that tells us something about what our viewers are interested in.

By the time Girard left in 2003, viewers' average income had fallen a bit but was still about $75,000 per year. Ray, who appeals by design to a less-wealthy audience, was part of Girard's legacy. Saving on the cost of food, while not as central as the time-saving element on *30 Minute Meals*, is an implicit agenda of the show (as it is explicitly on Ray's travel show, *$40 a Day*). Ray frequently makes a point of how the ingredients she's using can be purchased at any old grocery store, and the viewer can witness her taking the package of pre-shredded cheddar out of the fridge and dumping it into a bowl. As your girl-next-door, she does

Rachael Ray meets Americans in the middle.

not expect you to buy, other than extra virgin olive oil or EVOO (Ray's coinage was added to *The Oxford American College Dictionary* in 2007), the cream-of-the-crop brand. She doesn't want you to spend too much time or money on cooking. She just wants you to get your butt into the kitchen and do it.

Rachael Ray hit because she has all the elements needed to satisfy both the criteria of the Food Network and the needs of the zeitgeist. She has the personality and the performance chops. She is the midcult antidote to the haute cuisine, béchamel stance that seemed to be losing ground with viewers. Like Paula Deen, she is someone who seems amazed by her success and maintains that girl-next-door charm as a central facet of her appeal. She does not have the skills and experience of Emeril, but she makes no pretense of being a chef. She is likeably self-deprecating, and she does give Sara Moulton credit for the "garbage bowl."

As formulaic as it sounds, Ray's shows give viewers what they need to get the job done: get some food, heat it up, make it not too boring, eat it, move on. Don't forget to have fun and enjoy yourself, she seems to say. Hers is a far cry from the intricate, multi-page recipes that were all the rage in her mother's day. Ray cooks and talks and weighs like most of us do—she is not classically aspirational. Her sensibility seems to be what viewers want, at least as evidenced by the propagation of shows like hers. As Bill Buford wrote in *The New Yorker*, "The two essential premises of *30 Minute Meals*—no one knows how to cook and everyone is in a hurry—now inform most instructional cooking shows." It's not that we don't know how, it's that many of us choose not to do it.

Photofest

Martha Stewart—the quintessential do-it-yourself media maven—has been an aspirational and controversial model of homemaking since the 1980s.

There is a continuum, however, where aspirational and inspirational, Price Chopper and Whole Foods, organic and semi-homemade exist. On one end there are those shows that Buford describes, with Rachael Ray as the poster girl. On the other end is Martha Stewart. Stewart, who had turns as a model then a stockbroker before turning to catering in the late 1970s, is a guide to all "good things" related to home—cooking, gardening, decorating, and crafts. She smacks of a throwback to the old homemaking shows, but at the same time Stewart's cooking segments also correspond with the recent trends of an increased focus on health and the subsequent desire to control one's food. The latter is made explicit, however, and is certainly not in reaction to the current fashion since she was raised with a farm-to-table mentality. On her cooking, gardening, and homemaking show *Martha Stewart Living*, which predated the Food Network, she represents the idealized modern homemaker—for better or worse. Among other things, she is known for creating aesthetically pleasing, delicious, nutritious meals made from foods grown in her own garden, on a table she refinished herself, accompanied by napkins she has hand-decorated. She embodies the servantless upper-class American who appears to have it all and do it all with grace, style, and ease.

Stewart is in many ways a modern version of the woman-who-could-do-it-all-without-exertion, Dione Lucas. The ghost of Lucas that lurks within Stewart manifests itself in the same flawless execution and alleged unintended intimidation. In the early 1990s, Stewart, too, was a bit out of sync with her peers, encouraging women to go on and spend more time as domestic agents at a time when politically correct mainstream society was promoting the opposite. "What I've found is that even women working outside the home have a craving to spend time on their homes," Stewart told the *Chicago Tribune* in 1993. "It's what I call my backlash. They are responding favorably to do-it-yourself, do-it-at-home, being creative." Had Stewart and Lucas been contemporaries on the screen, they would either have been dueling perfectionists or partners in the art form. Stewart would express herself creatively in the earthy American way, putting up jams and pickles, going to the market, and digging in her garden; Lucas would stay in the kitchen, busily enacting inimitable feats, evoking a European sense of fine dining. They'd meet up in the dining nook at the end of the show, clink glasses, pretend to start eating, and then go home to their lonely towers of excellence.

During Stewart's ascendance as a domestic queen, average subjects perpetually whined and accused Stewart of making them feel inadequate because they couldn't replicate her stunts. It's easy to imagine disappointing Lucas and Stewart, not living up to their imagined judgmental expectations, and fearing their harsh criticism when you just didn't try hard enough or summon enough confidence.

In a 1996 article in *The New Republic*, Margaret Talbot wrote, "Every age gets the household goddess it deserves." Talbot compared the 1960s having Julia Child to the 1990s (and "probably well into the next century," she predicted) having Martha Stewart. Though Talbot wrote the article before Stewart was imprisoned for insider trading and before Rachael Ray was invented, her argument remains valid. Talbot referred to Martha as the "anti-Julia." Where Julia is "messy and forgiving," Martha is "Mildred Pierce in earth-toned Armani." Julia was true to her can-do mission, making viewers feel they could achieve, but Martha, with her unflappable calm and unfailing perfection, seems to make many viewers feel inadequate. Stewart is reminiscent of the ambiguous persona of Arlene Francis on *Home* and the projection of those "upper-middlebrow aspirations" as Marsha Cassidy described.

As the *New York Times*'s Kim Severson commented to Stewart, "It's an interesting world in which someone like you and someone like Rachael Ray can both be successful." Rachael Ray and Martha Stewart are both touchstones of our modern era. They represent the paradoxes and contradictions within ourselves and our complicated relationship with food, cooking, and living. Rachael is always in a hurry; Martha seems to have all the time in the world. Rachael wants to help us reduce the amount of work we do in the kitchen and, even though she acknowledges our incredibly busy lives, Martha does nothing if not prescribe more work.

Martha and Julia Child—who is still somewhere in constant motion on that continuum—shared the same goal for their subjects: living well. They both implicitly granted side-door access to upper-class worlds, Julia pooh-poohing the existence of the gate and Martha issuing a perceived set of conditions for entry. All of our lifestyle guides mean to do the same thing—make their endeavors seem both inspirational and accessible—but Martha can't seem to help but communicate that in a way that seems impossible, whereas Julia gave us detailed instructions, and Rachael goes all out to make it seem as if we could do better than her, no prob.

In 1997, host Bill Boggs interviewed Stewart on his Food Network show *Corner Table* while they dined at the illustrious New York restaurant Jean Georges. Boggs introduced Stewart as "queen of all media" and "topmost food and lifestyle authority" but also described her family as "very unwealthy, almost poor, with six children and a teacher father." Her upbringing is often trotted out as an attempt at an "I'm like you" approach, as if a humble background will soften her regal authority. But with her it never works. Boggs asked her about the wackiest thing that happened in front of the camera, and she told a story of the time she ate a nut, started to choke, and lost her voice. She called the incident "embarrassing and unacceptable." If she can't forgive herself for an automatic physiological response, what will she think of us floundering in our kitchens daring to try one of her recipes? We can imagine that if the nut incident happened upon Julia she would have silently admonished herself but laughed it off and likewise Rachael would gulp water, whack herself on the chest, smile hugely, and say, "Dontcha hate when that happens?"

As much as Stewart seems remote and not like people with whom most of us hang out, Rachael Ray strikes a nerve exactly because she is like us. "America loves Rachael because Rachael *is* America," her friend chef Mario Batali said of her on her Food Network *Chefography*. She makes us feel good about ourselves because she doesn't appear to be rich (though we know better) and is not skinny and could no sooner be called snobby than she could be mistaken for British. But don't we teach our children to strive, to aim high, to challenge themselves? Isn't that what boosts self-esteem? And aren't we allowed some escape and fantasy, even if it's only as far as Westport, Connecticut?

Rachael Ray was dubbed by *Newsweek* as "the most down-to-earth TV star on the planet" and by *Entertainment Weekly* as "the next domestic goddess." "What makes Rachael Ray so exciting to people," said Bob Tuschman, "is that she speaks their language, shops at the same places they shop, and uses the same ingredients." As Buford wrote, "Ray wants to be just like us." Not the other way around. We may secretly want to be just like Martha, but Rachael is attainable, so if she meets us where we are, we will respond. We're rewarded with success—her recipes are easy, she has low expectations. That seems to be pretty effective for self-esteem, too. Sandra Lee and Ray may be reviled by purists, but they are also the ones most people are likely to emulate, the ones more like who they really are. Their ratings and cookbook sales bear out their enormous popularity and their ability to speak to the masses.

"When you hit in this field," said Molly O'Neill, obliquely referring to no host in particular, "it's very easy to get the idea that your taste is representative of millions of people's taste. And in fact it's representative of millions of people's desire. That's a very big distinction." Since both Ray and Stewart have a vast media presence—they both host their own daytime talk shows airing in simultaneous time slots, too—millions have the luxury of being able to meet a wide range of needs and desires.

Democratization

If there is an emblematic buzzword that has been coopted for the era of user-generated content and reality programming, it's "democratizing." To some, perhaps those same viewers whose kitchens are mirrored on TV, Martha Stewart *is* perceived as an attainable ideal. On a 2008 episode of the reality show *Real Housewives of New York City*, the ambitiously entrepreneurial natural foods chef, Bethenny, declared, "Martha democratized style. I want to democratize health."

The Food Network's mission is of the people through and through. "We view food as one of the most democratic of mediums," said Bob Tuschman. "Everybody eats every day, and *any*body can cook. . . . Our goal is to open the doors of the food world wide and invite everyone in. There are a lot of people in certain parts of the food world who like the closed community. We want just the opposite."

The winning "If I can do this, you can" theme conveyed by Julia Child pervaded most recipe instruction shows in the 1990s and

2000s but with a zeal that Julia would never have felt compelled to exert. What we see now is an outright campaign to make viewers believe they can do it. This is in contrast to Julia and Dione and the Frug, who certainly wanted us to cook—but Julia's recipes were pages long, Dione's required great skill, and The Frug would even admit, "I know it's hard!" In the modern era, everything is about accessibility. Rachael Ray and Lagasse always reassure viewers that they don't need to worry if they don't know some shmancy jargon ("a genoise is just sponge cake," Emeril said comfortingly, and in so doing, like Julia, aligns himself with us, not *them*).

It would be difficult to improve on cultural studies scholar Toby Miller's summation of the popularization movement via television:

> In the 1960s this means a scion of the US gentry tolling up her jolly-hockey-mistress sleeves and being ordinary on non-profit television. In the 1990s it means multicultural chefs blending world cuisines on a money-hungry quasi-infotainment cable system. In the process, French food is demystified and rendered one amongst many forms of fine eating.

What was once considered a "trade" as opposed to a "profession," cooking is now a red-hot hobby and career path. It has cut across class lines in both directions. Kids from working-class families are now able to enter the high falutin' world of professional chefdom, and patrician offspring can now justifiably join the erstwhile low-rent world of cooking for a living. Television cooking shows, and the media in general, are largely responsible for glamorizing what will always be, in actuality, toiling, sweaty labor. Likewise, food TV has brought deserved attention to a previously uncelebrated class of laborers and artisans. "We are an egalitarian attempting society," said food and restaurant consultant Clark Wolf.

> One of the most wonderful things about this culture and about food [is] that a drunken stoned busboy can in three

to five years become a multimillionaire, multiple restaurant restaurateur, and a pillar of the community. I don't know of any other business or cultural place in our society that can do that. It's partly because of the necessary fluidity of food and food culture and the resonance, the power of it.

"Through food," wrote Duke University Romance Studies professor Alice Yaeger Kaplan, "access to aristocracy has been democratized, because unlike the Grand Tour, food is both accessible and interpretable by varying social milieux." She uses the example of the croissant as an item that is seen everywhere from "the menu at the Pierre to the strip mall Burger King." This is certainly doubly true of food television, given that the mass medium is a natural democratizer. "During the second half of the twentieth century, television has reached and sustained a position as the foremost medium for cross-demographic communication," wrote cultural and media studies scholar John Hartley of the concept he calls "democratainment." True enough, there are high-income viewers who take note of the food television show trappings and think, "They are speaking to me." There are also less wealthy people watching who see a relatively easy entrée into *that* world. "Food television normalizes the exotic for suburbia and exoticizes the normal for a hip elite, middle-class homeworkers, and late-night revelers," wrote Toby Miller. Food television is not necessarily, however, the great equalizer. Simply putting something on television doesn't make it accessible to all—just viewable by all. It is not so much a socially progressive public service as it is a handy marketing strategy.

The lowbrow medium of TV has gradually eased the distinctions between high and low culinary culture. Because most Americans own a TV, they have access to shows that tell them about arugula and EVOO. In theory, this gourmet cornucopia is available to anyone. But in practice, there are geographic and financial barriers to the foods and the lifestyles portrayed. Food television does allow a level of entrée to fancy foods and lifestyles, but it is still a tease. For a large element of society, time and money are obstacles to the cultural trading up that beckons us. While cooking became a hobby and a luxury for many, for many more it is still a chore. Julia Child is rightfully hailed as a true democratic force, having brought complex French cooking to the masses, debunking the myth that you had to be a chef or a certain kind of person of a certain class to cook and eat like a certain kind of person of a certain class. Child allowed people to turn prior generations' rigid mores and exclusive rituals on their head, as in "I, too, can cook French food." But at the same time, French food (and an implicit, immutable hierarchy) was retained as the standard.

The kind of cooking that is portrayed on food television is not the same kind that's carried out by a low paid immigrant workforce in restaurant kitchens or in the homes of a paycheck-to-paycheck striving family. The expensive ingredients, the well-equipped kitchens, a host's aesthetic—these elements imply a social status that is at odds with the buoyant words emitted by the host. It is not the food of basic needs, but at another level entirely, concentrating instead on pleasure, well-being, and self-fulfillment. But, as food studies scholar Krishnendu Ray wondered in his article "Domesticating Cuisine," "Should we restrict food to a narrow range of functions when we do not expect the same with shelter or clothing or a whole lot of other essential needs?" It is indeed curious that food is perhaps unfairly called out as being fetishized and aestheticized when so many other forms of basic needs—architecture, fashion—are treated as playthings without being labeled excessively libidinous or morally bereft.

Nevertheless, the food-as-lifestyle perspective is intrinsically exclusive. There always has been and always will be a divide in the world of food, not only because one needs to have a certain amount of disposable income in order to enjoy food as a leisure activity, but because even for those who do have the means, there will always be some new ingredient, restaurant, appliance, or health benefit that's unattainable because it is beyond the psychic reach of the culturally ignorant. What's portrayed on these shows, as populist as they claim to be, is still an elite world where having good knives in your kitchen is a basic assumption and eating fresh, local, and at home is the ideal. Are the *Top Chef* contestants charged with updating the Elks Club's members' American classics diets of meatloaf and tuna casserole with healthier versions performing a public service, or are they patronizing? Could food television be getting in its own populist way as it actually imposes elitist values? And does it really want democracy anyway?

"Knowing and using the language of cuisine, including exercising one's educated palate, separates those with cultural capital from ordinary eaters," wrote food scholar Pauline Adema. "As more people become familiar with gourmet foods, flavors, and preparation techniques the value of gourmet food and cooking as cultural capital decreases." In other words, once Oscar Madison is enjoying Yoplait or your midwestern mom is drinking hazelnut coffee as a matter of course, it's way past its chic prime. Once edamame is found in the local Stop & Shop, its secret shining moment in the province of the privileged is gone. Indeed, an egalitarian flattening is just what food snobs bristle about, professing a fear of the triumph of mediocrity. If people can, as sociologist Pierre Bourdieu argued, acquire taste, social classes are in grave danger. "Food has peaked as a cultural window. It's mainstream now," said Molly O'Neill. "Go to a book signing for Martha Stewart. There are truck drivers in that line with their books."

O'Neill has long observed the gradual mainstreaming of the postwar food reawakening.

> It went from the top five percent of the culture and in a very democratic fashion it trickled down from the $300,000 income households to the $30,000 income households. That is very exciting to mass marketers. It is not exciting to the top

five percent [the intelligent and the wealthy and the privileged in America]. They *must* distinguish themselves.

The divide is evident to all the players, even if we do not all have a language to describe it. What O'Neill refers to as the "top five percent" Sara Moulton calls by a different name. "I've always said there's two different sets of foodies in this country," said Moulton. "There's the haute foodies, and I don't mean it in the snobby sense but the more sophisticated sort of slow food movement interested in good ingredients and authentic cooking interested in real techniques. And then there's the hockey fan foodies. Those would be the ones who want to have fun." She invoked Emeril—who she acknowledged is a serious chef—and Rachael Ray as appealing to the "hockey fan foodies," the bottom 95 percent, or what Graham Kerr referred to as the "great unwashed."

For a member of any of the latter groups, the hope that one can find an affordable, relatively easy path to an upper-class way of life is constant. So, if the average home cook in Peoria cannot afford a kitchen re-do, at least she may assuage her desires with some of the trappings of her favorite on-air personalities. "Oh, how one aspires to Nigella-dom—to live so fully, to mouth the word 'succulently' so succulently," wrote Stephen Metcalf in *Slate*. We not only want to cook like the TV hosts, but we also want to live like them. Cooking shows, always having been how-to and instructional, have become lifestyle guides.

"The real tectonic shift in the food landscape," said Anthony Bourdain,

> was when Americans overcame their revulsion for raw fish and suddenly seemingly all at once decided that sushi was desirable. That changed everything for everybody. . . . The real question is why did they start seeing sushi as desirable? We were raised in an instinctive way to think that eating raw fish was like sleeping with your sister or your brother. It was

that fundamentally wrong. . . . It doesn't really matter why people start eating raw fish. Maybe they saw it on *Sex and the City*, maybe they saw the characters eating it and thought that looks like something hip maybe I should do.

Food scholar Kimberly Joy Orlijan wrote,

> Food TV's audience (and arguably all TV audiences) are buying an identity, whether that be "American" or "cook" or both. . . . Further, when the viewer of a cooking program learns what it means to "chiffonade" and to "canel," to "deglaze" and to "degorge," the viewer is acquiring another language—that of the kitchen, a language that creates an imagined community. . . . Attaining the language of cooking and purchasing an identity via acquiring products spawn communities that necessarily, by their very existence as communities, create and exclude others.

The imagined trading up that one can do with food TV means that we can vicariously become part of Martha Stewart's or Nigella Lawson's coterie or imagine ourselves in their lovely kitchens with them.

As *Something from the Oven* author Laura Shapiro wrote in *Slate*:

> Fantasy has always played a big part in beat-the-clock cookbooks; in fact, the category relies on it. . . . Despite the shopping lists, the step-by-step directions, the time-saving tips, and the authors who insist that this is exactly how they cook at home, there's little that reflects the real world in such books. Like those gigantic, glossy tomes with titles like *My Kitchen in the Wine Country* or *Tuscany at Table*, the quick-cook books are wish books. They're cheaper, friendlier, and far more portable than their $75 siblings, but they're wish books all the same. Open a quick-cook book and you're transported—not to some Provencal dreamscape but to your own kitchen. Why,

that's you at the counter, cheerfully putting together a charming meal for the family while your children set the table. You can practically see them storing up those all-important food memories that will accompany them through life like a St. Christopher medal.

Perhaps, just as Americans began to glorify the outdoors as they built themselves into suburban housing tracts in the 1950s and 1960s, so we have renewed our food obsession and at the same time are unknowingly losing touch with food and turning it into a fantasy. The gathering of takeaway information that shapes our behavior occurs on an individual and societal level. As drama scholar Martin Esslin wrote,

> [T]he identity of a culture, the self-image of a nation, is formed by the concepts, myths, beliefs, and patterns of conduct that are instantly recognized by the members of that social entity as being peculiarly theirs. No other single factor of our present-day civilization—not the educational system or religion or science or the arts—is so all-pervasive, so influential, so totally accessible to and shared by all individuals in society as is the world presented by television.

Just as Darryl Hannah's mermaid character in *Splash* learned how to speak from watching TV (and, as historian Mary McFeely described, cookbooks teach ethnic groups and working-class Americans "this is what you ought to aspire to"), so we collectively learn how to walk and talk and what is expected of us. And through food television, we learn, not just techniques and tips but cultural literacy.

Business/Culture of Food/Television

"Being on television brings democratization as surely as it brings commodification," wrote Toby Miller. Television has always been about selling, whether it's advertisers' products to consumers or viewers' eyeballs to advertisers. Consequently food television has always had as much (or more, some argue) to do with the business and culture of television as it has to do with food itself. If cooking shows are about the television business and television is about selling products, then cooking shows are inextricably tied to marketing and consumerism on a grand scale. Dione Lucas's line of canned soups in the 1950s are no match for the branding of today's hosts and their spin-off product lines. It's not just that Emeril, Mario, Nigella, Martha, Rachael, and compatriots have their own knives, cookware, dishware, spice rubs, and apparel that we can buy and use or just display in our own kitchens, but TV cooking show hosts sell most of the cookbooks in America and extend their popular reach via newspaper columns, websites, blogs, and entire magazines.

Over the past sixty years, we have witnessed a gradual transformation in cooking shows—from the dissemination of basic cooking methods by a home ec teacher in a standard kitchen to a celebrity host-centric, branded, living catalogue. But the behavior is not as conscious as choosing from a catalogue. The desire seeps in and does its number on us just as advertising does. The changing tone of cooking shows—rote recipe instruction to cascading cherries—correlates with the evolution of advertising over the history of television. Content that used to be just plain old information is now studied exhaustively as to its psychological effects. Advertisers in the 1950s figured out who their consumers were—women—and the influence of advertising has only increased since then.

Buying the lifestyle is made explicit with a show like *Shopping with Chefs*, which began on Fine Living in 2007. "Now you can cook like a pro and impress your family and friends" the show's website promises. Host-chefs Jill Davie and David Myers certainly offer helpful hints such as "[l]ook for peppermills that produce a fine grind, have a sturdy metal grinding mechanism, are easy to fill, and have a large peppercorn capacity," but it is up to the viewer to eventually come to terms with the fact that owning and using the suggested peppermill will only make him *look* like a professional, and only to his easily impressed family and friends. The urge to own the same equipment the professionals do is not confined to food and cooking. We also buy high-tech outerwear to commute to our office jobs during inclement weather. But it makes us feel good about ourselves to take the endeavor seriously.

America's Test Kitchen's Chris Kimball is not on television because he loves to ham it up on camera. "These days," he said, "if you're not on television in the food world you just don't exist. You really have to be on television just from a business point of view. If you look at Jacques Pépin before and after TV, his life completely changed." As Pépin himself said, "It's not that you get millions of dollars with PBS. The return for me is the fact that I'm selling books."

Cookbook authors and TV cooking hosts are often one and the same because TV is a magical marketing forum. Sometimes the show comes first (Graham Kerr, Rachael Ray, Jamie Oliver), sometimes the book comes first (Julia Child, Justin Wilson, Paula Deen, Martha Stewart). In a growing number of cases, it appears that the media forum comes first, then the food "chops" can be added later (though this was the case with Mary Lee Taylor, Monty Margetts, Sally Ogle, and LaDeva Davis in the 1930s, 40s, 60s, and 70s, respectively). This chef's moment of glory we are currently witnessing is actually not good for *all* chefs. "There are some really talented chefs who because they're just not interested or are just unable to talk about themselves on camera," said Anthony Bourdain, "their very deserving restaurants are suffering in an increasingly competitive marketplace because they're not willing to drink the media savvy Kool-Aid that everybody else is."

"When we started it was perfectly rational to say to the entrepreneur in the United States, 'all you need to do to be a success is to find a need and fill it,'" said Graham Kerr. "Today if you want to survive— because we're not talking about success anymore—if you want to survive in business, you have to find a want and *exploit* it."

CHAPTER 9

Evolution:
How Did We Get Here and What's On Next?

When man has satisfied his physical needs, then psychologically grounded desires take over. These can never be satisfied or, in any case, no progress can be proved. The concept of satiation has very little standing in economics. It is neither useful nor scientific to speculate on the comparative cravings of the stomach and the mind.

—John Kenneth Galbraith

The Air, the Water, the Kool-Aid

There is a tendency to perceive our current widespread fixation on food as an unprecedented trend. But it is not a new cultural interest— it is a perennial. "What's happening today has happened before and will happen again," said food writer Molly O'Neill. Extracurricular, supra-survival attention to food has waxed and waned in America from the nation's inception. There may have been a relative dry spell from Jeffersonian gastronomia to Kennedy Francophilia, and, from the 1960s to the 1990s, interest was on a low but gradually increasing simmer. Television was a crucial factor that turned up the heat, but not the only one.

The Providence Journal Company, customarily acting on some data and business sense in the early 1990s, could not have known the extent to which the topic they settled on was going to explode. Fortunately for the media company, at the same time they were pondering a strategic move, the culture was experiencing a culinary shift once again. Over the previous two pre–Food Network decades, Americans had not only been culinarily educated—in large part by television—but home cooking had been promoted from chore to fun. A fashionable foodist culture had been firmly established, and in certain social milieux to consider oneself a part of it was a badge of honor. The newest wave of food interest showed up in cultural expression everywhere. It was increasingly a focal point in movies—*Eat Drink Man Woman, Big Night, Mostly Martha, Ratatouille, Woman on Top,* and *No Reservations,* to name only a few. Food writing from all perspectives showed up on bestseller lists—Michael Pollan's *Omnivore's Dilemma,* Ruth Reichl's *Tender at the Bone,* and David Kamp's *The United States of Arugula.* In May 2006, *The New York Times Book Review* issued its first-ever "food issue." Magazines like *The Nation* and *The New Yorker* instituted annual issues devoted to food.

Once the 1980s quieted down, there was a sense of leaving the party and voluntarily going back inside. You don't have to go home, the decade seemed to say, but you can't stay here. But people did go home, and happily so. Though the opt-out mom has been criticized as a myth based on skewed data and the stay-at-home dad has been outed in part as a recession-dad, the *idea* of home gained considerable cachet in the 1990s. The attitude continued through the high-flying tech boom economy at the end of the decade and on into the new century. Erica Gruen's ideas for the Food Network in the mid-1990s had come partly from what she and her associates learned from focus groups that reflected these social trends but also from her own experience as part of the targeted viewing demographic.

"Baby boomers had to give up sex, drugs, and rock and roll, but they still had food," she said. "You don't go with your friends to see the Stones anymore. You have them come over and you make a big meal. Or you go out to dinner at a restaurant and you sit around and talk." Anthony Bourdain sees a generational divergence as well. When he was growing up, his parents and their peers would go out to dinner and, he said, "you'd talk about movies or books or television or the theater. Now you go out to dinner and you're talking about dinner."

In *Bobos in Paradise*, journalist David Brooks describes more of the boomer culture resettlement:

> Like so much else in this new cultural wave, [natural and organic supermarket] Fresh Fields has taken the ethos of California in the 1960s and selectively updated it. Gone are the sixties-era things that were fun and of interest to teenagers, like Free Love, and retained are all the things that might be of interest to middle-aged hypochondriacs, like whole grains. So in the information age, suburban customers can stroll amidst the radish sprouts, the bins of brown and basmati rice . . . and the vegetarian dog biscuits, basking in their reflected wholesomeness.

And as it turned out, Gruen noted, it wasn't just baby boomers gravitating to the nest. Generation X-ers, too, perhaps as a result of coming up during the slow simmer years of the current foodie-ism or being oversaturated with television glitz and glamour from their teen years, were interested in domestic pursuits at a surprisingly early age. "So we were able to appeal to both of those demographic groups," said Gruen. As is true for most cultural changes, much of what we saw in the 1990s was a reaction to what we experienced in the 1980s. Sociologist Juliet Schor observed a shift in priorities where young people were moving away, she wrote, from the "frenzied work ethic of the 1980s to more traditional values."

The Food Network both tapped into and created a market for Americans' interest in food. That interest ranges from wanting ideas for dinner to wanting a connection with home and comfort. With the number of shows about cooking, one might be given to believe that the whole nation has donned aprons and is whistling away in their kitchens. Not only is the downshifting work ethic illusory, however, but the emphasis on home is deceptive. As Bob Tuschman, among others, note (including Department of Energy data), fewer people cook at home than they used to. "They work a lot more, they see their families less, they see their friends less, they travel more, they're home less," Tuschman said. But he sees the Food Network as a surrogate. "I think cooking shows offer a lot of grounding and a sense of being at home, even if it's not your home, and a sense of the pleasure and comforts of being home and having food cooked for you." Likewise, food scholar Pauline Adema noted that "growing numbers of viewers are tuning in to and watching food television because it feeds a hunger for emotional and physical pleasures vicariously gratified by watching someone cook, talk about and eat food."

The Food Network can be one salve for the harried and fraught lives in which every one of us seems entangled. Unrealistic expectations of having and doing it all have made a gender-neutral comeback, reminding us of the double-duty load for 1950s homemakers. Today, we still watch cooking shows to learn new skills but increasingly—by virtue of the shows' entertainment levels and our exhausted selves— more to let someone else do the work and entertain us while we put up our feet for a bit and order take-out.

For the most part, cooking shows are and always have been reassuring, encouraging, and predictably optimistic. "You go for entertainment and relaxation," said cookbook author Barbara Kafka on the topic of why we watch food television. "You know the world isn't going to blow up in your face in the next ten minutes." As Reese Schonfeld said, "The Food Network is soothing. These other networks don't offer that." And Brooke Johnson said of the Food Network brand, "It enhances the media landscape whereas a lot of things don't. I like to be associated with things that are positive in a social way as opposed to negative." And Bob Tuschman said, "Our goal in everything we do is to bring a really positive, fun vibe to anything having to do with the food world." (*Hell's Kitchen* and *Top Chef*, in contrast, play on our penchant for drama and, while they serve as entertaining distraction, they are far from soothing.)

The retro home trend manifested itself in the form of home cooking shows like *Martha Stewart Living* and *Cooking Live* as well as programs that focused on the kitchen. Whereas the kitchen used to be a place for only domestics and women to spend their time, and then feminism either implicitly or explicitly urged women to vacate, ". . . today in the age of Bobo [bourgeois bohemian] reconciliation, everybody is back in the kitchen, albeit on his or her own terms," wrote David Brooks. "Indeed, in today's educated-class homes, the kitchen has become the symbol of domestic bliss, the way the hearth used to be for the bourgeoisie." One only needs to watch a few minutes of popular home design shows like DIY's *Kitchen Renovations*, Food Network's *Kitchen Accomplished*, HGTV's *Design on a Dime*, or TLC's *While You Were Out* to grasp the elevated stature of the kitchen itself. Americans are more willing than ever to spend time and money to make that room bigger and more functional, hospitable and beautiful.

By the mid-1990s, technology and globalization were ruling forces, affecting every aspect of American life. Men and women worked around the clock, both at home and in the office, and wanted it *all*—not just material wealth (though we quickly became adept at channeling that into soul-soothing, earth-friendly acquisitions), but information mastery, invincible physical health, a meaningful career and home life, and a friendly but convenient cohabitation with the environment. Technological advances—ATMs, VCRs, cell phones, and most notably the Internet—exacerbated Americans' ambition, impatience, consumption, insatiability, and endless desire for self-improvement and social and cultural advancement. While food can be an antidote to the chaos of modern life, it can also be part of the problem. Food has achieved a status worthy enough to be a controversial topic—from economic, political, and philosophical perspectives of the food industrial complex and E. coli, to school lunches and raw milk cheese. How we eat is equated with how we live, and, as consumers, how we live is manifested by the stove, blender, and chef's knife we own and the supermarket where we shop.

The (perceived) dialing down trend coupled with what Schor attributes to the late 1960s and 1970s "post-materialist values"— desires for personal fulfillment, self-expression, *meaning* in everything we do—is a broadly painted wrap-up of the 1990s to the present. However, it's not that simple. Traditional values mingle with consumerist ones. Where work had become play in the 1980s, in the 1990s play became work. Cooking was a hobby but a very serious one requiring a special vocabulary, a furrowed brow, and proper appliances. Americans may not view work in exactly the same way they did fifty years ago in part because it has crept into all areas of our lives, even leisure time. As David Brooks wrote, "[T]he Protesant Work Ethic has been replaced by the Bobo Play Ethic . . . where everything we do must serve the Life Mission, which is cultivation, progress, and self-improvement." The Food Network relies on this ethic to capture viewers who want to "veg out by learning" as Judy Girard said. We—specifically Bobos—must always be on the path to self-improvement, conscious of not wasting any moments.

We may be a nation of workaholics, but what many of us consider "work" today is far removed from that of our predecessors. The elbow grease that some hobbyists apply to cooking may be an unconscious attempt to replace the loss of industrial labor. The words historian Mary Drake McFeely used to describe cookbooks could be applied equally to cooking shows. "As fashion magazines sell body images, cookbooks sell images of the cook as scientist, artist, master chef, efficiency expert, perfecter of domestic bliss, earth protector, or patriot," she wrote. "In the face of a dwindling necessity for hard work in the kitchen, these images have encouraged consumerism and persuaded women to stay in the kitchen by proposing fantasy roles intended to make cooking provide some of the satisfaction we expect of paid work."

As the nature of cooking in our lives has changed over the past century, food media have taken on new roles. "Watching TV cooking shows can be understood as a form of productive leisure, as viewers invest their free time in the 'work of acquisition' of culinary cultural capital, as a means of improving the self through food knowledge," wrote Isabelle de Solier. As de Solier observed in the opening of *The Naked Chef*, host Jamie Oliver says, "Cooking's gotta be a laugh. It's gotta be simple. It's gotta be tasty. It's gotta be fun." That's an order. It's as if Oliver is channeling sociologist Pierre Bourdieu who argued that the new middle class is governed by "a morality of pleasure as a duty." Though the Bobo play ethic could be just as well interpreted as "duty as pleasure."

As Gruen and Bourdain suggest, cooking and food is even more of a focal point in our social lives than ever before. Cooking shows have reflected that by inviting more people in and making what used to be a private one-on-one cooking lesson into a social event. On *Molto Mario* and *Emeril Live*, the chefs hosted politely salivating guests seated at their counters and chatted with them as they prepared their dishes. Though there had been families (Jinx and Tex, Bontempis, Popes, and Romagnolis) cooking together on TV in the 1950s, 60s, and 70s, duets were more common in the 1990s: *Too Hot Tamales*, *Two Fat Ladies*, *Down Home with the Neelys*, Jacques Pépin and his daughter Claudine. Good friends Julia Child and Jacques Pépin mingled their "bon appetit!" and "happy cooking!" on *Julia and Jacques Cooking at Home*. They interacted by asking questions of each other ("why do you use that cut?" etc.) and helpfully handing each other various ingredients or tools. On the 1999 series premiere, the two legends bit into giant cheeseburgers. She made steak Diane. He made steak au poivre. She called him Jack. Priceless.

Groups in the kitchen (or by the outdoor grill or the fire pit) are more prevalent in the modern period, too. A photo spread in *Bon Appetit* typically portrays a garden party, laughing guests—not a single person eating breakfast alone. In our real lives, too, we tend to cook with people. For special occasions it's a group effort, much more so than in our mothers' day. Today's world is more interconnected and socially networked. We're supposedly not atomistic creatures watching alone, so the portrayal of a group mentality resonates. As the Barefoot Contessa, Nigella, Giada, and Jamie Oliver invite their friends to their homes, the intimate para-social bond between host and viewer is broken. But the format adds an attractive lifestyle element. The ultimate expression is found in the occasional omnibus dream team programs like the Thanksgiving day special Sara Moulton did on the Food Network in 2004 with Emeril, Tyler Florence, Giada, and Rachael (Moulton described it as "awkward") and the *Miami Grill Fest* on the Food Network in 2008 where Tyler Florence, Bobby Flay, Giada De Laurentiis, Paula Deen, and Alton Brown gathered in Miami to cook and hang out and chide each other and entertain and show us recipes. This only works, of course, because they are celebrities. A bunch of local cooking show hosts getting together in the 1950s would have just quintupled the pedantry. We might be missing the intimacy of the para-social relationship or perhaps feel left out, but the trade-off is that we get a little thrill from (what feels like) spying on our heroes interacting, and from seeing another side of a celebrity. It also promotes the positive happy loving family vibe of the Food Network.

Good for the Topic

Not only can much of food television be good for the soul but it's also good for the culture and status of food, and eating and cooking in general. Judy Girard bemoaned the fact that Food Network programs don't make much of a showing at the annual James Beard Awards. "Some years we didn't even get one," she said, "And all the PBS shows would sweep. . . . We're having an influence on the food industry that's enormous, and they don't recognize us for it. . . . We just never matched their criteria all that much." It seems to be the price food television must pay for aiming for "good television." (All those Emmys and Cable Ace awards ought to be nothing to complain about.)

Though not recognized by that venerable organization, they are recognized by the community at large. Rather than criticizing modern cooking television as arriviste, Pollyannish, insipid, or even culturally damaging (as some do), members of the elite (not the *elitist*) of the food world see it as a positive, socially educative force—just as Barnes and Noble, Amazon.com, and Oprah are good for reading. *America's Test Kitchen* host Chris Kimball, who credits Rachael Ray as a gateway TV cook, isn't the only "serious" cook who tips his hat to the Food Network. "There is a lot to be said for the Food Network and for their contribution," said Molly O'Neill. And despite his opinion that everything on the Food Network is too "cute," food and restaurant consultant Clark Wolf said, "It's all good. Even Rachael Ray who sounds like she's about to break into a smoker's cough and pull up her tube top. It's all good for the topic."

"By the time I was on the Food Network I'd been cooking for over twenty years. And I'd worked in restaurants for seven," said Sara Moulton.

So I knew my stuff inside and out. So it's upsetting to those of us—it's one of those old "I walked five miles to school"— that somebody's who's never professionally cooked or gone to cooking school or really learned how to cook goes on and becomes this hero in the cooking world. When Rachael Ray gets up there and said I don't know how to cook but I'm gonna teach you how to cook I would be scratching my head and say why would anybody think that was positive? But you know what? It is!

Food writer and culinary historian Andrew Smith said, "I think Rachael Ray does a beautiful job of entertaining. I sit back and say I know more about some things than she does, but she's on TV! She does a good job and she's got a magazine and she's making a go of it and more power to her. There's a public persona that foodies have to have, and to demonstrate that you're a true foodie you have to be able to condemn the Food Network programs. And there's good reason to condemn them. Yes, there are problems but they do good things and I think they should get credit for it."

"The Food Network has gotten people cooking and that's great. I think the Food Network's really gotten kids cooking and young people in general cooking, twenty year olds," said Moulton. "When I first started and would be on the road I'd meet people who'd say, oh I love you and I love so and so's show and I love so and so's show. Now they just say, I watch the Food Network 24/7. So it's more like it's their network and they're part of a club. I think that's all very positive."

The rise in popularity of food and cooking made the culinary field at first a decent career choice and then a glamorous one. "I think now if you went and surveyed five hundred high-end chefs I think most of them would say the Food Network has had a positive effect on their business and what they do," said Judy Girard. She added that the culinary school industry claims that the Food Network has had an enormous effect on people's interest in going to culinary school and, she said, "If you tracked the growth of culinary schools in the last ten years it matches the growth of the Food Network." According to national and local reports, both the number of and the enrollment in professional and recreational cooking schools has increased exponentially since the 1990s.

As Bourdain said, "Largely because of Food Network, *who's* cooking has become an important component for the first time in history. When you're talking about food you're mentioning who did it. That's a seismic change." He sees the fanfare as empowering for chefs.

Television absolutely changed the landscape of cooking. . . . Even just a few years ago . . . it would be customers who decided. The market drove what was on menus. You had to have steak. You had to have a chicken. You had to have a few fish selections. Nowadays chefs actually decide what you're gonna eat next year. You will eat pork belly. It's gonna be kidneys next year. And in fact you *will* eat it. So I think chefs are starting to use television and the media like politicians do. Repetition repetition. You know, the Goebbels model.

Bourdain also sees a benefit for diners. "I think a growing percentage [of the public] have higher expectations when they go in a restaurant, which leads to more pride in the kitchen because they have very real hope of getting somewhere in their lives, getting a little prestige." Likewise Judy Girard shared informal reports from the grocery store industry and another mutually beneficial effect of food TV. "The Food Network had quite an effect on people expecting that the products that they saw on the New York–based network would be on the shelf in Kansas City," she said, "and that helps to open and broaden the range of products that people expect in their daily lives around food."

In the early twenty-first century there is a thread of nostalgia among some serious food people for the Food Network pioneers, mostly as an indictment against current Food Network programming. Bloggers at food-centric watering holes like Chowhound. com decry the direction the Food Network has taken over the past decade. Many long for the days of the "nuts and bolts" cooking shows and serious treatment of food, which they find preferable to what is often deemed a dumbing down of the subject. Yet there are others who think the entertainment angle of food television has been an improvement. Sara Dickerman wrote in *Slate*,

> When was it, exactly, that home economists took over the Food Network? In a few years, it has gone from being a guilty pleasure to something far more tedious and less inspiring. Shows that feature the goofy erudition of professional chefs (like the Iron Chefs, Jacques Torres, or Mario Batali) have been shunted to the off hours of the schedule and replaced with a flood of truly hausfrau offerings.

She briefly disparaged hausfrau specimens Rachael Ray and Sandra Lee before she pointed to professional chef Gordon Ramsay as the possible savior of the genre in his attempts to rescue embattled restaurants on *Kitchen Nightmares*. While "hausfrau" is not a descriptor commonly applied to Rachael Ray, it goes to show that viewers want different things from food television, and the genre cannot help but be at cross-purposes as it tries to please everyone.

Back in the day, cooking shows were simple how-to's and what-you-see-is-what-you-get. There was nothing to deconstruct, or at least there was no one who deemed it worth doing. Talking and writing about food outside the kitchen these days is the stuff of scholarly discourse and a standard pastime for people from all walks of life, and now food television enjoys some of the same attention. Ever since the Food Network was created, and developing the food TV genre became a legitimate endeavor to which scores of professionals have dedicated themselves, we can now actually talk about anything from what makes a good cooking show to its gender subtext and textual structure—things we wouldn't have articulated or considered twenty years ago.

Evolution

Some argue that the modern cooking show is a different species altogether from earlier incarnations. As cookbook author Barbara Kafka contended, "These [current shows] are not its origins. Jim [Beard] and Dione [Lucas] were not the genesis. Theirs didn't work." Others see a continuum. I contend that the modern show is the sibling of even the old radio shows, and their continued existence adheres to the scientific theory of evolution. Cooking programs reproduce and replicate as in the cases of the multiple gene expressions of Bobby Flay, Rachael Ray, Emeril, et al. They interbreed—*Julia and Jacques Cooking at Home*, the aforementioned omnibus gatherings. Most importantly, they mutate in ways that promote their survival. Most early period programs died out because their producers were not yet aware of the importance of personality and "entertainment values." As television producers and audiences became more savvy and choosy, only the fittest (most watchable) survived. In accordance with "entertainment values," producers in the middle and modern periods introduced auspicious changes: "Galloping Gourmet" Graham Kerr pioneered the in-studio audience. Justin Wilson ("the Cajun Julia Child") possessed a highly imitable accent. Sara Moulton offered a call-in feature. Emeril Lagasse boasted an in-studio band and an exclamatory catch phrase ("bam!"). *The Two Fat Ladies'* motorcycle with sidecar, Martha Stewart's enviable kitchen, Giada De Laurentiis's dazzling smile, along with out of studio shows like Anthony Bourdain's, all proved favorable for the genre's virility.

The theory of natural selection has been illustrated not only by the number of cooking shows that come and go overall in the modern period but also on a micro level. Rapid reproduction of competition-style cooking shows is centered on the very notion of survival of the fittest. Those with harmful (e.g., whiny or arrogant) traits are eliminated one by excruciating one. While many of the contestants are competing for a post to run a restaurant, others are hoping to host their own cooking show. Because the Food Network ecosystem could not possibly support them all, the producers cleverly arranged for a controlled natural selection contest in *The Next Food Network Star.*

In 2005, scientists discovered that hidden genetic information unexpectedly reappears in later generations. This may explain why in the middle period, the Beard/Lucas gene reappeared, expressed in Julia Child, Graham Kerr, and a host of offspring. Two advantageous conditions were at last present: the widespread adoption of television values, and interest in food as cultural capital and a form of self-expression.

As *New York Times* restaurant critic Frank Bruni wrote of *Top Chef*, "Its narrative arc and razzmatazz editing may take it a long way from Julia Child's *The French Chef* and the beginnings of food television, but it's a recognizable member of the same family, an engine of culinary education and inspiration as well as *Ten Little Indians*–style suspense." He clearly understands the scientific underpinnings at work.

Marsha Cassidy, author of *What Women Watched*, said,

> What I find surprising is that the fundamental conventions and narrative arc of the genre look remarkably similar across the decades. The "expert cook" speaks directly to the viewer through the camera. The program is set in a natural-looking although well-appointed kitchen. The show spends a good deal of time demonstrating techniques and cooking steps, often in close-up and sometimes using the overhead camera. Viewers see the dish at various stages of preparation, and the end product is finally tasted and deemed delicious.

"This concept of the 'homemaker' is dated today," said Cassidy. "So contemporary cooking shows must appeal to versions of femininity—and masculinity—that have currency in today's culture." They have *evolved* to stay relevant. Bill Buford wrote: "Ours is a different audience from the one that watched Julia." While the genre has evolved, we have, too, and television must keep up with our changing needs and desires.

Not only did a whole genre survive, but specific elements have been preserved, embodied by their ideological offspring. Martha Stewart and Sandra Lee are descendants (or new expressions) of Dione Lucas and Poppy Cannon, respectively. Elements of the latter survived because they served a useful purpose. Beyond even the perseverance of particular conventions, cooking shows still perform the same service they always have—to teach us how to live. In the early days of cooking television, because we didn't look for such broad counsel from our cooking show hosts, their role was narrow. Now it's larger and—because we let it be so—layered with more meaning than it once was.

The Future of Food Television

In her 1968 *New York* magazine article about the rise of gourmet cooking, Nora Ephron asked several members of the "food establishment" about the future of the trend. "Of course it will last," responded Poppy Cannon. "Just in the way sculpture will last. We need it. It is a basic art. We ought to have a National Academy of the Arts to represent the art of cooking."

"Others are less sure," Ephron wrote. "They claim that the food of the future will be quite different: pre-cooked, reconstituted and frozen dishes with portion control." She quoted cookbook writer Nika Hazelton: "Ultimately cooking will be like an indoor sport, just like making lace and handiwork." Cannon and Hazelton were both right. Cannon, who died in 1975, would be pleased to know about the likes of the James Beard Foundation and *Gastronomica: The Journal of Food and Culture*. Hazelton's prediction of cooking as an indoor sport was on the money, given that culinary skill has become a competition for players as well as a spectator sport. And while we don't subsist on astronaut fare, doomsayers would have the bittersweet satisfaction of "I told you so" if they were still here to witness the prepared food industry's supremacy.

In 1992 Molly O'Neill interviewed George Rosenbaum, CEO of Leo J. Shapiro & Associates, a market research group in Chicago, who said, "We're growing a generation of cooks who will view prepared, microwaveable food as the norm. Food that requires conventional cooking will be perplexing and daunting." The Food Network—born just over a year after Rosenbaum made his claim—does everything it possibly can to remove the perplexing and the daunting from cooking. His prediction touches upon that paradox that rears its head time and again—the Generation X-ers, millennials, and most everyone else are much more fine food savvy than they used to be, but that doesn't mean we're not buying billions of dollars worth of frozen pizza.

In his *Corner Table* interview with Martha Stewart in 1997, Bill Boggs asked Stewart about the future of the American home. She said she hopes it's "more like what it used to be, center of family." She also said that she hoped that ten years from that day (which would be 2007) Jean Georges is alive and well and experimenting. And that "there are many people who rely on me for information . . . and that I can help them." All of her hopes came true, and, despite her own legal bumps, her recipes and creative ideas are still highly sought after via her omni-media presence.

"Just as we saw the discussion and writing about food expand from food magazines to some component of every publication of every kind," said Clark Wolf, "We are going to see it in television. The bottom line is that food is the largest industry in the world and whether we like to face it as Americans or not, the most important topic. . . . I don't think food has been done very well on television yet. It's still in its infancy. And I think we'll get there."

In 2001, one journalist wrote, "It's unclear how much more can be squeezed out of the nation's growing food fascination." Between the publishing of that statement and the publishing of this one, the answer is: a lot. Even if it's squeezing the same fruits over and over again, there is clearly a lot of juice. But there could still be changes in store for us that we cannot yet imagine, maybe nothing fantastical, but a spin. In 2007, Geoffrey Drummond said,

> I think you're going to start seeing the Food Network starting to develop sitcoms, licensing movies. *My Dinner with Andre* is probably too high end for them but things like *Dinner Rush.* You need to keep growing. The only way [is] to keep growing as other stations and other venues start doing cooking shows, someone's going to have the next big ratings pull in cooking.

Erica Gruen, who still recognizes the Food Network brand as the one that she and her team helped create over a decade ago, also acknowledged the need for change. "There's no reason why the Food Network can't keep growing and improving and it's really a matter of the talent and abilities of the creative staff," she said.

> There's going to be in the next several years a major consolidation in the television business both on the broadcasting

side and the network side, because the cost of running television, the margins are starting to decline as advertising on television moves to the Internet. At some point it seems likely that Food Network, HG, DIY, the whole group will be sold to some other entity, Fox or NBC or somebody like that. . . . So the long-term prospects for the Food Network have more to do with the macro factors in the television and advertising businesses than the network alone.

Anthony Bourdain said of the Food Network,

They're always floundering around in their own way trying to look for the hip, cutting-edge, new thing, trying to anticipate what's next. But really it's like watching your mother try to breakdance. They're caught in a situation where they're afraid of alienating their core audience of Paula Deen fans and yet very aware of the fact that their viewership has increased spectacularly, especially among that young male demographic that the advertisers really want. So they're trying to be both. And when you design shows by committee you get a predictable result.

In terms of financial success, he sees them doing all the right things, namely pleasing their stockholders. In terms of quality, he said, "They're clearly aiming lower and lower." Likewise Molly O'Neill, lamenting the current climate wherein "no one takes risks," described the Food Network as "totally derivative" and "committee-controlled."

As senior VP of programming Eileen Opatut told a reporter in 2001, like a good chef, "we're always experimenting." In his 2006 New Yorker article, Bill Buford described the Food Network as "basically a good-hearted organization still fundamentally clueless about itself (TV or non-TV?) [meaning TV values, i.e., production values] and its audience (cooks or noncooks?)." Given its very broad and therefore somewhat mysterious audience, the network was and still is unsure of its mission in many ways. While the Food Network's shows may reflect viewers, they don't reflect the nation. Ethnic food is still marginalized to some extent and still finds its more comfortable home on PBS (*Jewish Cooking in America with Joan Nathan, Hidden Korea, Hidden India, Lidia's Italy,* and Latin cooking with Daisy Martinez). Though it's changing—the Food Network's *Simply Delicioso,* hosted by Colombian restaurateur Ingrid Hoffman premiered in 2007 and *Down Home with Neelys,* hosted by African American husband and wife restaurateurs premiered in 2008—the program landscape is heavily white and non-Hispanic. Food Network president Brooke Johnson said, "There are a lot of ethnic cuisines that I foresee us exploring in the future."

Staying Power

Food and cooking continued to take on cultural capital as the 1990s progressed. At the same time, again in reaction to the excess of the 1980s, many Americans began to at least *think* about scaling back, to turn their backs on the elite high life and look at where food came from. At the end of the twentieth century, a resurgence of concerns about health, the global economy, the environment, and politics (trans fats, mad cow disease, and genetic modification, to name a few) have taken many Americans back to social issues brought to the fore in the 1960s and 1970s. Books like Eric Schlosser's *Fast Food Nation* and Marion Nestle's *What to Eat* and films like Morgan Spurlock's *Supersize Me* are testaments to socially conscious movements finally becoming mainstream. The current wave of food interest has attempted to capture more people (partly via television's cross-demographic power, as John Hartley described) cutting across a wider and deeper swath of the populace, not just the top 5 percent. Americans who can afford to are once again marrying food with ideology. We equate food choice—including where we shop—with morals and ethics. On most food television, this impulse is not explicit.

It's not unusual for hosts to mention free-range chicken or organic produce, though it is generally not a focus or explained.

This will likely change, said Molly O'Neill whose prognosticating is as philosophical as Erica Gruen's is fiscal. "People are reaching out for higher intellectual content. They want food to be more than show and tell and 'look at me, mom!'" She believes the future content—whether it be in food television or podcasting, video on demand or webcam-ing (Bourdain, likewise, thinks food blogging is the future)—will embrace regionality as opposed to panculturalism and will move away from chefs. That kind of shift, she said, is

> almost always about a person. Who did the Food Network? Sara Moulton and Emeril. End of story. Who will be the emblematic one? We don't know. I can predict one thing. It will be a person who has optimism and joy and is real. And it's not [someone] using food as a vehicle for something else. The cultural quest, yearning, is for real, tangible, not puffed up, not artificial. And I think that will very much shape what our next generation of television looks like.

As the American economy takes a beating, so our food television—a forum that is so closely tied with our consumer behavior—must continue to evolve. "Will the chefs come to the depression?" asked O'Neill. "How does entertainment work when people really are not sure they're going to pay their mortgage? All of that makes people want hope. That's the kind of message and kind of infectious spirit. . . . It's a powerful moment."

On the surface, watching cooking shows satisfies our desire to be entertained by a performer and to engage with a subject that has pleasurable and comfortable associations. They also operate on a deeper psychological level. Because food can be incorporated into and coupled with any subject matter, because it is everything, it can also be nothing, neutral, benign, and open to interpretation. Just as Julia Child served as a tabula rasa onto which viewers could project their needs, food television as a whole can be that, too, which helps to explain the genre's longevity. Such a canvas is useful for the financial stakeholders involved in programming, and, on the psychological side, it is the perfect screen to project ourselves onto.

O'Neill does not consider—nor has anyone else—even uttering the idea that such a frivolous pursuit as food television might lose its audience. The genre has withstood decades of economic highs and lows and will continue to respond in kind, but it might do so in ways we cannot yet imagine. As Laurence Jarvik wrote of cooking shows on public broadcasting: "They were available before the Corporation for Public Broadcasting was created in 1967 and would continue to be available were it to fade from the scene, because they fulfill a genuine need of the American television audience." It is a dramatic overstatement to call food television a basic need, but its connection with one of that triumvirate (or two, if we count shelter as the place that houses our kitchens) does help to explain why they are still with us.

Our needs and our wants are sometimes indistinguishable, especially when it comes to food. The desire surrounding food—while sometimes inflated and taken to bizarre extremes—is still ultimately borne of a basic need, one that will never disappear. This abets the staying power of cooking and food shows.

But why does it seem so important to all of these TV cooks that we get into the kitchen? And why does it matter if the Food Network is good for the topic? Why does knowing and learning about food matter? It matters because it brings us to a fuller understanding of ourselves. Cooking and knowing about food does more than help us get dates or keep pace with the times. Because they touch on the physical and the psychological, on pleasure, work, and creativity, they allow us to be fully engaged in life. Cooking and eating are positive life forces. This, too, helps to ensure their survival.

With food and television both central to our lives—one by design, the other by choice—we cannot ignore their impact. Though at times it may seem so, we are not just living and eating and watching mindlessly. We are consuming, and as consumers we are far from passive.

Just as food television has seduced us and affected our behavior in the marketplace, so it has affected us in our kitchens, in our relationships with friends and family, and in how we choose to spend our leisure time. And as consumers—the ones that programmers and advertisers are keen on attracting—we have power. The changes we have seen on television are a two-way street. They are partially a result of those advertisers and programmers heeding our desires.

At root, the cooking programs we have been watching for more than a half-century provide us with that potent combination of something we need as well as something we want. The evolution of the genre shows us that we—both as individuals and collectively—have a drive to move forward. It is not enough for us to simply subsist—be it on plain meat and potatoes or on bland instructional programs. The evolution has shown our ingenuity in that as a culture we can take something and make it better, adapt it, and make it work for us. We are interested in improving ourselves. We are forward looking and optimistic. We crave inspiration and adventure but don't always want to leave home to satisfy those needs. We need to eat but we want the task to be pleasurable. We strive to learn and grow but we want to be entertained. Because we, in collaboration with the media powers, have made it so that these needs and wants are satisfied, they are still here and continue to change with us.

REFERENCES

Epigraphs

Mintz, Sidney W. "Feeding, Eating, and Grazing: Some Speculations on Modern Food Habits." *Journal of Gastronomy* 7, no. 1 (1993).
Tyler, Anne. *Morgan's Passing.* New York: Random House, 1980.

Chapter 1

Interviews
Marion Cunningham, June 2004.
Barbara Kafka, July 2004.

Correspondence
Marsha Cassidy, email, August 2007.

Video/Audio
Excerpt from *Television Kitchen* with Florence Hanford, archived at Broadcast Pioneers of Philadelphia. © KYW-TV, Channel 3 in Philadelphia. http://www.broadcastpioneers.com/bp/tvkitchenvideo.html.
Excerpt from *The Mary Lee Taylor Show*, archived at the University of Virginia American Studies Department. http://xroads.virginia.edu/~1930s2/ Radio/day/10am.html.
Chef Milani Cooks episode, June 30, 1950, UCLA Film and Television Archive.
Hi, Mom! episode, December 11, 1957, Paley Center for Media, New York, NY.

Conversation with Julia Child, May 2000, Paley Center for Media, New York, NY.

Unpublished works/Archival material

Advertisements in *Variety*, August 8, 1951, and February 4, 1953, The Billy Rose Theatre Collection of the New York Public Library for the Performing Arts, clip file.

Television reviews of *Creative Cookery*, unidentified source, n.d., The Billy Rose Theatre Collection of the New York Public Library for the Performing Arts, clip file.

Roebuck, Tad, and Andy Lanset. *A Work in Progress: A History of WNYC*, n.d.

Stewart, Robert Hammel. "The Development of Network Television Program Types to January 1953." Ph.D. diss., Ohio State University, 1954 (cites *Television*, Spring 1944, p. 21).

Published works

Alexander, Kelly, and Cynthia Harris. *Hometown Appetites: The Story of Clementine Paddleford, the Forgotten Food Writer Who Chronicled How America Ate*. New York: Gotham Books, 2008.

"American Cookery Level Greatly Raised by Radio." *The Hartford Courant*, March 8, 1925.

"'Aunt Sammy' to be Introduced to Fans Tomorrow." *Chicago Daily Tribune*, October 3, 1926.

Beard, James. *Delights and Prejudices*. New York: Atheneum, 1964.

Clark, Robert. "Beard: Early Years in New York, 1937–1947." *Journal of Gastronomy* 4, no. 2 (1988).

"Cooking by Radio." *The Washington Post*, October 16, 1925.

"Cooking with Corris to Begin Third Decade." *Los Angeles Times*, November 30, 1967.

Curd, Dan. "All You Can Eat: 150 Years of Dining in Madison." *Madison Magazine*, April 2006.

"Doucette Returning as TV Chef on WNBQ." *Chicago Daily Tribune*, August 22, 1954.

Dunning, John. *On the Air: The Encyclopedia of Old-time Radio*. New York: Oxford University Press, 1998.

"Francois Pope: French Chef in a Business Suit." *Chicago Daily Tribune*, June 12, 1960.

Fussell, Betty Harper, and M. F. K. Fisher. *Masters of American Cookery: M. F. K. Fisher, James Andrew Beard, Raymond Craig Claiborne, Julia McWilliams Child*. At Table series. Lincoln: University of Nebraska Press, 2005.

General Mills of Minneapolis. "The Radio Made Betty." *Fortune*, April 1945.

Getz Rouse, Morleen. "Daytime Radio Programming for the Homemaker 1926–1956." *Journal of Popular Culture* 12, no. 2 (1979).

Goodwin, Doris Kearns. *No Ordinary Time: Franklin and Eleanor Roosevelt: The Home Front in World War II.* New York: Simon & Schuster, 1994.

Haskin, Frederic J. "Millions Aided by Aunt Sammy." *Los Angeles Times,* October 30, 1926.

Kaufman, William Irving. *Cooking with the Experts.* New York: Random House, 1955.

Kisseloff, Jeff. *The Box: An Oral History of Television, 1920–1961.* New York: Viking, 1995.

Kovitz, Ray. "When It Comes to Food, Chef Milani Cooks It, Talks About It, Sells It—All Successfully." *Los Angeles Times,* August 29, 1952.

Lape, Bob. "More Flash, Less Pan: The New Wave of TV Chefs." *Gastronome,* Winter 1990.

"Many Men Tune in on Betty Crocker's Recipes." *The Hartford Courant,* April 22, 1928.

McCarthy, Josephine Vercelli. *Josie McCarthy's Favorite TV Recipes.* Englewood Cliffs, NJ: Prentice-Hall, 1958.

McFeely, Mary Drake. *Can She Bake a Cherry Pie: American Women and the Kitchen in the Twentieth Century.* Amherst: University of Massachusetts Press, 2000.

McLuhan, Marshall. *Understanding Media: The Extensions of Man.* New York: McGraw-Hill, 1964.

Mendelson, Anne. "The 40s." *Gourmet,* September 2001.

Mueller, Edna Vance Adams, and Patty Vineyard MacDonald. *Long Lost Recipes of Aunt Susan.* Hot Spring Village, AR: P. V. MacDonald, 1989.

Neuhaus, Jessamyn. *Manly Meals and Mom's Home Cooking: Cookbooks and Gender in Modern America.* Baltimore: Johns Hopkins University Press, 2003.

"On the Kitchen Front." *Christian Science Monitor,* September 15, 1943.

Paddleford, Clementine. "Food Flashes." *Gourmet,* May 1941.

Pennell, Ellen La Verne. *Women on TV.* Minneapolis: Burgess Publishing Co, 1954.

"Radio Cooks." *The Hartford Courant,* December 12, 1944.

Rice, Robert. "Diary of a Viewer." *The New Yorker,* August 30, 1947.

Sarnoff, David. "Possible Social Effects of Television." *Annals of the American Academy of Political and Social Science* 213 (January 1941).

Sterling, Christopher H., and John M. Kittross. *Stay Tuned: A Concise History of American Broadcasting.* Belmont, CA: Wadsworth Publishing Co., 1990.

Stern, Jane, and Michael Stern. *American Gourmet: Classic Recipes, Deluxe Delights, Flamboyant Favorites, and Swank "Company" Food from the '50s and '60s.* New York: HarperCollins, 1991.

Stewart, R. W. "Television Goes into the Entertainment Field as a New Merchandising Medium." *New York Times,* July 6, 1941.

Taylor, Kiley. "Men All About Are Learning to Cook for Fun." *New York Times*, March 19, 1939.

United States Bureau of Human Nutrition and Home Economics, Ruth Van Deman, and Fanny Walker Yeatman. *Aunt Sammy's Radio Recipes*. New York: Universe Books, 1975.

United States Census Bureau. *Statistical Abstract of the United States: 2003*. Mini-historical statistics. No. HS-42. Selected Communications Media: 1920 to 2001. http://www.census.gov/statab/hist/HS-42.pdf.

"U. S. Housewives Resume Radio Cooking Lessons." *Chicago Daily Tribune*, September 26, 1926.

Williams, Mark. "Considering Monty Margett's Cook's Corner." In *Television, History, and American Culture: Feminist Critical Essays*, edited by Mary Beth Haralovich and Lauren Rabinovitz. Durham, NC: Duke University Press, 1999.

Work, Bob. "Chef Milani Lives by His Stomach and the Recipe Pays Off in TV Fans." *Los Angeles Times*, August 9, 1959.

Chapter 2

Interviews

Milly Abrams, June 2004.
Barbara Kafka, July 2004.

Video

Dione Lucas Show episodes viewed courtesy of Joe Langhan and Schlesinger Library.
Home episode, August 9, 1957, Paley Center for Media, New York, NY.

Unpublished works/Archival material

Dione Lucas Papers. Schlesinger Library, Radcliffe Institute, Harvard University.
James Beard memoir transcript, 1978. The James Beard Papers, Fales Library and Special Collections, New York University Libraries.
Les Dames d'Escoffier New York Chapter program, January 22, 1994, Dione Lucas Papers, Schlesinger Library.
Promotional package for Operation Blue Flame, 1953, Dione Lucas Papers, Schlesinger Library.
Stewart, Robert Hammel. "The Development of Network Television Program Types to January 1953." Ph.D. diss., Ohio State University, 1954.
Unidentified newspaper clipping containing "no ordinary cooking show" quote, Dione Lucas Papers, Schlesinger Library.

Published works

"A Panel Plus Soap Is What the Lady Ordered." *Los Angeles Times*, April 28, 1962.

"Blue Ribbon Cook." *Life*, April 4, 1949.

Brooks, Tim, and Earle Marsh. *The Complete Directory to Prime Time Network and Cable TV Shows, 1946–Present.* 6th ed. New York: Ballantine Books, 1995.

Burros, Marian Fox. *Cooking for Comfort: More Than 100 Wonderful Recipes That Are as Satisfying to Cook as They Are to Eat.* New York: Simon & Schuster, 2003.

Cannon, Poppy. "Can-Opener Cookbook." *Cosmopolitan*, January 1952.

———. *The New New Can-Opener Cookbook* [First published in 1951 as: *The Can-Opener Cookbook*]. New York: Crowell, 1968.

Cassidy, Marsha Francis. *What Women Watched: Daytime Television in the 1950s.* Austin: University of Texas Press, 2005.

———, and Mimi White. "Innovating Women's Television in Local and National Networks: Ruth Lyons and Arlene Francis." *Camera Obscura* 17, no. 3 (2002).

Claiborne, Craig. "Tools of Her Trade in Dione Lucas's Shop." *New York Times*, March 5, 1970.

Coppola, Jo. "The View from Here." *New York Post,* January 8, 1958.

Cowan, Ruth Schwartz. "Industrial Revolution in the Home." *Technology and Culture* 17, no. 1 (1976).

Curtis, Charlotte. "Women Breaking Away from Homey Role in TV." *New York Times,* May 6, 1961.

Donaldson, Gary A. *Abundance & Anxiety: America, 1945–1960.* Westport, CT: Praeger, 1997.

Dosti, Rose. "Learning to Cook First Courses Better Late Than Never." *Los Angeles Times*, October 17, 1991.

Fitch, Noel Riley. *Appetite for Life: The Biography of Julia Child.* New York: Doubleday, 1997.

Freiman, Jane Salzfass. "Before Julia, There Was This Great, Unheralded Teacher." *Chicago Tribune,* October 8, 1979.

Gibbs, Angelica. "With Palette Knife and Skillet." *The New Yorker*, May 28, 1949.

Gould, Jack. "TV: Suburban Revue." *New York Times,* January 15, 1958.

Gross, Ben. "What's On: Gourmet Club." *New York Daily News,* January 16, 1958.

Hoffman, Marilyn. "Oklahoma Wife Turns Her Talents into Career." *Christian Science Monitor*, June 23, 1952.

Laurent, Lawrence. "Monument to Piffle." *The Washington Post and Times Herald*, April 25, 1954.

Leblebici, Huseyin, Gerald R. Salancik, Anne Copay, and Tom King. "Institutional Change and the Transformation of Interorganizational Fields: An Organizational History of the U.S. Radio Broadcasting Industry." *Administrative Science Quarterly* 36, no. 3 (1991).

Levenstein, Harvey A. *Paradox of Plenty: A Social History of Eating in Modern America.* New York: Oxford University Press, 1993.

Lucas, Dione. *The Cordon Bleu Cook Book.* Boston: Little, Brown, 1981.

Mintz, Steven, and Susan Kellogg. *Domestic Revolutions: A Social History of American Family Life.* New York: Free Press, 1988.

The New Female Instructor: Or, Young Woman's Guide to Domestic Happiness. (Abridged facsimile of ed. published: London: Kelly, 1834.) London: Rosters, 1988.

New York Times, Home display advertisement, February 1, 1954.

Pennell, Ellen La Verne. *Women on TV.* Minneapolis: Burgess Publishing Co., 1954.

Prall, Robert. "TV's Galley Gals: Dione Lucas Abhors Jiffy Techniques in Cookery: Believes 'More Art and Less Chemistry' Makes for Finer Cooking." *NY World Telegram,* n.d. (clipping, Dione Lucas Papers).

Schor, Juliet. *The Overworked American: The Unexpected Decline of Leisure.* New York: Basic Books, 1991.

Shapiro, Laura. "Canned Heat." *Gourmet,* February 2004.

———. *Something from the Oven: Reinventing Dinner in 1950's America.* New York: Viking, 2004.

Snoddy, Aileen. "Old-Pro Dione Lucas Stages a Gourmet Comeback." *Newspaper Enterprise Association,* April 13, 1970.

Spigel, Lynn. *Make Room for TV: Television and the Family Ideal in Postwar America.* Chicago: University of Chicago Press, 1992.

Stein, Ben. "Those Fabulous Fifties." *Brill's Content,* February 1999.

Stern, Jane, and Michael Stern. *American Gourmet: Classic Recipes, Deluxe Delights, Flamboyant Favorites, and Swank "Company" Food from the '50s and '60s.* New York: HarperCollins, 1991.

Variety Television Reviews. New York: Garland Pub., 1950.

Chapter 3

Interviews
Stephen Chen, July 2007.
Geoffrey Drummond, June 2007.
Russ Morash, June 2007.
Jacques Pépin, September 2007.

Video
Conversation with Julia Child, May 2000, Paley Center for Media, New York, NY.
The French Chef episodes via commercially available DVDs.
Joyce Chen Cooks, episodes courtesy Stephen Chen.

Public programs
"Julia Child: Culinary Revolutionary," New School for Social Research, June 12, 2008.

"Julia Child in America," New York Public Library, Cullman Center for Scholars and Writers, October 10, 2007.

Unpublished works/Archival material

Armes, Ashley R. "Image of Nation, Image of Culture: France and French Cooking in the American Press, 1918–1969." M.A. thesis, Texas Tech University, 2006.

Brost, Lori F. "Television Cooking Shows: Defining the Genre." Ph.D. diss., Indiana University, 2000.

Julia Child Papers. Schlesinger Library, Radcliffe Institute, Harvard University.

Published works

"Boston TV." *Christian Science Monitor*, February 6, 1967.

Bracken, Peg. *The I Hate to Cook Book*. New York: Harcourt, Brace, 1960.

Child, Julia. *The French Chef Cookbook*. New York: Knopf, 1968.

———, and Alex Prud'homme. *My Life in France*. New York: Alfred A. Knopf, 2006.

Claiborne, Craig. "American Interest in Chinese Cuisine Grows Like Bamboo Shoot in Spring." *New York Times*, February 13, 1964.

Dutton, Walt. "Everybody Cooks Except the Hostess." *Los Angeles Times*, August 2, 1967.

Ephron, Nora. "Critics in the World of the Rising Soufflé (Or Is It the Rising Meringue?)". *New York*, September 30, 1968.

"Everyone's in the Kitchen." *Time*, November 25, 1966.

Fitch, Noel Riley. *Appetite for Life: The Biography of Julia Child*. New York: Doubleday, 1997.

Fussell, Betty Harper, and M. F. K. Fisher. *Masters of American Cookery: M. F. K. Fisher, James Andrew Beard, Raymond Craig Claiborne, Julia McWilliams Child*. At Table Series. Lincoln: University of Nebraska Press, 2005.

Graham, Lee. "Women Don't Like to Look at Women." *New York Times*, May 24, 1964.

Jarvik, Laurence Ariel. *PBS, Behind the Screen*. Rocklin, CA: Forum, 1997.

Kaplan, Alice Yaeger. "Taste Wars: American Professions of French Culture." *Yale French Studies* no. 73 (1987).

Lehrman, Karen. "What Julia Started." *U.S. News World Report*, September 22, 1997.

Levenstein, Harvey A. *Paradox of Plenty: A Social History of Eating in Modern America*. New York: Oxford University Press, 1993.

Lovegren, Sylvia. *Fashionable Food: Seven Decades of Food Fads*. New York: Macmillan, 1995.

Miller, Toby. "From Brahmin Julia to Working-Class Emeril: The Evolution of Television Cooking." In *High-Pop: Making Culture into Popular*

Entertainment, edited by Jim Collins. Malden, MA: Blackwell Publishers, 2002.

Mintz, Steven, and Susan Kellogg. *Domestic Revolutions: A Social History of American Family Life.* New York: Free Press, 1988.

Public Broadcasting Service. "Corporate facts: The PBS Audience," August 2006. http://www.pbs.org/aboutpbs/aboutpbs_corp_audience.html.

Shapiro, Laura. *Julia Child.* Penguin Lives series. New York: Lipper/Viking, 2007.

Smilgis, Martha. "A Ms. Visit with Julia Child: 'Live! Eat! Enjoy!'" *Ms.*, Summer 2003.

Symons, Michael. "Grandmas to Gourmets: The Revolution of 1963." *Food, Culture & Society* 9, no. 2 (Summer 2006).

"Television as an Educator." *Chicago Tribune*, May 12, 1968.

Weiland, Joanne. "Joyce Chen Inc. Founder and First to Introduce Authentic Chinese Cooking to U.S. Restaurants." *Nation's Restaurant News*, February 1996.

Will, Joanne. "Men Talk about Food, Too; They Want Variety in Meals." *Chicago Tribune*, September 24, 1965.

Chapter 4

Interviews
LaDeva Davis, May 2008.
Graham and Treena Kerr, May 2005.
Bob Lape, June 2007.

Correspondence
Jinx Morgan, email, July 2008.

Video
Biography: Graham Kerr The Galloping Gourmet. New York: A&E Television Networks. Marketed and distributed in the U.S. by New Video, 2000.
The Mike Douglas Show, 1975–76, episodes viewed courtesy LaDeva Davis.
Saucepans and the Single Girl, pilot episode, November 16, 1968, UCLA Film and Television Archive.

Unpublished works/Archival material
James Beard memoir transcript, 1978. The James Beard Papers, Fales Library and Special Collections, New York University Libraries.

Published works
Adema, Pauline. "Vicarious Consumption: Food, Television and the Ambiguity of Modernity." *Journal of American & Comparative Cultures* 23, no. 3 (Fall 2000).

Belasco, Warren James. *Appetite for Change: How the Counterculture Took on the Food Industry, 1966–1988.* New York: Pantheon Books, 1989.

Collin, Dorothy. "People." *Chicago Tribune,* December 28, 1975.

Dunham, Wayne. "The Galloping Gourmet Is Here to Take Kerr." *Chicago Tribune,* March 23, 1975.

Gould, Jack. "TV: A Panel Talk Program with Real Discussions." *New York Times,* May 22, 1969.

Kennedy, Shawn G. "Everyone's in the Kitchen with La Deva." *New York Times,* March 26, 1976.

"Kitchen: America's Playroom." *Forbes,* March 15, 1976.

"Kitsch in the Kitchen." *Time,* February 28, 1969.

Laurent, Lawrence. "Talk, Food, Sewing, Art, Music—and Dinah." *The Washington Post,* July 2, 1972.

Miller, Toby. "From Brahmin Julia to Working-Class Emeril: The Evolution of Television Cooking." In *High-Pop: Making Culture into Popular Entertainment,* edited by Jim Collins. Malden, MA: Blackwell Publishers, 2002.

Ness, Margaret. "Galloping Gourmet Spices TV." *Christian Science Monitor,* May 22, 1969.

Pépin, Jacques. "Women Are Now in Restaurants, Men in Homes." *Los Angeles Times,* April 24, 1978.

Polak, Maralyn Lois. "Interview: LaDeva Davis—She's a Shoo-in for Stardom." *Philadelphia Inquirer,* October 5, 1975.

Quinn, Sally. "Chef Beard." *The Washington Post,* March 14, 1970.

Shapiro, Harriet. "TV's Newest Star Chef: He's 20 Times Quicker than the 'Galloping Gourmet.'" *People,* December 12, 1979.

Smith, Cecil. "Galloping Gourmet Whips Up Laughs." *Los Angeles Times,* October 23, 1969.

Snoddy, Aileen. "Old-Pro Dione Lucas Stages a Gourmet Comeback." *Newspaper Enterprise Association,* April 13, 1970.

Telfer, Elizabeth. *Food for Thought: Philosophy and Food.* New York: Routledge, 1996.

Wade, David. *Dining with David Wade.* Dallas, TX: David Wade Industries, 1967.

Warga, Wayne. "He's Cute: Wives Charmed by TV Cook." *Los Angeles Times,* June 21, 1969.

Chapter 5

Interviews

Geoffrey Drummond, June 2007.
Sara Wilson Easterly, January 2008.
Lynne Rossetto Kasper, November 2007.

Video
Conversation with Julia Child, May 2000, Paley Center for Media, New York, NY.
The Frugal Gourmet episodes viewed via New York Public Library circulating collection.

Unpublished works/Archival material
"News from Random House: *Betty Cocker's Working Woman Cookbook*," 1982. The Cecily Brownstone Papers, Fales Library and Special Collections, New York University Libraries.

Published works
Barr, Ann, and Paul Levy. *The Official Foodie Handbook: Be Modern—Worship Food*. New York: Timbre Books, 1984.
Chao, Phebe Shih. "TV Cook shows: Gendered Cooking." *Jump Cut* 42 December 1998.
Collins, Glenn. "'Frugal Gourmet': A Minister Makes Food His Mission." *New York Times*, February 10, 1988.
Crocker, Betty. *Betty Crocker's Working Woman's Cookbook*. New York: Random House, 1982.
Davidson, Alan. *The Oxford Companion to Food*. Oxford: Oxford University Press, 1999.
Dwan, Lois. "Restaurants." *Los Angeles Times*, September 17, 1978.
Ferguson, Priscilla Parkhurst, and Sharon Zukin. "The Career of Chefs." In *Eating Culture*, edited by Ron Scapp and Brian Seitz. Albany: State University of New York Press, 1998.
Gray, Tom. "Money Changes Everything." *The Brains*. Mercury Records, 1980.
Guenthner, Joseph F., Biing-Hwan Lin, and Annette E. Levi. "The Influence of Microwave Ovens on the Demand for Fresh and Frozen Potatoes." *Journal of Food Distribution Research* 22, no. 3 (September 1991).
Hall, Trish. "A New Spectator Sport: Looking, Not Cooking." *New York Times*, January 4, 1989.
Hanes, Phyllis. "A Culinary Success Story: The Saga of Television's Chef Tell." *Christian Science Monitor*, February 11, 1987.
Hansen, Barbara. "Kitchen Wit of 'The Frugal Gourmet' TV Series Host Whips Up Some Humor with Ingredients." *Los Angeles Times*, August 1, 1985.
Harrison, Barbara Grizzuti. "P.C. on the Grill." *Harper's Magazine*, June 1992.
Kuh, Patric. *The Last Days of Haute Cuisine*. New York: Viking, 2001.
Leete, Laura, and Juliet B. Schor. "Assessing the Time-Squeeze Hypothesis: Hours Worked in the United States, 1969–89." *Industrial Relations* 33, no. 1 (Winter 1994).

Locin, Mitchell. "The Cajun Julia Child Cooks Up Crawfish and Controversy, He Garontees!" *Chicago Tribune*, August 4, 1985.

McGrath, Charles. "Is PBS Still Necessary?" *New York Times*, February 17, 2008.

Miller, Bryan. "Rating TV Chefs: Cooks Beware." *New York Times*, May 5, 1993.

Miller, Toby. "From Brahmin Julia to Working-Class Emeril: The Evolution of Television Cooking." In *High-Pop: Making Culture into Popular Entertainment*, edited by Jim Collins. Malden, MA: Blackwell Publishers, 2002.

Mintz, Sidney W. "Feeding, Eating, and Grazing: Some Speculations on Modern Food Habits." *Journal of Gastronomy* 7, no. 1 (1993).

O'Neill, Molly. "Grocery Wars: Good-for-You Vs. Indulge!" *New York Times*, February 26, 1992.

———. "Convenience in the Kitchen: The Way Mama Used to Heat." *New York Times*, March 4, 1992.

Rubenstein, Hal. "The Hunger: Justin Wilson's Louisiana Cookin'." *Interview*, July 1995.

Smith, Andrew F. "Microwave Oven." In *Encyclopedia of Food and Culture*, vol. 2, edited by Solomon H. Katz. New York: Charles Scribner's Sons, 2003.

Smith, Jeff. *The Frugal Gourmet*. New York: Morrow, 1984.

United States Public Health Service, Office of the Surgeon General. *The Surgeon General's Report on Nutrition and Health*. Washington, DC: U.S. Dept. of Health and Human Services, Public Health Service, 1988.

Weaver, William Woys. *America Eats: Forms of Edible Folk Art*. New York: Museum of American Folk Art: Perennial Library, 1989.

Wilson, Justin. *Justin Wilson Looking Back: A Cajun Cookbook*. Gretna, LA: Pelican Publishing, 1997.

Zibart, Eve. "PBS' Feeding Frenzy; A Raging Appetite for Cooking Shows." *The Washington Post*, April 30, 1989.

Chapter 6

Interviews

Anthony Bourdain, August 2007.
Geoffrey Drummond, June 2007.
Erica Gruen, August 2007.
Lynne Rossetto Kasper, November 2007.
Joe Langhan, May 2004.
Sara Moulton, June 2008.
Trygve Myhren, August 2007.
Molly O'Neill, April 2008.
Reese Schonfeld, June 2007.

Bob Tuschman, October 2007.
Clark Wolf, August 2007.

Correspondence
Joe Langhan, email, August 2008.
Andrew Smith, email, June 2008.

Video
Early Food Network programs (*Cooking Live, Cooking With Master Chefs, Dining Around, Emeril Live, In Food Today, Taste, Too Hot Tamales*), Paley Center for Media, New York, NY.

Public programs
"The Edible Airwaves: How to Cook for Television," March 1, 2005, Paley Center for Media, New York, NY.

Published works
Cassidy, Marsha Francis. *What Women Watched: Daytime Television in the 1950s.* Austin: University of Texas Press, 2005.
Conover, Kirsten A. "Food Channel Delivers 'Round the Clock." *Christian Science Monitor*, December 24, 1993.
Eddy, Kristin. "Chefs Right at Home: The Food Network, Now a Decade Old, Has Given Us Culinary Heroes and the Confidence to Star in Our Own Kitchens." *Newsday*, October 29, 2003.
Edgerton, Gary R., and Brian Geoffrey Rose. *Thinking Outside the Box: A Contemporary Television Genre Reader.* Lexington: University Press of Kentucky, 2005.
Essex, Andrew. "Recipe for Success." *Entertainment Weekly*, November 13, 1998.
Esslin, Martin. *The Age of Television.* New Brunswick, NJ: Transaction Publishers, 2002.
"Food Channel Has Programs for all Tastes." *Charleston Daily Mail*, June 1, 1995.
Grimes, William. "Can't Stand the Heat? Change the Channel." *New York Times*, August 23, 1998.
Hansen, Signe. "Society of the Appetite: Celebrity Chefs Deliver Consumers." *Food, Culture & Society* 11, no. 1 (March 2008).
Matus, Victorino. "Bam!: Making Sense of America's Celebrity-Chef Culture." *The Weekly Standard*, August 20–27, 2007.
Meyrowitz, Joshua. *No Sense of Place: The Impact of Electronic Media on Social Behavior.* New York: Oxford University Press, 1985.
Poniewozik, James. "Full Metal Skillet." *Salon*, September 3, 1997. http://www.salon.com/sept97/media/media970903.html.
Siegel, Lee. "Why *Iron Chef* is so popular." *The New Republic* Online, January 10, 2006.

Turner, Marcia Layton. *Emeril!: Inside the Amazing Success of Today's Most Popular Chef.* Hoboken, NJ: Wiley, 2004.

Unger, Arthur. "Home on the Range—the Boom in Cooking Programs." *Television Quarterly* 30, no. 1 (1999).

Wheaton, Ken, and Matthew Creamer. "Real-Life Adventure: Trapped in an Elevator with PR People!" *Advertising Age*, February 26, 2007.

Chapter 7

Interviews
Anthony Bourdain, August 2007.
Geoffrey Drummond, June 2007.
Judy Girard, August 2007.
Erica Gruen, August 2007.
Brooke Johnson, July 2007.
Christopher Kimball, October 2007.
Sara Moulton, June 2008.
Adam Ried, December 2007.
Reese Schonfeld, June 2007.

Public programs
"Julia Child in America," New York Public Library, Cullman Center for Scholars and Writers, October 10, 2007.

"Times Talks," January 11, 2008, Martha Stewart interviewed by *New York Times* writer Kim Severson, produced by New York Times Television and CUNY–TV, viewed on CUNY–TV, June 2008.

Published works
Becker, Ron. "Horribly Guilty Television." *FlowTV* 7, no. 12 (April 24, 2008). http://flowtv.org/?p=1273.

Bell, David, and Gill Valentine. *Consuming Geographies: We Are Where We Eat.* New York: Routledge, 1997.

Bittman, Mark. "101 Summer Express: Simple Meals Ready in 10 Minutes or Less." *New York Times*, July 18, 2007.

Booker, Katrina. "Selling Cooking to Non-Cooks." *Fortune*, July 6, 1998.

Bourdain, Anthony. "Nobody Asked Me But . . ." Post on *Ruhlman.com*, February 8, 2007. http://blog.ruhlman.com/2007/02/guest_blogging_.html.

Bruni, Frank. "Cooking Under Pressure, That's Reality." *New York Times*, January 31, 2007.

Buford, Bill. "TV Dinners; Notes of a Gastronome." *The New Yorker*, October 2, 2006.

Chan, Andrew. "'La Grande Bouffe'." *Gastronomica* 3, no. 4 (Fall 2003).

Esslin, Martin. *The Age of Television.* New Brunswick, NJ: Transaction Publishers, 2002.

Franklin, Nancy. "Women's Work; Sunday Night on Lifetime." *The New Yorker*, August 13, 2007.

Fusco, Mary Ann Castronovo. "Top-Rated TV Dinners; Entertaining Fare." *Bergen Record*, February 15, 1989.

Grimes, William. "Can't Stand the Heat? Change the Channel." *New York Times*, August 23, 1998.

Hancock, Noelle. "Food Fight." *New York Observer*, November 1, 2004.

Kaufman, Frederick. "Debbie Does Salad." *Harper's Magazine*, October 2005.

Littlejohn, Janice Rhoshalle. "Food Network Is Now a Daily Requirement." *USA Today*, December 11, 2003.

MacVean, Mary. "Coming Soon to a TV Screen Near You: An All-Food Channel." *The Associated Press*, May 5, 1993.

Ray, Krishnendu. "Domesticating Cuisine: Food and Aesthetics on American Television." *Gastronomica* 7, no. 1 (Winter 2007).

Waxman, Nahum. "Cooking Dumb, Eating Dumb." In *Dumbing Down: Essays on the Strip Mining of American Culture*, edited by Katharine Washburn, John F. Thornton and John Ivan Simon. New York: W. W. Norton, 1996.

Chapter 8

Interviews
Anthony Bourdain, August 2007.
Geoffrey Drummond, June 2007.
Erica Gruen, August 2007.
Graham Kerr, May 2005.
Chris Kimball, October 2007.
Sara Moulton, June 2008.
Molly O'Neill, April 2008.
Jacques Pépin, September 2007.
Reese Schonfeld, June 2007.
Bob Tuschman, October 2007.
Clark Wolf, August 2007.

Correspondence
Marsha Cassidy, email, August 2007.

Video
Bill Bogg's Corner Table, 1997 episode, Paley Center for Media, New York, NY.

Public programs
"Times Talks," January 11, 2008, Martha Stewart interviewed by *New York Times* writer Kim Severon, produced by New York Times Television and CUNY–TV, viewed on CUNY–TV, June 2008.

Unpublished works/Archival material
Orlijan, Kimberly Joy. "Consuming Subjects: Cultural Productions of Food and Eating." Ph.D. diss, University of California, Riverside, 1999.

Published works
Adema, Pauline. "Vicarious Consumption: Food, Television and the Ambiguity of Modernity." *Journal of American & Comparative Cultures* 23, no. 3 (Fall 2000).
Allen, Robert Clyde, and Annette Hill. *The Television Studies Reader.* New York: Routledge, 2004.
Buford, Bill. "TV Dinners; Notes of a Gastronome." *The New Yorker*, October 2, 2006.
Cassidy, Marsha Francis. *What Women Watched: Daytime Television in the 1950s.* Austin: University of Texas Press, 2005.
Esslin, Martin. *The Age of Television.* New Brunswick, NJ: Transaction Publishers, 2002.
Forkan, Jim. "Fox News Scores Branding Points." *Multichannel News*, April 22, 2002.
Fussell, Betty Harper. *My Kitchen Wars.* New York: North Point Press, 1999.
Hartley, John. *Uses of Television.* New York: Routledge, 1999.
Kaplan, Alice Yaeger. "Taste Wars: American Professions of French Culture." *Yale French Studies* no. 73 (1987).
Lavin, Cheryl. "Fast Track. Q&A. [Martha Stewart]." *Chicago Tribune*, September 12, 1993.
McConville, Jim. "TV's Changing Demographics: Narrowing their Aim: Cable Advertisers Want Well-to-do Viewers." *Electronic Media*, April 20, 1998.
Metcalf, Stephen. "Sexy Food Nerds: Cooking Geeks Get Hot on *America's Test Kitchen.*" *Slate*, October 13, 2003. http://www.slate.com/id/2089461/.
Miller, Toby. "From Brahmin Julia to Working-Class Emeril: The Evolution of Television Cooking." In *High-Pop: Making Culture into Popular Entertainment*, edited by Jim Collins. Malden, MA: Blackwell Publishers, 2002.
Poniewozik, James. "Full Metal Skillet." *Salon*, September 3, 1997. http://www.salon.com/sept97/media/media970903.html.
Ray, Krishnendu. "Domesticating Cuisine: Food and Aesthetics on American Television." *Gastronomica* 7, no. 1 (Winter 2007).

Reynolds, Mike. "Cooking Up Entertainment: Food Net Gathers Ingredients for a Less Recipe-Laden Primetime Lineup." *Multichannel News*, April 10, 2006.

Shapiro, Laura. "The Myth of the 30-Minute Meal." *Slate*, April 28, 2008. http://www.slate.com/id/2189694/.

Talbot, Margaret. "Les Tres Riches Heures De Martha Stewart." *The New Republic*, May 13, 1996.

Chapter 9

Interviews
Anthony Bourdain, August 2007.
Judy Girard, August 2007.
Erica Gruen, August 2007.
Barbara Kafka, July 2004.
Sara Moulton, June 2008.
Jacques Pépin, September 2007.
Reese Schonfeld, June 2007.
Bob Tuschman, October 2007.
Clark Wolf, August 2007.

Correspondence
Marsha Cassidy, email, August 2007.
Andrew Smith, email, June 2008.

Video
Bill Bogg's Corner Table, 1997 episode, Paley Center for Media, New York, NY.
Julia Child in America, New York Public Library, Cullman Center for Scholars and Writers, October 10, 2007.

Public programs
"Julia Child: Culinary Revolutionary," New School for Social Research, June 12, 2008.

Published works
Adema, Pauline. "Vicarious Consumption: Food, Television and the Ambiguity of Modernity." *Journal of American & Comparative Cultures* 23, no. 3 (Fall, 2000).

Bourdieu, Pierre. *Distinction: A Social Critique of the Judgment of Taste.* Cambridge, MA: Harvard University Press, 1984.

Brooks, David. *Bobos in Paradise: The New Upper Class and How They Got*

There. New York: Simon & Schuster, 2000.

Bruni, Frank. "Cooking Under Pressure, That's Reality." *New York Times*, January 31, 2007.

Buford, Bill. "TV Dinners; Notes of a Gastronome." *The New Yorker*, October 2, 2006.

Curtis, Kim. "Culinary School Enrollment Is Up Amid Celebrity Chef Craze, but Low-Paying Jobs, Debt Await." *The Associated Press*, January 1, 2007.

de Solier, Isabelle. "TV Dinners: Culinary Television, Education and Distinction." *Continuum: Journal of Media & Cultural Studies* 19, no. 4 (December 2005).

Dickerman, Sara. "Bloody Hell's Kitchen: The Foul-Mouthed British Chef Who Could Save Food TV." *Slate*, January 5, 2005. http://www.slate.com/id/2111851/.

Ephron, Nora. "Critics in the World of the Rising Soufflé (Or Is It the Rising Meringue?)." *New York*, September 30, 1968.

Galbraith, John Kenneth. *The Affluent Society*. Boston: Houghton Mifflin, 1958.

Jarvik, Laurence Ariel. *PBS, Behind the Screen*. Rocklin, CA: Forum, 1997.

Lehrman, Karen. "What Julia Started." *U.S. News World Report*, September 22, 1997.

McFeely, Mary Drake. *Can She Bake a Cherry Pie: American Women and the Kitchen in the Twentieth Century*. Amherst: University of Massachusetts Press, 2000.

O'Neill, Molly. "Convenience in the Kitchen: The Way Mama Used to Heat." *New York Times*, March 4, 1992.

Schor, Juliet. *The Overworked American: The Unexpected Decline of Leisure*. New York: Basic Books, 1991.

Sutel, Seth. "Food Network Builds Audience Beyond Soufflé-and-Truffles Set." *ABC news.com*, January 19, 2001. http://abcnews.go.com/print?id=88743.

SELECTED BIBLIOGRAPHY

In addition to sources listed by chapter, this bibliography includes resources on which I relied for background research.

Allen, Patricia, and Carolyn Sachs. "Women and Food Chains: The Gendered Politics of Food." *International Journal of Sociology of Food and Agriculture* 15, no. 1 (April 2007).

Bowers, Douglas E. "Cooking Trends Echo Changing Roles of Women." *FoodReview* 23, no. 1 (2000).

Brenner, Leslie. *American Appetite: The Coming of Age of a Cuisine*. New York: Bard, 1999.

Brunsdon, Charlotte. "Feminism, Postfeminism, Martha, Martha, and Nigella." *Cinema Journal* 44, no. 2 (Winter 2005).

Buford, Bill. *Heat: An Amateur's Adventures as Kitchen Slave, Line Cook, Pasta Maker, and Apprentice to a Dante-Quoting Butcher in Tuscany*. New York: Alfred A. Knopf, 2006.

Cohen, Lizabeth. *A Consumers' Republic: The Politics of Mass Consumption in Postwar America*. New York: Vintage Books, 2003.

Erickson, Hal. *Syndicated Television: The First Forty Years, 1947–1987*. Jefferson, NC: McFarland, 1989.

Goldstein, Darra, ed. *Gastronomica: A Tribute to Julia Child* 3, no. 5 (Summer 2005).

Goldstein, David B. "Recipes for Living Martha Stewart and the New American Subject." In *Ordinary Lifestyles: Popular Media, Consumption and Taste*, edited by David Bell and Joanne Hollows. Berkshire, Great Britain: McGraw-Hill Education, 2005.

Hess, John L., and Karen Hess. *The Taste of America*. Urbana: University of Illinois Press, 2000.

Hyatt, Wesley. *The Encyclopedia of Daytime Television*. New York: Billboard Books, 1997.

Inness, Sherrie A. *Dinner Roles: American Women and Culinary Culture*. Iowa City, IA: University of Iowa City, 2001.

―――. *Secret Ingredients: Race, Gender, and Class at the Dinner Table*. New York: Palgrave Macmillan, 2006.

Johnson, Lesley, and Justine Lloyd. *Sentenced to Everyday Life: Feminism and the Housewife*. Oxford: Berg, 2004.

Jones, Evan. *American Food: The Gastronomic Story*. Woodstock, NY: Overlook Press, 1990.

Kamp, David. *The United States of Arugula: How We Became a Gourmet Nation*. New York: Broadway Books, 2006.

Kaufman, Frederick. *A Short History of the American Stomach*. Orlando, FL: Harcourt, 2008.

Ketchum, Cheri. "The Essence of Cooking Shows: How the Food Network Constructs Consumer Fantasies." *Journal of Communication Inquiry* 29, no. 3 (July 2005).

Lapham, Lewis H. "Everyone's in the Kitchen with Julia." *Saturday Evening Post*, August 8, 1964.

Mariani, John F. *The Dictionary of American Food and Drink*. New Haven: Ticknor & Fields, 1983.

Marks, Susan. *Finding Betty Crocker: The Secret Life of America's First Lady of Food*. New York: Simon & Schuster, 2005.

May, Elaine Tyler. *Homeward Bound: American Families in the Cold War Era*. New York: Basic Books, 1988.

Miller, Toby. *Cultural Citizenship: Cosmopolitanism, Consumerism, and Television in a Neoliberal Age*. Philadelphia: Temple University Press, 2007.

Mittell, Jason. *Genre and Television: From Cop Shows to Cartoons in American Culture*. New York: Routledge, 2004.

Modleski, Tania. "The Rhythms of Reception: Daytime Television and Women's Work." In *Regarding Television: Critical Approaches—An Anthology*, edited by E. Ann Kaplan. Frederick, MD: University Publications of America, 1983.

Murray, Michael D., and Donald G. Godfrey. *Television in America: Local Station History from Across the Nation*. Ames: Iowa State University Press, 1997.

O'Neill, Molly. "Food Porn." *Columbia Journalism Review*, September/October 2003.

Pépin, Jacques. *The Apprentice: My Life in the Kitchen*. Boston: Houghton Mifflin, 2003.

Reichl, Ruth, ed. *Gourmet: Special Anniversary Issue. 60 Years of Fabulous Food*. September 2001.

Samuel, Lawrence R. *Brought to You By: Postwar Television Advertising and the American Dream*. Austin: University of Texas Press, 2001.

Savan, Leslie. *The Sponsored Life: Ads, TV, and American Culture*. Philadelphia: Temple University Press, 1994.

Schwartz, Tony. *The Responsive Chord*. Garden City, NY: Anchor Press, 1973.

Sies, Leora M., and Luther F. Sies. *The Encyclopedia of Women in Radio, 1920–1960*. Jefferson, NC: McFarland & Co., 2003.

Smith, Andrew F. *The Oxford Encyclopedia of Food and Drink in America*. Oxford: Oxford University Press, 2004.

Stern, Jane, and Michael Stern. *Jane & Michael Stern's Encyclopedia of Pop Culture: An A to Z Guide of Who's Who and What's What, from Aerobics and Bubble Gum to Valley of the Dolls and Moon Unit Zappa*. New York: HarperPerennial, 1992.

Stole, Inger L. "The *Kate Smith Hour* and the Struggle for Control of Television Programming in the Early 1950s." *Historical Journal of Film, Radio and Television* 20, no. 4 (October 2000).

Terrace, Vincent. *Encyclopedia of Television Subjects, Themes and Settings*. Jefferson, NC: McFarland & Co., 2007.

Timberg, Bernard, and Robert Erler. *Television Talk: A History of the TV Talk Show*. Austin: University of Texas Press, 2002.

Toossi, Mitra. "A Century of Change: U.S. Labor Force from 1950 to 2050." *Monthly Labor Review* 125 (May 2002).

Unger, Arthur. "Guess Who's Coming to Dinner? Television!" *Television Quarterly* 30, no. 1 (1999).

INDEX

television program format, 60–62, 118
Margetts, Monty, 42–43, 84, 231
marketing of TV shows/networks, 59, 85,
    152–153, 182, 188, 212, 215, 224
Martinez, Daisy, 249
Mastering the Art of French Cooking. See
    Child, Julia
McCarthy, Josephine, 39–40
McCarthy, Joseph, 45, 65
McCrary, Tex, 34
McDavid, Jack, 164
McDonald's, 133, 152
McLuhan, Marshall, 15
men
    and cooking, 18–19, 27, 50–51, 88–89,
        96–98, 115–17, 137, 143, 212–14
    as hosts, 35–36, 97, 116–17
    See also gender roles
Metzger, Mary, 139
microwaves, 132, 140, 246
middle class, American, 21, 30, 44, 67, 77, 79,
    85, 96, 128, 135, 141, 224, 238
Milani, Chef (Joseph), 35, 40–41, 116
Milliken, Mary Sue. *See Too Hot Tamales*
Morash, Russ, 72–74, 77, 83–91 passim, 152
Morimoto, Masaharu, 198, 239–41 passim
Moulton, Sara, 172–75, 200, 202, 213, 218,
    227, 250
MTV, 137, 163, 166, 192
Myhren, Trygve, 159–167 passim

Naked Chef, The, 178, 238
narrative structure, 191–92
Nathan, Joan, 249
NBC, 26–29 passim, 39, 42, 47, 62, 64–65, 160
networks, broadcast and cable
    control of programming, 38, 60, 85–86,
        99–100, 111, 137, 159, 192, 211
New York Times, coverage of food/cooking,
    84, 136, 233
niche programming, 86, 155, 159, 163,
    192–93, 206
Nielsen ratings, 49, 164, 216
Nivens, Sue Ann, 123
nutrition. *See* health
O'Neill, Molly, 84, 85, 100, 134–40 passim,
    182, 202, 222, 226–27, 232, 240, 248, 250–51
Ogle, Sally, 84, 231
Oliver, Jamie, 178–79, 183, 184, 203, 213, 231,
    238, 239
Opatut, Eileen, 196, 248
organic food, 84, 203, 218, 250
Oshinsky, Carl, 139

Paddleford, Clementine, 23–24
Palmer, Charles, 164, 214
Paterson, Jennifer. *See Two Fat Ladies*
Paula's Home Cooking, 182, 193, 200
Pennell, Ellen, 34–37 passim, 64
Pépin, Jacques, 80–87 passim, 103, 116,
    137–38, 162, 231, 238
performance in cooking shows, 28, 78, 177, 217
personality, and cooking show hosts, 42–43,
    79, 94, 109, 124, 153, 175–78

Peyroux, Earl, 139
Pope, Francois, 35–36, 97, 116, 238
populism in cooking shows, 79–80, 104,
    222–227
porn, food, 188–192
post-World War II era, 19, 37, 39, 44–48
    passim, 67, 81, 226
    See also World War II
Powell, Julie, 90, 104
Prescott, Allen, 26, 34
prime-time programming, 49–50, 164, 170–
    71, 174, 177, 185, 193, 195, 213, 215
product lines, show hosts', 58, 152, 230,
product promotion, 20, 26, 30, 57, 87, 229–30
production values, 37, 186, 248
Providence Journal Company, 159–167
    passim, 192, 199, 233
Prudhomme, Paul, 135, 142, 165
psychological aspect of food/cooking shows,
    96, 151, 183, 230, 235, 250–51
public broadcasting, 86–90, 99, 125, 128,
    138–141, 145, 147, 154–55, 185, 193, 209,
    231, 239, 251
    audience, 72, 77, 115, 146
    vs. commercial, 85–87, 115, 123, 165,
        188, 205–206
    diversity and innovation on, 100, 139,
        249
Puck, Wolfgang, 85, 135, 146, 180, 181, 193

Queer Eye for the Straight Guy, 194, 214

race, 21, 103, 127
    audience demographics, 88
    and cooking show hosts, 35, 124–25, 249
radio, 60, 62
    early cooking programs, 13–23, 26, 243
Ramsay, Gordon, 197, 199, 242
Ray, Rachael, 55, 78, 153, 171, 173, 177, 181,
    183–85 passim, 190–95 passim, 200, 203,
    207, 209–11 passim, 213, 217–223, 227,
    230, 231, 240–43 passim
reality television, 182, 184, 191, 192, 197, 222
recipes, delivery method of
    explicit vs. vague, 55, 110, 137, 175, 206
    in newspapers and magazines, 14
    on TV and radio, 14, 20, 32, 61, 67
Rector, George, 19, 26
regionality, 13, 127, 128, 135, 142, 195, 250
Reichl, Ruth, 162, 233
Richard, Michel, 164
Richman, Alan, 162, 163
Ried, Adam, 207, 209
Romagnoli, Margaret and Franco, 127, 238
Roosevelt, Franklin D., 24, 140
Rosengarten, David, 163, 189
Rosie the Riveter, 19, 44
Ruth, Helen, 31

Sarnoff, David, 24–25
Saturday Night Live, 91, 107
Schonfeld, Reese, 161–63 passim, 165–66,
    168, 171, 180, 187, 192, 214–16 passim, 235
Scripps Network, 169, 211